Preface

Mankind has known about the power of the printed word for centuries. Until recently, however, achieving a professional look required special training and special equipment, equipment costing as much as $100,000 or more.

Now Ventura Publisher puts that power right on your desk — and makes it easy enough for anyone to use. The same personal computer you already own for word processing or accounting is now your personal design studio/typesetter/print shop. That means you'll save money. Lots of money.

Xerox Ventura Publisher lets you use the tools of publishing— tools like typography, artwork and graphic design— to give your words more power, more weight, more impact. Ventura Publisher can make your documents seem professional and important. That can make you and your company seem more important.

We have been fortunate to use Xerox Ventura Publisher since its first incarnation. Since November 1985, when we first saw the product, we have watched it progress in a very short time to become the most powerful desktop publishing program available for personal computers. We have used it to produce a variety of publications, including newsletters, brochures, proposals, reports, press releases— and this book, as explained in Appendix B.

And now we are passing along what we've discovered— the tips, the tricks, the shortcuts, and the advanced techniques that turn Xerox Ventura Publisher into a desktop publishing powerhouse. Just by spending a few hours with this book you will see how easily you can adapt Xerox Ventura Publisher to your own business. When you understand how powerful it is, how simple it is to operate, how inexpensively it produces top-quality documents, we think you'll share our enthusiasm for this remarkable product.

The power to publish lies waiting for you. All you need is this book, a personal computer with printer, and an amazing piece of software called Xerox Ventura Publisher.

Jesse Berst
James Cavuoto
April, 1987

INSIDE
XEROX VENTURA
PUBLISHER

A Guide to Professional-Quality
Desktop Publishing on the IBM PC

By James Cavuoto and Jesse Berst

Micro Publishing, Torrance, California

and

New Riders Publishing, Thousand Oaks, California

Inside Xerox Ventura Publisher

A Guide to Professional-Quality Desktop Publishing on the IBM PC

by James Cavuoto and Jesse Berst

Published by:
Micro Publishing
21150 Hawthorne Blvd., Suite 104
Torrance, CA 90503
and
New Riders Publishing
P.O. Box 4846-V
Thousand Oaks, CA 91360

Copyright © 1987 by Micro Publishing

First Printing, April 1987

Printed in the United States of America

Library of Congress Card Catalog Number: 87-090425
ISBN 0-934035-13-X

Acknowledgments

We would like to thank the individuals and organizations who helped make this book possible. Representatives of Xerox Corporation were instrumental in encouraging us to write this book and in helping to get it published. These include Larry Spelhaug, Terry Dillman, Ravi Sahay, Randi Doeker, James Brown, Carolyn Grossman, Doug Heineman, Jan Powell, Barry Nickerson, Carol Clement, and Barry Sulpor.

John Meyer of Ventura Software, Inc. devoted considerable effort to examining the manuscript for technical accuracy— despite the enormous demands on his time. Marcela Murman proofread the pages and made editorial suggestions. And our thanks to the entire staff of New Riders Publishing, who pitched in with editorial and design help.

The following companies loaned us hardware or software that we used to produce the book:

Xerox Corp.	Full Page Display
AST Research	Premium Publisher computer
Conographic Corp	ConoVision 2800 display
Sigma Designs Inc.	Laserview Display System

Z-Soft, Inc.	PC Paintbrush Plus
WordPerfect Corp.	WordPerfect
Microsoft Corp.	Word 3.0
MicroPro International Corp.	WordStar 4.0
SymSoft Inc.	HotShot
Digital Research, Inc.	GEM Draw Plus
Dest Corp.	PC Scan Plus
Three D Corp.	Perspective
IMSI	Desktop Publisher's Graphics
Conographic Corp.	Conofonts
Autodesk Inc.	AutoCAD

Finally, we would like to express our thanks and admiration to the programmers at Ventura Software, Inc. who wrote Ventura Publisher: Don Heiskell, Lee Lorenzen, and John Grant.

Table of Contents

Acknowledgments   **iii**

Preface   **v**

Chapter One: Introduction to Desktop Publishing   **1**

Desktop Publishing Defined...3

How To Benefit From Desktop Publishing 4

The Shortcomings of Desktop Publishing 7

Ventura Publisher vs. Other Programs...7

Chapter Two: Introduction to Ventura Publisher   **13**

Before You Start 14

Ten Minutes to Ventura Publisher 15

Understanding Ventura Publisher...24

The Ventura Formula 43

Chapter Three: Creating Text   **49**

The Ventura Publisher Approach to Text..50

General Rules for Creating Text 50

Formatting ASCII Files...58

Using Word Processor Files...60

Creating Text with Other Programs 62

Creating Text With Ventura Publisher..67

Editing Text After Using Ventura Publisher...68

Preformatting Ventura Publisher Files 69

Chapter Four: Creating Pictures   89

The Ventura Approach to Pictures 90
Two Kinds of Pictures 91
Creating Line-Art 94
Creating Images 100
Creating Images with Scanners 104
Screen Capture Utilities 110
Converting File Formats 113
Ventura Conversion Utilities 116

Chapter Five: Working with Style Sheets   119

Loading a Style Sheet 119
Applying a Style Sheet 121
Changing a Style Sheet 128
Working with the Menus 130
Style Sheet Maintenance 155

Chapter Six: Document Design and Layout   159

A Game Plan for Laying Out Pages 159
Loading the Style Sheet 161
Working with Text 162
Working with Pictures 184
Saving the Chapter 205

Chapter Seven: Producing Output   207

Printing Options 208
Printing a Single Chapter 212
Multi-Chapter Operations 213
Using More Than One Printer 221
Fonts 226
Printing to a Disk File 229
Binding Pages 230
Guidelines for Offset Printing 231

Chapter Eight: Advanced Functions   239

Typographic Functions 239
Unusual or Difficult Formats 255
Numbering Functions 271
File Management Functions 282

Chapter Nine: Special Tips & Techniques   287

Frame Techniques 288
Graphic Techniques 295
Memory Management Techniques 302
Notes on Different Document Types 307

Appendix A: Manufacturers and Products   317

Appendix B: Colophon   321

Index   324

Chapter One

Introduction to Desktop Publishing

Welcome to the revolution. A movement is underway that is revolutionizing the way businesspeople produce printed pages. This book will show you how to profit from that trend using a remarkable software program called Xerox Ventura Publisher.

To gain perspective, let's harken back to an earlier revolution and an event that dramatically illustrates the power of the printed word. In January, 1776, Thomas Paine published *Common Sense,* a vivid call for the formation of a republic. His 50-page pamphlet led directly to the Declaration of Independence a few months later.

Common Sense was an immediate bestseller (120,000 copies in three months—equivalent to 10 million today). Paine's problems lay not with writing or selling, but with the publisher/printer, who delayed him, overcharged him and generally disregarded his wishes.

Sound familiar?

Two hundred years after Paine's manifesto, the printing process is more sophisticated, but it certainly isn't any simpler. Two hundred years later, we're still complaining that

COMMON SENSE:

ADDRESSED TO THE

INHABITANTS

OF

A M E R I C A.

On the following interesting

S U B J E C T S.

I Of the Origin and Design of Government in general,
    with concise Remarks on the English Constitution.

II. Of Monarchy and Hereditary Succession.

III Thoughts on the present State of American Affairs.

IV. Of the present Ability of America, with some miscellaneous
     Reflections.

Written by an ENGLISHMAN.

Man knows no Master save creating HEAVEN,
Or those whom choice and common good ordain.
                                    THOMSON.

PHILADELPHIA, Printed
And Sold by R. BELL, in Third Street, 1776.

10 Weeks on the Colonial Best-Seller List!

*C*ommon
*S*ense

THOMAS PAINE

The Blockbuster All America Is Talking About

Figure 1-1
Thomas Paine's Common Sense as it appeared originally (left), and how it might
have appeared if Ventura Publisher had been available (right).

the people who produce our pages are delaying us, overcharging us, and generally disregarding our wishes.

It doesn't have to be that way.

Which brings us back to our modern-day revolution. Desktop publishing is transforming the process of producing pages. If Thomas Paine were alive today, we think he would have been one of the first to use it. That cantankerous rebel could not have resisted the freedom it provides and the control it allows. Using a product like Xerox Ventura Publisher, Paine could have saved time. He could have experimented until he got things right (see Figure 1-1). And he could have saved money— something the penniless writer certainly would have appreciated.

It's too late for Thomas Paine. But those of us who are around today can cash in on desktop publishing, thanks to

Xerox Ventura Publisher, a product that gives an inexpensive personal computer the power of a print shop.

Desktop Publishing Defined

We're anxious to show you how Ventura Publisher can pay off. First you need to understand where this exceptional product fits into the scheme of things.

Let's begin by defining the term desktop publishing. Quite simply, it's the use of a personal computer for most or all of the stages of publishing. Both desktop and traditional publishing have the same basic steps: creation (of text and pictures), assembly (into pages), and printing. But the traditional method is a tedious, detail-oriented process involving expensive equipment and highly-trained personnel (see the Box at the end of this chapter for a comparison).

Desktop publishing had its beginnings in the 1970s, when Xerox Corporation introduced the Star workstation. This computer was the first to offer a high-resolution display that could integrate text and pictures on screen. It also incorporated a revolutionary device called a mouse, which let users move around the screen by sliding a hand-held controller. This user interface was subsequently borrowed by other manufacturers. It's evident in products such as the Apple Macintosh, Microsoft Windows, Digital Research Inc.'s GEM environment, and the Documenter system from Xerox itself.

The second major component of desktop publishing was the laser printer, first put to use by Xerox in the 1970s. Just as the Star workstation offered the ability to merge text and graphics on screen, laser printers offered the capability to merge text and graphics on the printed page.

Prices have fallen in the years since Xerox's pioneering efforts. As a result, many of the capabilities present in the early Star/laser printer system are now available for less than $10,000.

How To Benefit From Desktop Publishing

Desktop publishing offers a host of benefits to the savvy businessperson. We've listed a few examples below.

Save Money

Desktop publishing saves on equipment and on labor. Even low-end typesetters cost $25,000 to $50,000. Many cost more than $100,000. And labor costs continue to climb for the skilled personnel required to manually layout, illustrate, code, paste-up, and print. It takes significantly fewer man-hours to produce a page on a personal computer than it would using traditional methods. Desktop publishing also cuts paper costs when compared to typewritten pages. Typesetting fits up to 30% more on a page. Merging graphics with text also saves space (a picture's worth a thousand words, remember?).

When you add it all up, desktop publishing can cut a printing bill almost in half. Now consider that American corporations spend an estimated $200 billion to produce 2.5 *trillion*

Task	Before Desktop Publishing	After Desktop Publishing	Savings
Writing	$126	$110	$16
Editing	75	18	57
Keyboard	34	0	34
Proofread	31	6	25
Typesetting	35	0	35
Revisions	15	0	15
Illustrations	150	0	150
Halftones	15	15	0
Paste-Up	19	0	19
Correct	14	0	14
Total	$514	$149	$365

Figure 1-2
The cost justification for a desktop publishing system for each issue of a 24-page in-house magazine at a typical corporation.

pages each year. Quite simply, desktop publishing is an easy computer application to cost-justify (see Figure 1-2).

Save Time

Many desktop publishing installations can pay for themselves in less than a year through reduced labor costs alone. But there's another side to saving time that's difficult to quantify.

In many cases, getting a document out sooner provides a competitive advantage. A newsletter publisher, for instance, can wait right up to deadline before assembling the final pages. News is fresher and more timely. Result: satisfied customers and more subscriptions. Likewise, contractors might gain an edge by being the first to submit a professional-looking bid; scientists by getting a monograph out ahead of time; managers by getting a report to top brass before their rivals; consultants by beating the competition to the punch with a top-notch proposal.

More Control

Now, for the first time, you govern when your work gets done and how it will look. That translates to freedom. Freedom from high-priced type shops that charge a lot for simple jobs. Freedom from artists and layout people who don't understand what you want. Freedom from outside companies who have no motivation to get it done right and on time. It also translates to fewer mistakes. Traditional publishing can involve as many as ten people:

- Writer
- Editor
- Designer/art director
- Typographer
- Illustrator
- Paste-up artist
- Proofreader
- Camera operator
- Negative stripper
- Printer

With a personal computer, a laser printer, and Xerox Ventura Publisher, one person can take the place of all these ex-

PROPOSAL TO ACME INSURANCE CORPORATION

Corporate Training

The Corporate Training department has identified an objective to redesign and reformat over 9000 pages of textual and graphic information which constitutes the company's training documentation elements. In addition to redesigning this substantial amount of information, the department will also add new sections to the current training curriculum. The training documentation is currently available in a variety of media, mostly on much copied papers. The documentation is somewhat out of date since the collection of materials dates back ten years. According to the Corporate Director of Training, there is no orderly fashion or design for this information. The corporation has hired a consultant, Ms. Joan Belden who has designed a specific format and process for the training documentation. Ms. Belden will become a member of the Acme Insurance staff to coordinate the processes of rewriting the documentation.

Currently, there is an in-house printing and type-setting shop. Because of delays and priorities, the training department does not have ready access to this facility. Due to the size and nature of this project, a decision has been made to evaluate departmental or work-group desk-top publishing solutions specifically for the training facility. Having an departmental facility for documentation will give the training operation the following benefits:

• Fast turn-around time without having to depend on another corporate department to print

documentation.

• Ability to make immediate changes and update training modules.

• Ability to use already installed Personal Computers and Word Processing equipment in association with the new publishing equipment.

Figure 1-1   The caption for this figure.

• Ability to incorporate the new machinery directly into the day-to-day operations of the department.

The TXN Solution
It is the recommendation of TXN Corporation that Acme Insurance consider the 3544 graphic workstation as the input terminal for the redesign/reformat processes in the training facility. TXN was the first company to offer this unique type of

Title of Report   1-1

PROPOSAL TO ACME INSURANCE CORPORATION

Corporate Training

The Corporate Training department has identified an objective to redesign and reformat over 9000 pages of textual and graphic information which constitutes the company's training documentation elements. In addition to redesigning this substantial amount of information, the department will also add new sections to the current training curriculum. The training documentation is currently available in a variety of media, mostly on much copied papers. The documentation is somewhat out of date since the collection of materials dates back ten years. According to the Corporate Director of Training, there is no orderly fashion or design for this information. The corporation has hired a consultant, Ms. Joan Belden who has designed a specific format and process for the training documentation. Ms. Belden will become a member of the Acme Insurance staff to coordinate the processes of rewriting the documentation.

Figure 1-3
The typewritten document on the right lacks the power to persuade that the published page on the left enjoys.

perts. Okay—one ambitious, hard-working person. But you get the point: The fewer the middlemen, the fewer the errors.

More Power to Persuade

There's a big difference between a typewritten document and one that's been professionally produced (see Figure 1-3). This difference means you'll have more *power to persuade*. Power to grab the reader's attention and keep it. Power to influence through words, graphics, and design. Power to create documents that look important, professional, expensive.

People judge you by what you produce. The old way of doing things discouraged experimentation. With desktop publishing you see the final result immediately, right on the screen. You preview multiple options in seconds. You have the time to try things out until everything looks right. If you put words on paper—resumes, reports, proposals, memos, viewgraphs, presentations, whatever—desktop publishing can help you create a better image.

A Competitive Edge

Millions will be using desktop publishing within a few years. Those who start early will have an advantage. Their proposals will look better. Their reports will appear more polished. Their brochures and advertisements will have a sophisticated veneer. Put simply, they'll have a jump on the competition.

The Shortcomings of Desktop Publishing

We wouldn't be doing our job if we didn't warn you that current desktop technology has several limitations. It doesn't provide as full a range of typestyles as professional typesetters. It doesn't yet do a good job with halftones (photos), which usually need to be stripped in the old-fashioned way. And it usually relies on laser printing, which is not adequate for certain jobs. (However, you can always send the final result to a phototypesetter).

Not all problems arise from the technology. Some of them come from human limitations. Desktop publishing software has a learning curve. Then there's the "temptation curve." You'll probably be less productive for a brief period because you'll be tempted to fiddle with every document until it is "just right" (we know about this problem first-hand). And finally, be aware that desktop publishing can't turn you into a graphic designer. Beginners will be wise to study and imitate professionally-prepared pages. Otherwise, they may find that desktop publishing does nothing more than make them a lot faster at producing very ugly documents.

Ventura Publisher vs. Other Programs

Given that desktop publishing provides the benefits outlined above, why pick Xerox Ventura Publisher? Several features distinguish this product from the rest of the pack:

- A true "What You See Is What You Get" display

- More than 5,000 pages per document, as many as 36,000 pages by linking at print time (if your disk is big enough)

- Compatibility with the inexpensive IBM PC/XT (other brands require the more costly AT-style or Macintosh computers)

- Compatibility with leading software. Ventura works seamlessly with your favorite programs. It even uses the same files, avoiding space-wasting duplication.

- Batch processing for long documents. Format and print hundreds of pages in one pass. Xerox Ventura Publisher is ideally suited for long documents such as books, catalogs, reports, and technical manuals.

- Style sheets, reusable formats for different documents.

Style sheets are important enough to deserve additional comment. A style sheet is a separate file containing format rules. A different style sheet creates a different look. It's a simple idea, but one that's extremely powerful.

If you know how—and we'll show you—you can reformat a document in seconds by loading a new style sheet. You can even build a library of styles, then try out dozens of design alternatives with a few clicks of the mouse (see Figure 1-4).

But perhaps the single greatest selling point of Xerox Ventura Publisher is its amazing combination of simplicity and power. Make no mistake—Ventura is a feature-packed program that takes many hours to master completely. Yet almost anyone can learn to format simple documents in 10 minutes. We'll prove it to you in Chapter Two.

Despite this ease of use, Ventura can create almost any kind of document. Today, many corporations produce pages in a dozen different ways depending on time, complexity, and cost, from hand-lettering to typewriters to press-on lettering all the way to phototypesetting. Ventura Publisher is so flexible and cost-efficient that most corporations can abandon this mish-

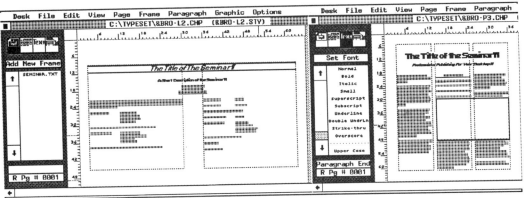

Figure 1-4
Two different style sheets applied to the same Ventura Publisher document.

mash of approaches. This one program can accomplish virtually all publishing tasks:

- Advertisements
- Brochures
- Directories
- Financial Reports
- Instruction Manuals
- Memos
- Overhead Transparencies
- Press Releases
- Reports

- Books
- Catalogs
- Documentation
- Forms
- Labels
- Newsletters
- Parts Lists
- Proposals
- Technical Manuals

By now it's obvious we're big fans of Xerox Ventura Publisher. We could continue for many more pages on the advantages it offers. Instead, we'd prefer to start showing you the ins and outs of putting Ventura to work.

The first step is to gain an overall understanding of Ventura Publisher and the way it approaches page makeup. That's precisely what we'll do in the next chapter. But first, you may want to read over the Box on the following two pages, which examines the traditional methods of publishing documents.

The Stages of Traditional Publishing

Throughout this book, we refer to traditional publishing methods. For those who do not have wide experience in manual page makeup, the following rundown explains the fundamentals.

Traditional publishing involves nine steps. The exact order differs from publication to publication, but the list below is typical of a monthly magazine. It closely parallels the process for other complex documents.

1. Writing

Authors create text on typewriters or word processors and give printed copies to editors.

2. Editing/Revision

Editors make pen and ink changes on the typewritten pages. If changes are extensive, the manuscript is retyped. If minor, the marked-up copy goes straight to the typesetter.

The editing process may go through several rounds of revisions until both writer and editor agree that the manuscript is finished.

3. Typesetting

The operator rekeys the manuscript into the typesetter, following the editor's marginal instructions about size and selection of type faces. The text is typeset into galleys. Galleys are the correct column width, but not the right length.

4. Illustration

An artist creates charts, graphs, drawings, or other illustrations for the article.

5. Page Design

Most publications have standard layouts or grids they reuse for most pages. Sometimes the designer creates special, unique layouts for certain articles.

The page design is represented on a layout sheet. The designer draws vertical and horizontal lines to show where the columns should be. He uses a blue pencil. These lines guide the paste-up artist, but the special color does not show up when the final page is photographed. Along with the lines, layout boards usually include repeating elements like logos and page numbers that appear on every page.

6. Paste-up

The paste-up artist cuts the galleys lengthwise into strips one column wide. He applies hot wax to the back. Some publications use rubber cement, but hot wax is easier to move—and there's almost always lots of moving to do when pages are created manually. The paste-up artist sticks the text into column one. When he reaches the bottom, he cuts the galley off and moves the remainder to another column or page.

Sometimes artwork is pasted onto the page like text. But often the paste-up artist leaves a space, or "window" for the illustration instead. Photos require a window because they are added to the page in a separate stage called "stripping."

Either way, the paste-up artist must decide how much space to leave for the illustration. Then he takes the original art and resizes it to fit the window. He may crop it (eliminate a portion of the picture), scale it (enlarge or reduce it), or a combination. The artist places rules, boxes or grids by hand using a pen or special tape. Finally he pastes down the captions.

Revisions are the worst thing that can happen to the paste-up artist. A small change of only a few words may have a "ripple effect" changing not only that page but the next, which changes the next and so on. To change a page, he must physically lift the waxed text off the page, recut it and reposition it.

7. Negatives

When everything has been pasted up into camera ready art (often referred to as mechanicals or boards) a camera operator shoots a negative of each page. Blank spaces appear on the negative where photos are to appear. The camera operator makes separate negatives of photos (and sometimes of drawings, too). These negatives are shot at the exact size and scale specified. This is one area where it is particularly easy to make mistakes.

8. Stripping

In a laborious process called stripping, negatives of artwork are overlaid onto the negatives of the page and matched to fit the blank windows that were left.

9. Printing

The combined negative from the preceding step is used to make a plate for a printing press, and the document is printed.

Contrast the stages of traditional publishing to desktop publishing. It's easy to see why desktop publishing with Ventura Publisher offers such dramatic time and cost savings.

Chapter Two

Introduction to Ventura Publisher

C hapter One explained the concept of desktop publishing. Now we're going to give you an overall understanding of Xerox Ventura Publisher. Don't worry about details yet. Later chapters will provide in-depth particulars, but first you need to get the big picture. Here are some of the things you'll understand by the time you finish this chapter:

- How to get a simple application up and running.

- The terminology used by Ventura Publisher and this book.

- The user interface and where to find basic functions.

- The Ventura Formula and how it applies to every document you create.

We'll begin with a brief, 10-minute test-drive. Although easy to operate, Ventura is very sophisticated. You might be overwhelmed if we plunged right into explanations of that sophistication. So we're going to start out with a quick, hands-on tryout. After you've experienced the *what* of Ventura, the second half of this chapter will explain the *how* and *why*.

Before You Start

Ventura Publisher runs on a wide range of MS-DOS computer systems. You can get full details from any authorized dealer. A hard disk drive is essential. You can get by with as little as two to three available megabytes, but we recommend 20 or more megabytes if you intend to do large-scale technical documentation or long documents combining many different graphics and text files.

For the moment, it doesn't matter which hardware configuration you own, or what additional software you may plan to use with Ventura. We will conduct the test-drive using sample files found on the original Ventura disks.

We have assumed that you have already installed Ventura Publisher. If not, do so now using the built-in, step-by-step program called VPPREP, which configures Ventura for your particular setup. Boot the system using MS-DOS 2.1 or higher. At the A prompt, put the #1 Ventura disk into drive A: (the disk labeled Ventura Publisher Application Disk). Type VPPREP and press Enter.

The installation program will take over from here. First it will ask questions. Your answers determine which specific files Ventura needs to transfer from the floppies onto your hard disk. Next VPPREP will tell you when to insert other disks. It will automatically create two new subdirectories on your hard disk. Then it will copy all the necessary programs and files into these subdirectories. It should take you less than 20 minutes from start to finish. If you make an error or change your hardware configuration, simply start from scratch and redo the installation.

Ventura 1.1 supports incremental installation. If you later want to change one portion of the program (to add a different printer or monitor, for instance) answer "No" when VPPREP asks if this is your first time. Then you can add only the files you need without bothering with the whole installation.

We have also assumed that you understand the basic terminology of page design. If you're a newcomer to this topic, refer to the Box at the end of this chapter. This Box demonstrates the specialized publishing and printing terms you need to know to operate Ventura.

Ten Minutes to Ventura Publisher

Once you've installed Ventura Publisher, you're ready for our 10-minute test drive. The purpose of this brief tutorial is to experience the features and concepts explained in the second half of this chapter. Don't concern yourself if you fail to understand the details. Nor should you be disturbed if you make a wrong choice and the tutorial doesn't go quite as planned. Your goal is simply to get a feel for Ventura and the way it operates.

And don't worry about meeting our 10-minute deadline. Although you can easily accomplish the test-drive in 10 minutes or less, feel free to explore on your own. When you're ready, come back to the second half of the chapter for a clarification of what you've been seeing.

Starting the Program

To load Ventura, go to the root directory of your hard disk. For most users, this will be accomplished by getting to the C prompt, then typing CD\. Now type VP (for Ventura Publisher). The built-in batch program will take over, automatically loading the files you need. Watch what happens—we'll be explaining later. When the program is finished loading, you will have a blank document with no text, no pictures, and the default style (whatever style was used last). In our tutorial, you'll do four things with this document:

- Load a text file

- Load a picture

- Load a new style sheet (a new format)

- Apply the new style sheet to the text

Loading Text

Adding text to a document takes place in two stages: (1) loading it and (2) placing it on the page. Let's bring in a text file called SAMPLE.TXT:

Touch the mouse cursor to the file menu at the top left of the screen. The menu will drop down.

Move the cursor down the list until LOAD TEXT/PICTURE is highlighted.

Press the mouse button once.

The dialog box shown in Figure 2-1 will appear. Notice the three darkened boxes, TEXT, ASCII, and ONE. If your dialog box does not look like this, change it by starting from the top of the box and moving the mouse cursor over the correct boxes and pressing once. Once the dialog box looks like Figure 2-1, move the cursor over the OK box and click once.

The dialog box will be replaced by the item selector shown in Figure 2-2. You should see the text cursor (a thin vertical cursor) on the line labeled selection. (If you do not, move the mouse cursor anywhere on the line and press once.)

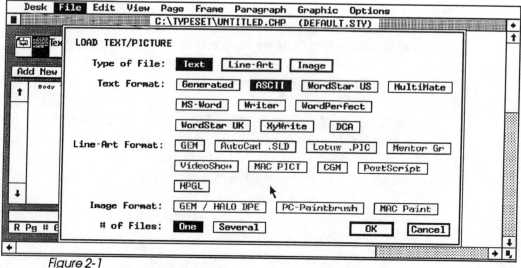

Figure 2-1
The load text/picture dialog box.

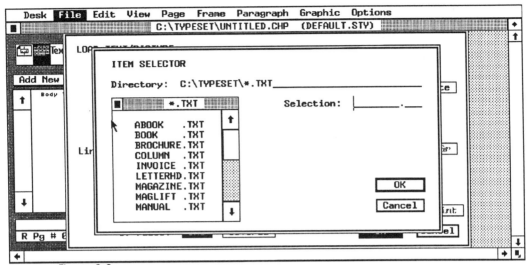

Figure 2-2
An item selector is used to choose among several files.

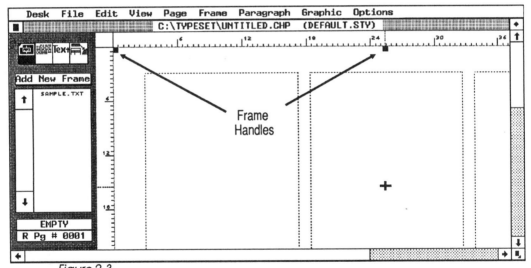

Figure 2-3
Small black handles on the edges of the frame let you know it is currently selected.

Click on the downward arrow at the lower right side of the item selector. The list of files will scroll down one line.

Continue clicking and scrolling until the filename SAMPLE.TXT appears.

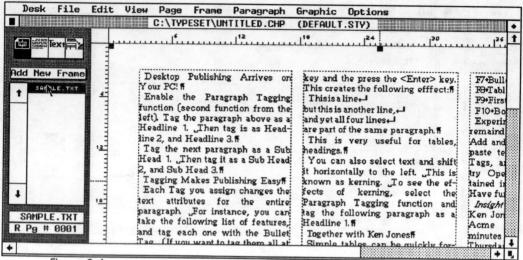

Figure 2-4
The text file SAMPLE.TXT has flowed onto the page.

Click once on SAMPLE.TXT to select it.

Click once on the OK button.

Ventura Publisher will respond with a screen message telling you it is loading the file.

Placing Text

You've loaded the text file SAMPLE.TXT. To place it on the page, first make sure you are in the correct mode. Ventura's four modes are represented by the four icons in the function selector at the top of the sidebar (see Figure 2-3). We need the frame setting mode at the moment.

Click once on the left-most icon in the function selector.

Now that you're in frame setting mode, tell Ventura where to put the text file.

Move the mouse cursor anywhere onto the Workspace and click once.

When you've finished, the screen will look like Figure 2-3. Look at the function selector. The frame setting icon is dark to

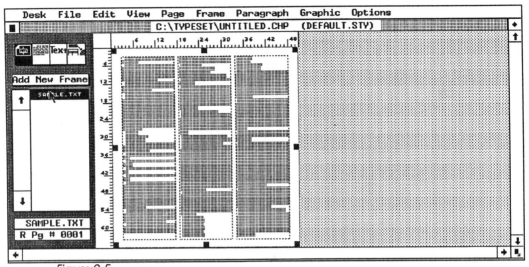

Figure 2-5
In reduced view, the entire page is visible in reduced form.

confirm which mode you are in. And notice the small black "handles" at the top of the workspace. They tell you that this area has been selected and is ready to accept text or graphics.

Now look at the assignment list, which shows the file SAMPLE.TXT. To pour this file onto the page:

Move the mouse cursor until it touches the name SAMPLE.TXT and click once.

The file will flow onto the page (Figure 2-4). If you like, take a few moments to explore this page. You can move around using the scroll bars at the right and bottom of the screen. To move down the page, for example, move the mouse cursor to the gray area below the scroll bar and click once. The display will move down the page one screen. You can move up and sideways in the same fashion.

♦ *Note: If you had the underlying page selected before you loaded the file, Ventura will automatically place SAMPLE.TXT on the page without any intervening steps.*

Loading and Placing a Picture
Let's move to reduced view so we can see the entire page.

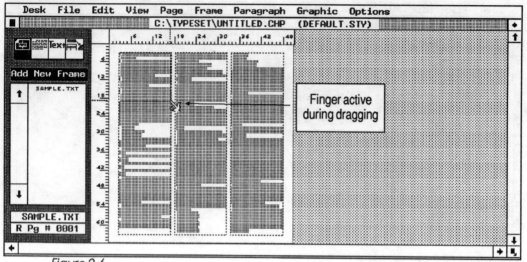

Figure 2-6
To add a new frame, click on Add New Frame and then drag the mouse where
you want the frame to be placed.

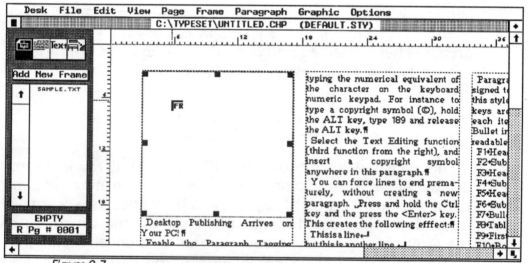

Figure 2-7
When a new frame is placed on the page, text previously there flows around the
new frame.

Pull down the view menu.

**Move down the list until REDUCED VIEW is
highlighted and click once.**

The display will change to look like Figure 2-5. Before we can load a graphics file, we need a place to put it. To create a frame:

Move to the addition button and click once. (This button reads "Add New Frame.")

Move the cursor to the upper left of the page.

Press the mouse button down and *without releasing the button* drag the mouse diagonally downwards as illustrated in Figure 2-6.

Release the button when you've created a new frame about the size of the one shown.

You have just created a new frame. As you can see in the reduced view, the text has automatically flowed around this picture. Now go to the view menu and change back to NORMAL VIEW. You should be able to see the upper left corner of the new frame as shown in Figure 2-7.

Let's place a picture into this blank space. Check to make sure that the new frame has "handles" around the edges. If it does not, place the cursor anywhere inside the blank frame and click once to select it.

Return to the file menu and choose the LOAD TEXT/PICTURE option again. When the dialog box appears, click on the buttons for LINE ART, GEM, and ONE, in that order. This tells Ventura that you want to load one line art image in the GEM Draw file format. When you finish the changes, click on the OK Button.

An item selector will appear. As we have done previously, select the name of the file you wish to load:

Scroll in the item selector until the filename COLUMBIA.GEM appears.

Click once on COLUMBIA.GEM.

Click on OK.

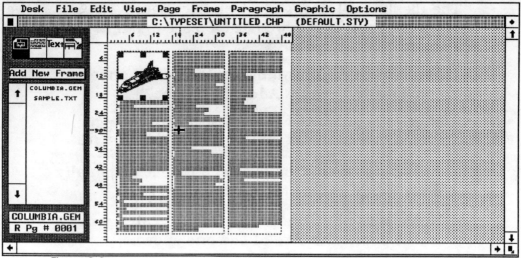

Figure 2-8
A reduced view of the page with the graphic image in place.

Ventura will load the picture file and place it into the previously blank frame. A reduced view of the page will look something like Figure 2-8. Notice that the file name of the picture file now appears on the assignment list along with the text file.

Loading a New Style Sheet

Now that we have text and a picture in the document, let's add a new format (a new style sheet):

> **Return to the file menu and select LOAD DIFF. STYLE. Ventura will display an item selector.**
>
> **Scroll until you see SAMPLE1.STY.**
>
> **Click on SAMPLE1.STY.**
>
> **Click on OK.**

Applying a Style Sheet

By loading a new style sheet, you immediately change page attributes such as margins, columns, headers, and so on. But to see the full result of this new style sheet, you must apply it to the text. This process is called "tagging."

To tag a document, switch to paragraph tagging mode by clicking on the second icon at the top of the sidebar. You'll know you're in the proper mode if the icon turns dark, the addition button changes to read "add new tag" and the assignment list changes to show tags names like headline and Subhead. Once you're in the proper mode, tagging is a simple two-step process.

This is a good place to define the word *paragraph* as used by Ventura. In common usage, a paragraph is a collection of sentences in a longer document, usually set off by indenting the first line. As used by Ventura and this book, a paragraph is any separate text element. It can be a single word, or hundreds of words. A Ventura paragraph, no matter how short or how long, is ended by placing a Return after the final character. Anytime you place a Return, you are telling Ventura to start a new paragraph.

Applying the style sheet to the text involves telling Ventura which paragraphs should use which tags. For instance, here's how to tell the program to apply the Headline tag to the first paragraph of the document.

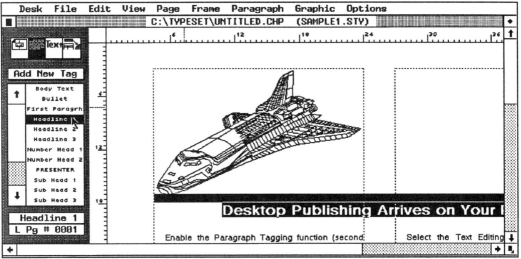

Figure 2-9
The headline style has been applied to the first paragraph.

> **Move the cursor until it touches any part of the
> first line and click once.**
>
> **Move to the assignment list and click once on
> the word Headline 1.**

The headline style will immediately be applied to the first
line (Figure 2-9). The sample document we loaded for this
tutorial contains instructions for tagging different sections of
the text. If you wish, take a few moments to follow the instructions and tag some more of the document. Experiment to see
the results of different choices and combinations.

You've finished the test-drive. To stop using the program,
choose QUIT from the file menu. To save the document under
a new name and continue your experiments later, choose SAVE
AS... from the file menu. If you use SAVE AS..., Ventura will ask
you for the name of the new document. Choose something like
LEARN or PRACTICE so you'll remember to delete the file after
you've finished. If you want to start over with a blank page,
select NEW from the file menu.

Understanding Ventura Publisher

Now you've seen Ventura Publisher for yourself. In a few
short minutes you've accomplished publishing tasks that require hours manually. (And you've only experienced a fraction
of Ventura's power and versatility!). Let's spend some time ex-
ploring and explaining what you saw on the screen.

The Ventura User Interface

The *user interface* is the means by which the operator and
the program communicate. If you understand the rules by
which Ventura operates, you'll have an easier time putting its
power to work.

The Role of GEM

Many of Ventura's interface features are actually provided
by a software system from Digital Research, Inc., known as

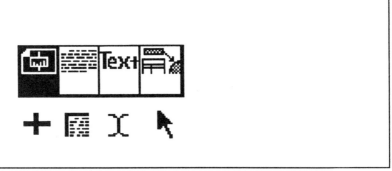

Figure 1-10
The four functions used in Ventura Publisher, with the corresponding mouse
shapes beneath each.

the Graphics Environment Manager (GEM for short). GEM
belongs in a software category called "windows managers" or
"graphics environments." When you first set Ventura up, the
installation program put GEM on the disk for you. The core
GEM modules reside on the subdirectory called \VENTURA,
which was automatically created during the installation
process.

♦ *Warning: Do not delete this directory or the files on them or
you will have to reinstall Ventura.*

When you start, a batch program automatically loads GEM,
and then loads Ventura as an application under GEM. This is
transparent to the user. When you type VP, the rest is done
automatically. Basically, GEM controls the mouse, display
adapter, and the dialog boxes from which the user makes
selections. Every application program running under GEM,
including Ventura Publisher, GEM Paint, and GEM Draw,
uses this same basic interface.

Digital Research also sells a separate GEM Desktop, which
serves as a shell for the disk operating system. However, you
need not have the GEM Desktop to run Ventura Publisher.
You can continue to start the program by typing VP from the
DOS prompt.

Ventura Publisher and the Mouse

Each time you move the mouse, the cursor moves cor-
respondingly on the screen. The shape of the cursor changes

according to the part of the screen you're on and the function you're using. Figure 2-10 shows the different shapes. You'll be seeing these cursors over and over again, and you'll soon learn them without realizing it.

Selecting with the Mouse

The main function of the mouse is to select. This is always done in the same fashion: by touching the item with the cursor and pressing the mouse button once. (If the mouse has more than one button, Ventura Publisher uses the left one.) When selecting from menus, the item is *highlighted* (turns dark) the moment the cursor touches it. The mouse works the same in item selectors and dialog boxes (described below) with one slight difference: Choices are highlighted *after* you press the mouse button to indicate the selection was made successfully.

Dragging with the Mouse

Dragging is used to move something around or change its size, as when we added a frame in our tutorial. Whenever we use the term *drag*, we are referring to the process of moving the mouse *while holding the button down*. After you finish the movement, release the button.

Moving Around the Page with the Mouse

The mouse is also used to move around the page, with the help of the scroll bars at the right edge and bottom edge of the screen. To move one line at a time, move the cursor to the arrow box and click. To move a screen at a time, put the cursor anywhere in the gray area and click. To move a distance of your own choosing, place the cursor on the white scroll bar and drag it to the new position. Figure 2-11 shows how to use these three movement options.

In addition to the scroll bars on the side of the screen, you'll also see scroll bars in the sidebar, and in the item selectors. These smaller scroll bars operate in precisely the same manner, except that they move you up and down a list of files or other items.

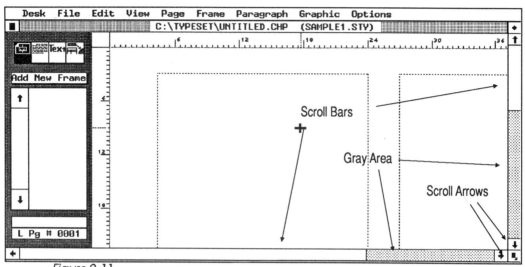

Figure 2-11
The three scroll options in Ventura Publisher.

While we're talking about moving around, let's discuss two ways to move to another page. You can (1) press the Page Up and Page Down keys on the numeric keypad which moves one page at a time or (2) use the GO TO PAGE function in the paragraph menu, which allows you to move to a page number of your choice.

Menus

Ventura has an abundance of features scattered amongst its nine menus. Learning these menus and what they control is one of the biggest challenges to mastering the program. Although the name of a Ventura menu is not always a good guide to what it's used for, Table 2-1 will give you a general idea of where to find things. Later chapters will go into greater depth about menus and their functions.

As you move through the menus, you'll notice some items listed in gray rather than black. This means they're not currently available for use. If, for example, you are *not* in the graphic drawing mode and you pull down the graphics menu, you'll find all the items shown in gray. You will be unable to highlight and select any of them. But change to graphics

Table 2-1
Ventura Publisher's Menus

Menu	Purpose
Desk	Used only if you add the GEM Desktop
File	To open and close certain kinds of files
Edit	Cutting, copying, and pasting text and graphics. Also contains certain footnote, indexing, and file functions
View	Selecting different ways of viewing the document and different modes of operation
Page	Functions that apply to every page in the document (page numbers, headers and footers, etc.)
Frame	Functions that apply to a Frame as a whole (margins, columns, background colors, etc.)
Paragraph	Functions that apply to the text within the Frame (fonts, line spacing, etc.)
Graphic	Drawing functions
Options	Functions that alter Ventura to suit you, or that expand its utility

drawing mode and you'll find the menu items in black. They are now be available for use.

Keys

Although you can accomplish most functions with the mouse and the menus, Ventura does assign special functions to certain keys. In addition, Ventura provides keyboard shortcuts for some functions. These shortcuts are listed to the right of the name when the menu drops down. Figure 2-12 lists Ventura's key assignments for general functions and its keyboard shortcuts.

Dialog Boxes

Ventura is a rich, full-featured program with many options. Dialog boxes choose and control those options. Dialog boxes appear after you make a selection from a menu (see Figure 2-13).

In our brief tutorial, we saw the dialog box for loading text and pictures. You may have noticed that some of its buttons were shown in gray type. As with Ventura's menus, gray type

Key	Purpose
Arrow keys on keypad	In text editing function, controls the movement of the text cursor (blinking vertical line). The arrow keys move the text cursor any direction without erasing the characters it passes over.
Alt	Used in conjunction with other keys. In the frame setting function, press and hold Alt while pressing and holding the mouse button to move images behind a frame. In Text editing function, press and hold the Alt key to type the numeric equivalent of a character that does not appear on the keyboard.
Backspace	Deletes the character to the left of the text cursor—a "destructive backspace."
Ctrl	Used in conjunction with other keys. See below for a list of control key combinations for keyboard shortcuts. in text editing, press and hold while pressing the space bar to insert a non- breaking space. Press and hold while pressing the hyphen to insert a discretionary hyphen..in graphic drawing, press and hold while pressing the mouse button to select graphics that are hidden behind others.
Del	In the frame setting function, deletes the frame that is currently selected. In the text editing function and in dialog boxes and item selectors, deletes the character to the right of the text cursor. in the graphic drawing function, deletes the selected graphic from the page.
End	Goes to the last page of the document.
Esc	In dialog boxes, deletes all characters on the line. Also used to halt printing and Go To Page operations. At all other times, pressing the Escape key redraws the screen.
Home	Goes to the first page of the document. If a mouse is not present, then pressing Home becomes the equivalent of clicking the mouse button once.
Ins	Pastes the item that is currently on the clipboard. In the frame setting function, pastes a frame to the current page. In the text editing function, pastes text. In the graphic drawing function, pastes a graphic.
Shift	In all four functions, used in conjunction with the mouse to select more than one item at a time. In frame setting and graphic drawing functions, pressing Shift keeps the tool enabled so you can draw several in a row.
Shift Del	In the frame setting, text editing and graphic drawing functions, copies the selected item.
Function Keys	Each of the 10 function keys can be assigned to one of the tags from the paragraph menu. These function key equivalents can be used to tag paragraphs while in the text editing function. (Normally, you must return to the paragraph tagging function and use the mouse to tag a paragraph).
Tab	In the text editing function, inserts tab characters. In dialog boxes and item selectors, moves the text cursor to the next line or the next place where text could be inserted.

Figure 2-12
The key assignments within Ventura Publisher.

Keyboard Shortcuts

Modes

^I	Paragraph Tagging
^O	Text Editing
^P	Graphic Drawing
^U	Frame Setting

General

^B	Renumber chapter
^S	Save
Del	Cut
Ins	Paste
Shift	Del Copy
^2	Addition button

Graphics

^A	Bring to front
^F	Fill attributes
^L	Line attributes
^Q	Select all
^Z	Send to back

Movement

^G	Go to page
Pg Up	Go to previous page
Pg Dn	Go to next page
End	Go to last page of document
Home	Go to first page of document

Viewing

^E	Enlarged view
^N	Normal view
^R	Reduced view
^T	Show/Hide Tabs & Returns
^W	Show/Hide Side-Bar

Figure 2-12 (continued)

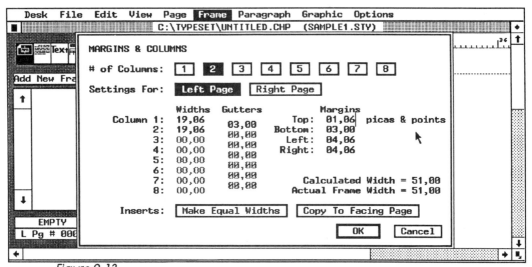

Figure 2-13
Clicking on the measurement units in a dialog box (e.g. "Picas & Points") changes
to another unit of measure.

means the item is not currently available for selection. To
choose a grayed item, you must first enable that feature. Occasionally you must go to another menu or to the sidebar to
turn on a feature, but usually you'll find a button in the same
dialog box.

Tips for Working with Dialog Boxes

Dialog boxes are prepared to accept information as soon as
the box appears on the screen. Normally the text cursor is
already blinking on the first line in the dialog box.

You can move the text cursor in three ways. First, simply
point to the new space and click once with the mouse.
Second, use the arrow keys on the numerical keypad—just
press the direction you want to move. Or third, move with
the tab key. Each time you press Tab, the text cursor jumps
to the next space.

However you move the text cursor, it usually jumps to the
end of the space. If the space is empty, you can start typing
and Ventura will fill in from the front. You can erase characters simply by backspacing over them. You can also clear the
entire line by pressing Escape.

♦ *Note: Do not mistake the backspace key (located at the upper right of the keyboard) with the left arrow key (located on the numeric keypad). The former deletes characters as it moves left; the latter merely passes over them.*

Ventura uses Enter as a shortcut for clicking on the OK Button. If you press Enter, the program will assume you are finished using the dialog box.

If you change your mind, click on the cancel button to return to where you were. Don't worry about clearing the settings— if you select Cancel, Ventura will ignore any changes made in the dialog box.

To change the units of measurement touch the name of the units with the mouse cursor and click once (see Figure 2-13). Click again, and the units will change again. At any time, you can toggle between these four choices:

- Inches
- Centimeters
- Picas & Points
- Fractional Points

When you reach the end, the cycle starts over. As you change, the program automatically recalculates the values. Inches are converted to centimeters; centimeters to picas & points, etc. Once in a while you may see ~ (the tilde character). The measurement has not been lost. It is simply too big, or too small, to display in the space. Convert to different units to see it reappear.

Be careful when entering picas & points. Consider, for example, the measurement 4 1/2 picas. You might be tempted to enter 4,5. In actuality, Ventura will interpret this as 4 picas and 50 points. Since 1 pica equals 12 points, the correct way to enter 4 1/2 picas is as 4 picas and 6 points. This is written as 4,06.

♦ *Warning: Don't forget the all-important zero when entering picas & points. If you enter 4,6 in the example above, Ventura will interpret it as 4 picas and 60 points. You must precede the points with a zero: 4,06.*

Refer to the Box at the end of this chapter for more information on picas, points, and other basics of printing terminology.

Item Selectors

Dialog Boxes are used to choose options and enter measurements. To choose *files*, Ventura uses a special type of dialog box called an *item selector*. When you see the phrase item selector, think file selector and you'll be on the right track.

An item selector shows up anytime Ventura needs to know which file you want to use. To use item selectors, you must understand four concepts: (1) how to choose files with the mouse, (2) how to choose files directly by typing their names, (3) how to filter files, and (4) how to change subdirectories and disk drives.

Choosing A file with the Mouse

Make sure the file name appears on the item selector list. If you don't see it, use the scroll bar or scroll buttons until it shows. Select it by clicking on the name. Notice how the file name appears in the previously blank selection line as soon as you click. This is your confirmation that you've chosen the correct file. Once you've got the right file, click OK.

Choosing Files Directly

To bypass the mouse, simply type in the file name directly. When the item selector appears, you'll see that the blinking text cursor is already on the selection line. To enter a file name, just start typing. Click OK when you're done. If you type the wrong name, press Backspace to erase the characters, or press Escape to clear the entire line and start over. If you change your mind, click on Cancel and Ventura will return you to the document.

Use the selection line to bypass the mouse, to name a file that does not yet exist, or to create a new name for an existing file.

File Filtering

Filtering excludes files that would otherwise clutter up the item selector. Look again at Figure 2-2. This item selector appeared when we loaded text during our tutorial. Notice the three-word file extension .TXT on the directory line. Ventura knows that ASCII graphics files should carry this extension. When you tell it to load a TXT file, it automatically filters out all others.

Although you can enter your own filters, Ventura has a list of file extensions it prefers to use. When you tell Ventura that you want to load, for example, a MultiMate text file, it remembers the subdirectory and the file extension you used last time. If you change either of these, Ventura will remember the changes the next time you load MultiMate files.

How do you change the file filter? Simply by placing the text cursor on the directory line, typing in the new extension and clicking OK. Ventura will immediately filter out all files except those that match the new extension.

So far we've been talking about filtering with file extensions. Those familiar with MS-DOS have probably guessed that you can also use the standard MS-DOS conventions to make further filters. For example, when writing this book, we started all our files with the two-letter code VP. Anytime we wanted to see only the chapters for our book, we had only to type in VP*.CHP to eliminate any files that did not start with VP and end with .CHP.

Changing Subdirectories and Disk Drives

Ventura Publisher is an intelligent program. When it places an item selector on the screen, it guesses which type of file you want and where it is likely to be found. You can see the result of its guess on the directory line. If you now choose a different subdirectory, Ventura will remember. The next time it opens this item selector, Ventura will start off with the last subdirectory you used.

It's easy to change subdirectories and disk drives. One simple method is identical to the way we changed file filters: Place the text cursor on the directory line and type in the name of the new subdirectory (and/or the new disk drive). As soon as you click OK, Ventura will switch to the new subdirectory.

Another method uses the backup button (see Figure 2-14). Clicking the backup button takes you to the next highest level directory. Suppose the directory line now shows C:\TYPESET\ARTICLES. Pressing the backup button will move up one level and the directory line will now read C:\TYPESET. Pressing it again will move up to the final, root level, and the directory line will read C:\.

When you click the backup button, the list of files will change to show what is available in the new subdirectory. As you browse through the list, you may see names preceded with a diamond character (see Figure 2-14). These are subdirectories. To move to a new subdirectory, click once on the name, as if selecting a file. The directory line will change, and you will find yourself in the new subdirectory.

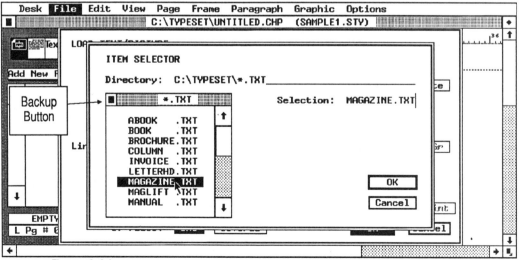

Figure 2-14
Clicking on the backup button in an item selector causes Ventura Publisher to move up one level from the current directory.

If you backup enough times, you will eventually see only the disk drive letters in the list. To move to a new drive, click on the one you want.

You can also type in the letter of the new drive on the directory line and click OK. If your disk drive does not appear, this is the only way to reach it. Type the drive and the subdirectory name on the directory line and then select OK.

Tips for Using Item Selectors

To make files appear at the top of the item selector list for quick and easy reference, simply precede the file name with a symbol. The file list is displayed alphabetically, and symbols are placed before the letters of the alphabet.

Dialog boxes will sometimes refuse to accept a filename without a three-letter extension. To select a file without an extension, type a period followed by three spaces.

You can also activate the OK Button by pressing the Enter key. You'll see the OK button turn dark just as if you'd selected it with the mouse. This shortcut works in dialog boxes, too. Anytime you see an OK button, you can select it by pressing Enter.

To make file selection faster, move the cursor over the file name and click twice rapidly instead of once. If you press twice in a row without a pause, the second click will activate the OK button. This method is faster, but it does have one slight disadvantage. If you've slipped and selected the wrong file by mistake, you won't have any opportunity to check your choice by looking at the selection line.

You can vary the speed of the double click option using SET PREFERENCES from the options menu. If you choose fast, you must click very rapidly to invoke the double click shortcut. If you choose slow you can wait longer between clicks and Ventura will still recognize it as a double click shortcut.

The Sidebar

We've learned a good deal about Ventura's user interface already. We've seen how it uses the mouse, the keys, and dialog boxes. These elements were pioneered by the research done at Xerox Palo Alto Research Center. They have become more or less standard in "graphic environments."

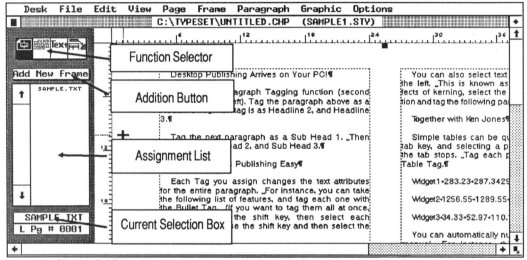

Figure 2-15
The elements of the sidebar.

But there's one portion of the Ventura interface that's not like anything else— the sidebar. This unique feature gives Ventura much of its power, flexibility, and speed.

The Function Selector

Figure 2-15 shows the sidebar with its parts labeled. At the top is the function selector, whose four icons control Ventura's four modes of operation:

Mode	Purpose
Frame setting	Create or select a frame to place text or pictures
Paragraph tagging	Change a style sheet and apply it to text
Text editing	Create or modify text
Graphic drawing	Create or modify pictures

You can change modes in three ways. You can select the
proper icon from the function selector. You can choose the
mode from the view menu. Or you can use the keyboard
shortcuts. These shortcuts are shown on the view menu next
to the names of the modes.

The four icons at the top of the sidebar do not change.
Likewise, the page number box at the bottom always shows
which page you are on. But the rest of the sidebar changes according to the mode you are in. Spend some time familiarizing
yourself with the information found in the sidebar. Often it's
the key to figuring out what's going on in the workspace.

Frame setting is the mode in which you select and operate
on frames, the containers into which we pour text and pictures. In this mode you can choose which frame you want,
load text and pictures into it, change its size, add a new
frame, or change frame attributes such as margins and
columns.

In the frame setting mode:

- The addition button reads "add new frame." Select this
  button to draw a new frame on a page (as we
  demonstrated in the test drive).

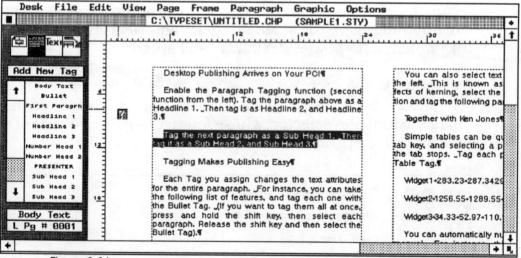

Figure 2-16
The sidebar in paragraph tagging mode. The assignment list shows the tags
available for use.

- The assignment list changes to display all the files currently available to be placed onto the page, whether text or pictures. If you don't see any names in the assignment list, you have not yet loaded a file.

- The current selection box shows the name of the file in the active frame. If the frame contains no files yet, it shows the word Empty. If you have not selected a frame, it is blank.

Paragraph tagging is the mode in which you apply tags from the style sheet to text.

- The addition button reads "add new tag." Select it to create an entirely new tag that is not already listed.

- The assignment list displays all the tags for the current style sheet.

- The current selection box remains blank until you select a paragraph from the document. Then it shows the tag assigned to that paragraph, as shown in Figure 2-16.

Text editing mode is used to alter text files that have been loaded into the document (See Figure 2-17).

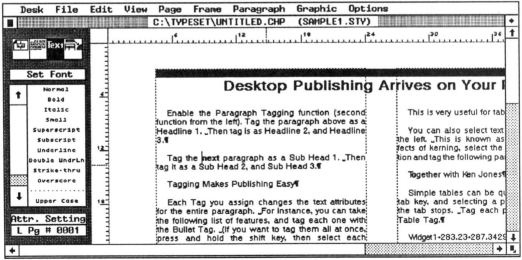

Figure 2-17
The sidebar in text editing mode. The assignment list shows the attributes available to be applied to text.

Figure 2-18
The sidebar in graphics drawing mode.

- The addition button shows "set font." Use it to change
  the font attributes of a few words within a paragraph (to
  change the entire paragraph, use the paragraph menu
  while in paragraph tagging mode).

- The assignment list displays the attributes (normal,
  bold, italic, etc.) available to apply to the text.

- The current selection box is empty when the cursor is
  over normal text. But text files also include marks that
  are usually not visible, such as the signals to turn
  italics on or off, to end a paragraph, to create a tab, and
  so on. When you move the cursor over one of these
  "invisible" marks, the term "attr. setting" appears in the
  current selection box.

Graphics drawing mode is used to create and modify drawings (see Figure 2-18).

- The addition button and the assignment list disappear
  to be replaced by six buttons. These buttons represent
  Ventura's six drawing tools.

- The current selection box shows the name of the tool now in use.

Frames and Pages

Think of frames as containers for text and graphics. In addition, frames specify attributes like margins and columns. Ventura's frame menu lists these attributes and lets you change them as you want.

Ventura makes things even easier by automatically drawing the first frame in a special frame is called the underlying page. Its boundaries are the edges of the paper and it automatically repeats itself for every page of the document. Most of the rules of ordinary frames apply to the underlying page, which differs only in these ways:

- It is created automatically.

- Its boundaries are the edges of the paper.

- It repeats on each page.

- Text flows automatically from page to page.

- It cannot be moved or copied.

If every page of your document has the same format, you won't need anything more than the underlying page frame. Usually, however, you'll want to modify certain pages. For example, you might want to place a picture onto a page, as we did in the tutorial. Or you might want to create a newsletter or magazine where virtually every page has a different layout. Chapter Six, Document Design and Layout, explains the layout process and the use of frames.

Chapter Files

The chapter file is the blueprint for the document. It lists all the elements and where they belong:

- Which text files to use and where to put them.

- Which graphics files to include.

- Which style sheet to apply.

In short, the chapter file stores a description of the document, the "addresses" of the files on the disk, and the order and manner in which they appear. Here is a list of the information stored in chapter files:

- File information
  - File names and locations
  - File placement

- Frame information
  - Frame margins
  - Frame columns
  - Frame ruling lines
  - Frame size
  - Frame background

- Numbering information
  - Starting page number
  - Starting chapter number
  - Starting table/figure number

- Other information
  - Headers and footers
  - Footnote settings

The first time you save a document, Ventura automatically builds a chapter file with this information. This file always has the extension CHP. When you load an existing document, do so by selecting OPEN CHAPTER from the file menu. Although you could achieve the same effect by loading the text, pictures and style sheet separately, there's no need to go to the trouble. Simply load the chapter file, and Ventura will use it to reload all the files and rebuild the document in its entirety.

Text + Pictures + Style Sheet = Document

Figure 2-19
The Ventura Formula.

The Ventura Formula

We've now concluded our look at Ventura's basic concepts and terminology. You need only one more fundamental principle before you're ready to tackle the rest of this book: The Ventura Formula.

As Figure 2-19 shows, the formula is a simple one: Text plus pictures plus style sheet equals a document. No matter what kind of documents you produce, the Ventura formula always holds true. The next few chapters explain each part of the formula in depth. Here's a preview:

Text

Ventura Publisher works directly with text files from leading word processors (it can also produce text files on its own). Ventura uses text files for two purposes. The first is to store text and its attributes (boldface, italicized, underlined, etc.). The second is to store tags, the special codes that tell Ventura what part of the document each text element represents—whether it's a headline, body text, a subheading, and so on.

Pictures

Most Ventura pictures come from outside files (it can also produce simple pictures on its own). Those files may be created by graphics programs, or by scanners (devices which scan pictures on paper to create an electronic description suitable for use by a computer). As with text, Ventura deals with the original file. But it does not change or modify that file, no matter what changes you make to the image after you bring it into Ventura. Rather, Ventura uses its own separate chapter file to store a *pointer* to the original picture, along with instructions on how to display it.

Style Sheets

Style sheets are the key to unlocking Ventura's advanced functions. As mentioned above, Ventura places tags into the original text files. These tags are notes that tell Ventura things like "Make these three words a headline" or "make the next five items into a list," and so on.

How does Ventura know how to format these tags? Simple—it creates a separate file known as the *style sheet*. This style sheet contains the format rules for the tags. For example: "Set all headlines in 36 point Helvetica Bold type with a 1 point rule underneath" or "Indent list items 1/2 inch and precede them with a bullet character."

This chapter has outlined the basic structure of Ventura Publisher. Now it's time to learn how to become productive. We'll start that process in the next chapter, which explores the first part of the Ventura formula: Text.

The Language of Pages and Typography

For those who are new to publishing, we are concluding this chapter with a special section on the terminology of page design. Even those with experience in printing and publishing may want to glance through this brief section, because it defines key words and terms *as used by Ventura Publisher and this book.* In a few cases, there may be differences between the traditional meanings and the definitions used by Ventura.

Measuring a Page

Ventura is outstanding in its ability to measure in different ways. You can choose from three methods: (1) inches, (2) centimeters, or (3) picas and points.

You're probably more familiar with inches or centimeters, but we suggest you learn to use picas and points, which are part of a system called *printer's measure.* Since type sizes are always specified this way, it makes sense to use printer's measure for everything on the page. Otherwise you spend too much time converting back and forth.

Points and Picas

Points are very small units, about 1/72 of an inch, but they are very important. They are used to measure the size of type, the size of rules and the spacing between lines. You'll use them constantly as you work with Ventura Publisher.

The point size of a typeface is determined by its lowercase letters. It is roughly the measurement from the highest ascender (the top of a "b" for instance) to the lowest descender (the bottom of a "g").

The best way to get comfortable with points is simply to start using them in practice. As we move through this book, we'll constantly be mentioning the sizes of type we use for our various examples. And as you use Ventura, you'll constantly be specifying sizes on your own. Since Ventura lets you see the results of your changes instantly, it only takes a few weeks before you can spot type sizes at a glance.

Picas are larger units, equal to 12 points or about 1/6 of an inch. (Don't confuse picas with the typewriter style of the same name.) Printers use picas to measure lines, margins and columns. Once again, the best way to get comfortable with picas is simply to start using them. Soon they'll become second nature. If you get confused, you can always switch Ventura's rulers or dialog boxes back to inches or centimeters.

One of the advantages of using picas to measure distances in Ventura Publisher is that the number 6 (as in picas per inch) is divisible by 3. Thus, if you are working with a three-column layout, you will end up with even values on your ruler and in your dialog boxes. For example, if you wish to divide a live area of 7 inches (42 picas) into three equal columns, you would end up with three columns of 13 picas with 1 1/2 picas space between each column. Using inches or centimeters, it would be impossible to express 13 picas exactly; you would need to approximate it with decimals.

Ems and Ens

Ems and ens are two other units of traditional printer's measure. They are used to measure blank space, and they vary according to the size of the type. The em space is always equal to the point size. In 12-point type, the em space is 12 points. In 18 point type it is 18, and so on. An en is 1/2 the em. In 12-point type, then, the en is 6 points; in 18-point type it is 9 points, and so on.

Typographical Terminology

Although ems and ens are not very important when it comes to measuring the page, they are used to describe to describe indents and dashes. They are two of the half dozen or so typographical terms you should know to work efficiently with Ventura.

Em dashes are equal to the em size—12 points in 12-point type, 18 points in 18-point type, and so on. Em dashes are used to separate two words in a sentence, as in the first sentence of this paragraph. The standard computer keyboard does not include a character for the em dash. Chapter Three explains how to insert em dashes and other special characters into your text files so they will be properly printed in Ventura.

En dashes are half the size of the em. They are used to separate numbers in a range, such as 1967–1969.

There are several other typographical characters you should learn to recognize if you want your pages to look truly professional.

Open and close quotes are among the most important new characters you should learn. A typewriter uses a single set of marks for quotations, whether those marks come at the beginning (open) or the end (close) of the quote. But true typeset materials have two separate symbols, one for opening quotes and one for closing quotes. Take a good look at this next phrase: "sample typeset quotation." Notice how the marks slant in a different direction at the beginning and the end? Now look at this typewritten version: "sample typewritten quotation." The marks are upright and identical.

Unfortunately, computer keyboards have only the one quote mark key left over from typewriter days. Chapter Three explains how to overcome this limitation and insert true open and close quotes into your text. It also explains how to insert other special symbols, even if they do not show up on your computer keyboard.

Thin and figure spaces are two additional space characters. The thin space is half the size of the en space. The figure space is equal to the width of a numeral. It is useful when typesetting tabular or financial material.

Font is another important typographical term you will see constantly when using Ventura. It refers to the size and style of type.

Printers use several different terms to describe different kinds of type: typestyles, typefaces, type families, type fonts. Ventura Publisher uses the word font. When you choose the set font option, Ventura allows you to change the *size*, the *style*, and the *attributes* of the type.

The size of the type is measured in points, as explained above. The style of the type is determined in part by the printer you use. Ventura will let you select from any of the typestyles supported by your printer.

Different type designs are called *typefaces* or *typestyles*. There are upwards of 3,000 typefaces, each of which has a name, such as Century, Helvetica, Times Roman, Souvenir and so on. One particular variety of a typeface is called a *font*. Helvetica is a typeface. Twelve point Helvetica Bold is a font.

Typefaces fall into several categories. The two most important are *Serif* and *sans serif*. Serifs are the curlicues that decorate the ends of letters. A serif typestyle is one that contains these curlicues. "Sans" is the French word for *without*, so a sans serif typeface is one that does not have them.

You will also encounter *pi and symbol fonts*. These are typefaces composed of pi characters, which are special symbols such as stars, bullets, ampersands, dingbats, math symbols and so on.

A single typeface can have many *attributes*. Attributes refer to the weight and slope of the type. Think of the weight of type as the thickness of the letterstrokes, or the amount of ink.

Another way to modify type is to change its slope. Normal type is straight up and down. If we slant the type, we refer to the new version as *italics*. Italics are often used to call attention to words within a sentence.

Ventura lets you combine attributes. You can, for example, choose to make a typestyle both bold and italics. Remember that Ventura "knows" which printer you are using. If that printer cannot support certain attributes or combinations of attributes, they will be shown in gray in the Dialog Box and you will be unable to select them.

Spacing is one final typographical definition you should understand before working with Ventura Publisher. In the old days, space between lines was called leading (pronounced ledding). The term came from the practice of putting strips of lead between lines to create extra space.

Ventura very logically refers to this as line spacing. You specify line spacing by selecting SPACING from the paragraph menu. If you do not specify anything, Ventura will automatically space the lines according to an internal formula.

With the definitions and explanations of this special section, you have the basic nomenclature you need to start work with Ventura. To simplify matters, we are ending this section with a short list of Ventura terms that might be confusing to a first time user.

Term	How Ventura Uses This Term
Attribute	The weight and slope of a typestyle, as in bold, light, normal, italics.
Chapter	Any single document that is edited at one time. Chapters can be printed in sequence to form longer documents.
Document	The Ventura manual uses this word to refer to a chapter. This book uses the word to mean a publication in the everyday sense.
Font	A particular variety of type, including the size, style, weight and slope, e.g. 12 point Times Roman Bold Italics.
Frame	A box or container which provides boundaries for text and graphics. A frame can be any size up to the size of the entire page.
Item Selector	A special kind of dialog box used to select files.
Paragraph	Any unique element of the document that can be described with a tag.
Tag	An element of a Ventura Publisher style sheet containing a consistent set of type and format specifications.
Underlying Page	A special frame automatically created whenever you start a new document in Ventura. Its boundaries are the edge of the page.

Chapter Three

Creating Text

Ventura Publisher possesses a rich set of features for creating impressive documents. But the most important element of any document is the text. After all, it is the written word that conveys the message.

A desktop publishing program, even one as powerful as Ventura Publisher, cannot produce well-written text. What it *can* do is make text creation as simple as possible. That way, you can concentrate on perfecting your writing rather than on mastering a new and confusing tool. Ventura Publisher was created with this philosophy in mind.

Sounds good. I just use my word processor like always—right? Not quite. There are several tricks you should know, simple techniques that smooth the process. This chapter includes general instructions, plus comments on specific word processing, spreadsheet, and database programs. At the end of the chapter, we've added a section that offers a quick, painless way to "preformat" word processing files so layout is even simpler.

This chapter focuses on creating text *before* you bring it into Ventura Publisher. Chapter Six, Document Design and

Layout, discusses how to bring text in, lay it out on the page, and make changes to this text using Ventura's built-in editing functions.

The Ventura Publisher Approach to Text

Most writers are comfortable with a particular word processing program. They have mastered its features and can create text files quickly, painlessly, and reliably. With Ventura Publisher, there's no need to throw away this investment of time and effort. Ventura Publisher works directly with most leading word processing programs. It can even work with database software, spreadsheet software, and programming languages.

There's another important benefit to Ventura Publisher's approach. Few documents are created, formatted, and printed in one pass. Revisions are almost always required. Fortunately, Ventura Publisher preserves all changes in the original text file. So go ahead and make corrections *during* page layout—those corrections will automatically be saved to the text file. And feel free to edit word processing files *after* they've been formatted with Ventura Publisher. Your edits will be incorporated the next time you bring that document into Ventura.

General Rules for Creating Text

As we've already seen, Ventura Publisher views writing, illustration and layout as three separate tasks:

Text + Pictures + Style Sheet = Document.

Consequently, when creating text for Ventura Publisher, you should concentrate on writing, not on formatting. Do not consider final attributes such as fonts, margins, columns, indents, footers, and so on. These factors will be taken care of later, when you bring the text into Ventura.

What's that mean while writing? Just this: Although your word processor has commands for margins, headers, indents, and other formatting options, don't use them. Formatting decisions made with the word processor will only be overridden by Ventura Publisher anyway.

Ventura Publisher also ignores extra spaces between words, if those spaces were inserted by the word processor to justify the margins. (These spaces are called "soft" or "discretionary" spaces to distinguish them from the "hard" spaces you insert when you touch the space bar.) It is thus of little use to justify text with the word processor. Ventura Publisher adjusts lines according to the fonts and column widths of the actual printed page, not those of the word processor. In fact, justifying text in the word processor can throw off certain Ventura tab functions.

It is also important to remember *not* to insert spaces or tabs at the beginning of a paragraph— even if you want the first line of each paragraph indented in the printed document. Let Ventura Publisher create the indent. That way you'll have the luxury of changing your mind. With a single Ventura command, you will be able to change the amount of the indent or turn it off entirely throughout the document.

Since Ventura Publisher handles spacing, there is one adjustment you should make in your typing style. Touch typists are trained to insert two spaces after a period or a colon. Instead, you should type only one space. Otherwise, the extra space causes *rivers*, unsightly gaps of white space that spoil the look of a page.

Tab Stops

We do not recommend using tab stops in the text files you create for Ventura. Chapter Nine, Special Tips & Techniques, gives suggestions on how to format tables using separate tags instead of tab stops.

Nevertheless, there are certain occasions that demand the use of tab stops. You must take two steps to make them work successfully with Ventura: (1) insert true tab characters and (2) insert only one tab stop between columns.

Ventura Publisher recognizes tabs as long as they are "real" tabs. When you press the tab key, some word processors insert the actual ASCII tab character, ^I (control I). Others simp-

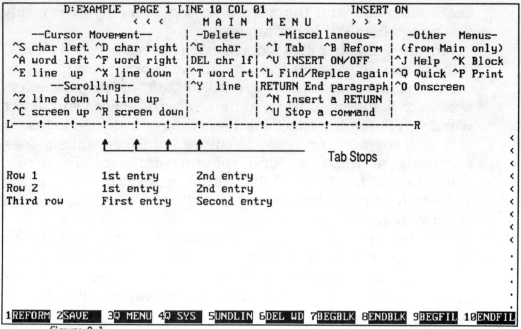

Figure 3-1
Formatting a table within your word processor often requires you to hit the tab key
several times. Tables in Ventura Publisher should have only one tab between
columns.

ly insert a string of spaces. Still others— like WordStar 3.3— let
you choose. Ventura Publisher will not recognize a string of
spaces as a tab, even if those spaces were inserted by pressing the tab key. If your word processor cannot insert the true
tab character, you must insert ^I manually into the file.

♦ *In WordStar 4 document mode, you must press ^P^I or ^P-Tab
to insert a true tab character.*

Inserting true tab characters is the first hurdle. The second
problem is inserting one and only one tab stop between
columns. Here's what often goes wrong: Many word processors have predefined tab settings at regular intervals. When
typing a simple two-column list, as in Figure 3-1, you press
the tab key several times to get the cursor over to the right
column. Each time you press the key, you are inserting
another tab stop. When you later use Ventura Publisher to
format that two-column list, Ventura expects to find only one

tab stop between the left column and the right. Instead, the file may contain as many as five or six.

So the second rule for tabular material is to insert one and *only* one tab stop between each column.

If you want to go to the trouble, you can set the tab stops on the screen so they approximate the final appearance on the page. Do so if this makes it easier for you or your typists. But the screen appearance doesn't matter to Ventura Publisher. All that matters is that you (1) insert a true tab character instead of spaces and (2) insert only one tab between columns.

Underlining, Italics, and Other Text Attributes

Ventura Publisher supports certain text attributes entered directly in the word processor. If you enter the word processing command to make a word boldface, for example, the word will also appear bold when the file is loaded into Ventura.

Feel free to use these attributes, but only to create an effect for one or two words within a paragraph. If you want an entire paragraph to be bold, type it normally. After bringing the file into Ventura, you will tag this entire paragraph with a bold font. When creating a large, bold headline, for example, don't bother to use the bold command from the word processor. Instead, choose a large, bold font in Ventura.

On the other hand, if you want a single bold word or phrase within an otherwise normal paragraph, use the word processor command. You can also wait and use Ventura's text editing mode to create the same effect, but it's generally best for authors to specify special text effects as they are typing. Otherwise it is easy to overlook or forget which words are intended for special emphasis.

This brings up the subject of italics, one of the most widely used text attributes. Although Ventura supports italics, many word processors, including WordStar 3.3, do not have an italics function. Nearly all word processors support underlining. But be aware that words are generally not underlined in typeset text. Instead, underlined words from typewritten manuscripts are converted to italics.

How should authors handle italics while creating text? One method is to continue the standard practice of using underlines to represent italics. Ventura supports underlining, so the words and phrases will still be underlined on the Ventura screen. The editor can then find and convert them to italics. A second method is to insert Ventura's italics command directly into the word processing file as it is typed. This method is explained in the advanced section at the end of the chapter.

Non-Breaking Spaces

Ventura Publisher will recognize non-breaking spaces from most word processors. Nonbreaking spaces are useful when you don't want words separated. Examples include brand names, like Lotus 1-2-3 and measurements, such as 43.8 cm. The unit of measurement (cm) should always be on the same line with the numerical value. An ordinary space inserted would allow the two to become separated if 43.8 came at the end of the line— the "cm" would be dropped to the beginning of the next line. To prevent this, enter a non-breaking space. This appears on the printed page as a normal space, but it forces the two words to remain on the same line.

The word processors supported by Ventura have commands for non-breaking spaces. Enter the command in the text file to create a non-breaking space in Ventura. You can also create non-breaking spaces while in Ventura Publisher's built-in text editing mode.

Discretionary Hyphens

Ventura Publisher will recognize "soft" or discretionary hyphens from most word processors. It will use these hyphenation points if necessary to justify a line. However, Ventura automatically hyphenates files as it loads them, making the use of discretionary hyphens somewhat redundant. It is true, however, that the Ventura hyphenation routine will occasionally miss opportunities for hyphenation. It sometimes inserts fewer discretionary hyphens than possible (but it will rarely insert too many). Some people may wish to add extra hyphenation points to certain words to improve the appearance of justified lines. However, we recommend that these hyphenation points be permanently added to the hyphenation dictionary as explained in Chapter Eight, Advanced Functions. For this reason, it is unlikely you will have much use for discretionary hyphens while creating text with a word processor.

♦ *Note: You can suppress automatic hyphenation for an individual word by placing a discretionary hyphen after the word.*

Spell Checking

We recommend using a spelling checker *before* loading word processing files into Ventura. Ventura inserts special codes into the word processing document to indicate tags, text attributes, fonts and so on. If you check the file after it has been loaded and saved by Ventura, the spell checking software will report these codes as misspelled words.

If you do heavy editing while in Ventura, however, you may feel you need to spell check afterwards. Since Ventura uses the original word processing files, you won't have any compatibility problems with the spell checker. You will, however, need to add the tag names and codes to the user dictionary so the spell checker will realize they are not misspellings.

Naming Files

Ventura Publisher uses default file extensions for different word processing programs. This does have some value for those who routinely use files from different word processing programs. A glance at the extension will show which format the file is in. We suggest you develop naming conventions to help manage large batches of files. For example, the extension TXT could be used to indicate ASCII text files while WP could indicate a WordPerfect file.

Converting File Formats

Ventura can be used to convert text files from one word processor format to another. Editors might, for example, collect material from several different authors using several different word processors. To facilitate copy editing or spell checking, they might want to convert them all to a common format.

To convert a file, bring it into Ventura using the procedures spelled out in Chapter Six. With frame setting still enabled, choose FILE TYPE/RENAME from the edit menu. When the dialog box appears, pick out the new file format (if you choose a new name as well you will preserve the old file in the old format).

That's all there is to it. The file will be saved to the new format the next time you save the chapter.

Tips for Creating Text

Let's summarize what we've learned so far about creating text for Ventura Publisher. Remember, these are general rules that apply to any text file, regardless of the word processing program:

Don't worry about formatting commands. You will create margins, columns, headers and do all the other formatting in Ventura Publisher. Just type the text flush left with any margins you like.

♦ *Note: The authors of this book often create word processing files for books and newsletters that will later be formatted with Ventura Publisher. We like to set our word processing margins to approximate the amount of text in the final column. For instance, when producing this book, we discovered that a word processing column 52 characters wide was roughly equivalent to one line on the printed page. Although only an approximation, this technique helps writers gauge the proper length for sentences and paragraphs.*

Don't indent the first line of a paragraph, even if you want an indent on the printed page. You'll do the indenting in Ventura Publisher.

Do not justify the text. Ventura Publisher will handle the justification. At best you are wasting your time to justify

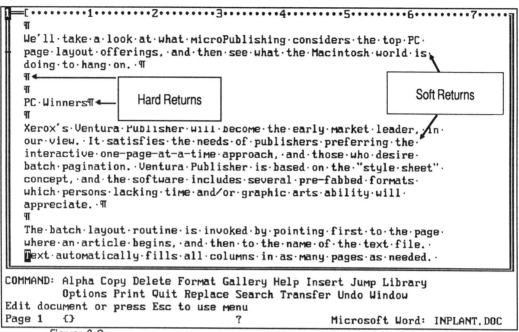

Figure 3-2
In Microsoft Word, soft returns are placed at the end of each screen line.

while using the word processor. At worst, you could cause problems with certain tabular functions.

Do not center text. You are only creating extra work for yourself. You'll have to remove the extra spaces before using Ventura Publisher's built-in centering command to place it accurately in the middle of the printed page, or centered across a column.

Insert only one space after periods and colons. Double-spacing will detract from the appearance of the final document.

Don't insert spaces after the last sentence in a paragraph. It is possible that these spaces could create an unwanted empty line in your document.

Insert only one tab stop between columns in a table. Make sure your word processor inserts the actual ^I tab character, not just spaces.

The tips listed above apply to all word processing programs. Some techniques, however, vary slightly from program to program. Let's explore some of the different word processing, database, and spreadsheet programs you can use to create text for Ventura Publisher.

Formatting ASCII Files

ASCII is the most widely accepted text standard for personal computers. Think of ASCII as a generic brand—the plain vanilla version of text. ASCII does not support sophisticated text or document formatting, but this is only a minor shortcoming since Ventura Publisher ignores most word processor commands anyway.

We're starting with ASCII because it's the lowest common denominator. Even if your word processor isn't directly supported by Ventura Publisher, you can translate files into ASCII format.

ASCII files require one special condition not necessary in any of the other word processing formats. To understand this requirement, we must introduce the concept of hard and soft returns.

A hard return starts a new line. Your word processor inserts a hard return whenever you press the key marked Enter, Return, or ↵. Hard returns show up as special symbols in the margin or the end of a line (see Figure 3-2). They are very important to Ventura Publisher, because they differentiate paragraphs.

Soft returns start a new line *only if there's no more room on the screen.* Think of them as "temporary display returns." Take a look at Figure 3-2. In the Microsoft Word example, the first line of the first paragraph ends with the word "PC." The second line ends with the word "is." You'll notice that there is nothing in the margin to the right of these words. That's because Word has inserted a *soft* return at the end of the lines. If we were to add some words to these sentences and reformat the paragraph, Word would ignore its original soft returns and create new ones as needed.

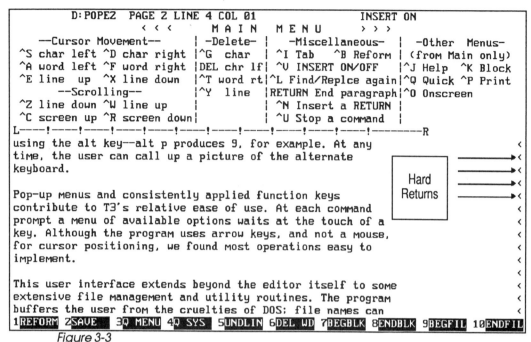

Figure 3-3
In an ASCII text file, two consecutive returns should separate each paragraph.

But ASCII doesn't support soft returns. Every time it sees the edge of the screen, it creates a hard return. If you were to bring a straight ASCII file into your word processor, you'd see a hard return symbol at the end of every line. Ventura Publisher knows about this quirk of ASCII. When you tell Ventura Publisher to load an ASCII file, it translates a single hard return into a soft return. How does it know when to end a paragraph? Simple—Ventura Publisher interprets *two consecutive* hard returns as the command for a new paragraph.

This explanation is leading up to an important rule: Always hit the Enter key twice between paragraphs in an ASCII file (see Figure 3-3). If you fail to use double returns to end paragraphs, Ventura Publisher will run them together.

♦ *Caution: This rule applies to ASCII text files only.*

Creating ASCII Text with Other Programs

ASCII is a very important and versatile text standard. It is the key to working with word processors, database managers and spreadsheet software that are not directly supported by Ventura Publisher. By converting their file formats to ASCII, you can use them to create text for Ventura.

Many programs have a special conversion utility. If that's the case, simply use it to change from the original file format to an ASCII file usable by Ventura.

Even if the program doesn't have a conversion utility, you can *still* create ASCII files. Just use the print function, but print to disk instead of to a printer. When a program sends text to a printer, it strips out special commands and converts the text to standard ASCII. Once again, many programs have special commands to allow printing to disk. Consult your user's manual.

♦ *Warning: If you print to disk, be sure to set all margins to zero in the word processor. This will prevent the appearance of unwanted space characters at the beginning of lines and between lines.*

One final note about ASCII files. Some word processors have an option that creates ASCII files directly. WordStar, for example, has a Document mode (D from the main menu) and a Nondocument mode (N from the main menu). WordStar's nondocument text files are straight ASCII files. Some users might choose to use ASCII files as a common denominator in companies that have not standardized on one word processing program.

♦ *Caution: you cannot convert an existing WordStar document to ASCII simply by opening it in nondocument mode. The exact method of converting to ASCII varies between WordStar 3.3 and WordStar 4.0 but perhaps the simplest way is to print to a disk file.*

Using Word Processor Files

Having finished with our discussion of ASCII files, let's turn our attention to the word processing programs supported by Ventura Publisher. All of them have one thing in common:

Table 3-1
Word Processing Codes Supported by Ventura Publisher

	Bold	Superscript	Subscript	Strikethrough	Underline	Disc Hyphen
Microsoft Word	Alt b	Alt +	Alt -	Alt s	Alt u	Ctrl -
MultiMate	Alt Z	Alt Q	Alt W	NA	Shift _	Shift F7
WordPerfect	F6	Shift F1 1	Shift F1 2	Alt F5 4	F8	Ctrl -
WordStar	^B	^T	^V	^X	^S	^OE -
Xerox Writer	Alt 9	Alt 4	Alt 5	NA	Alt 7	Hyph Fcn
XyWrite	Ctrl 2	Ctrl 7	Ctrl 8	NA	Ctrl 3	Shift ~

They support soft returns. It is thus not necessary to place two returns between paragraphs. A single return is all that is necessary to identify and separate paragraphs for Ventura's use. (If you prefer two returns between paragraphs, use the @PARAFILTR ON technique explained at the end of the chapter.)

♦ *Key note: There is one major difference between ASCII files and word processing files. ASCII files require two returns between paragraphs. Word processing files require only one.*

Ventura Publisher works with word processor files much the same way it works with ASCII files, with a few exceptions explained below.

As we mentioned above, Ventura requires true tab characters between columns. Some programs, such as WordStar, can insert either spaces or true tab characters. If you use WordStar to create text for Ventura Publisher, turn off the Vari-Tab feature by hitting ^OV (Control O-Control V). This ensures that actual tab characters, and not strings of spaces, will be inserted when you press the tab key.

Ventura Publisher ignores the dot commands and other codes a word processor uses to specify print formats. Don't bother with them in files created for Ventura Publisher. Likewise, justification has no positive effect, so make sure that justification is off before you start typing.

Word processors normally insert soft, or discretionary, hyphens to accomplish justification. Since Ventura Publisher disregards these soft hyphens, it makes sense to disable hyphenation if you can.

Ventura Publisher recognizes several word processor commands for text attributes. Text given one of these attributes within the word processor will automatically retain these attributes in Ventura Publisher. Table 3-1 offers a list of the word processing commands from each program that are recognized by Ventura.

In addition to the word processor commands supported directly by Ventura, you can also insert other effects using the techniques in the final section of this chapter.

Tips for Working with Word Processors

Put a single hard return between paragraphs. If you prefer two returns, use the @PARAFILTR ON technique explained at the end of the chapter.

Don't use dot commands or formatting codes since they will only be ignored by Ventura.

In WordStar, turn soft hyphens off at the beginning of every editing session. Also, turn hyphen-help off at the beginning of every editing session, or reinstall WordStar so that hyphen-help is off by default.

In WordStar 3.3, turn vari-tabs off at the beginning of every editing session.

Turn justification off at the beginning of every editing session.

Creating Text with Other Programs

Up to this point, we have talked about word processors. But you can also create text for Ventura Publisher with other programs.

Using a Database Program

Database management programs are powerful text-generating tools for Ventura Publisher. Database software is much more practical than word processing software for storing cer-

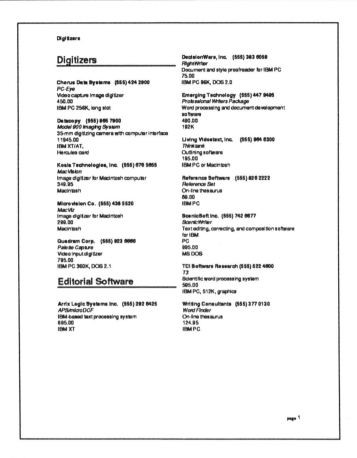

Figure 3-4
Database software is useful for creating directories such as this one.

tain kinds of information. It is particularly useful for directories, catalogs, price lists, phone books, and specification sheets (see Figure 3-4). Virtually all database programs, including best-sellers like dBase III, Rbase 5000, and DataFlex, can create ASCII files. When you combine the information-handling of a database with the batch processing of Ventura Publisher, you have a powerful team for creating large directories.

To achieve a simple coordination between the two, program the database as normal to accept and store the data you need. Then print a "report" to disk. This will create an ASCII file that can be loaded into Ventura and formatted.

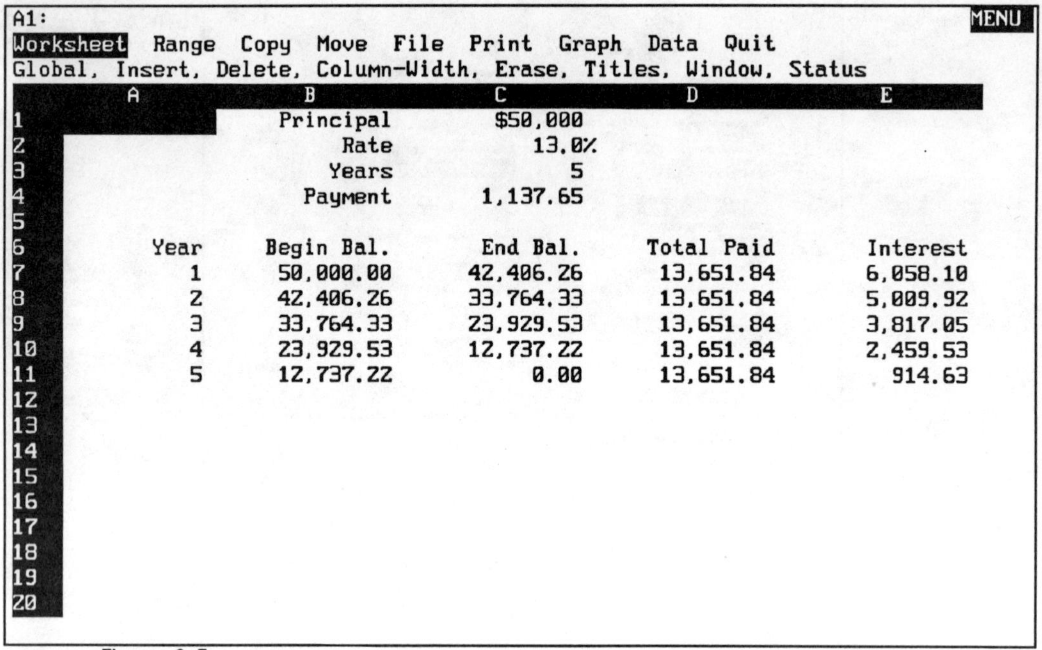

```
A1:                                                                  MENU
Worksheet  Range  Copy  Move  File  Print  Graph  Data  Quit
Global,  Insert,  Delete,  Column-Width,  Erase,  Titles,  Window,  Status
        A              B              C              D              E
1                   Principal      $50,000
2                        Rate        13.0%
3                       Years           5
4                     Payment    1,137.65
5
6        Year     Begin Bal.      End Bal.     Total Paid      Interest
7           1      50,000.00     42,406.26      13,651.84      6,058.10
8           2      42,406.26     33,764.33      13,651.84      5,009.92
9           3      33,764.33     23,929.53      13,651.84      3,817.05
10          4      23,929.53     12,737.22      13,651.84      2,459.53
11          5      12,737.22          0.00      13,651.84        914.63
12
13
14
15
16
17
18
19
20
```

Figure 3-5
A spreadsheet program can be used to create financial tables for Ventura Publisher.

For the ultimate in automated database publishing, read the final section in this chapter. It describes how to insert tags, text attributes, and other formatting information directly into text files *before* they are brought into Ventura. Using this technique, you can program a database to produce reports that automatically insert formatting codes into the text file. The result will be a "preformatted" text file. Using this method, you can cut days or even weeks from the process of publishing large directories. (See Chapter Nine, Special Tips & Techniques, for information on live headers and other sophisticated formatting techniques for directories and catalogs.)

Spreadsheet Programs

Spreadsheet programs like Lotus 1-2-3 and SuperCalc 4 can also create text for Ventura Publisher. Spreadsheet software is most useful for financial tables, comparison charts, and other tabular material (see Figure 3-5). For certain applications, you may prefer a spreadsheet. If the balance sheets already exist in Lotus 1-2-3, why bother to retype them for the annual report? And why use a word processor to create a complex financial table when a spreadsheet will do it faster while doing the math for you?

The precise steps to convert a spreadsheet file into a Ventura Publisher text file depend on the particular spreadsheet program. Some have a built-in ASCII option. If not, use the technique we learned above: print the worksheet, but send it to a disk file instead of the printer.

Conversion to ASCII presents few problems. A hurdle arises, however, when importing these ASCII files into Ventura Publisher. Spreadsheet programs use spaces to separate columns. As we saw earlier, Ventura Publisher requires the actual ^I tab character, not spaces.

The solution is to strip out those spaces and replace them with the tab character. One way to "clean up" the spreadsheet file is to transfer it into your word processor. Then you can use the search and replace function to remove multiple spaces and substitute tab characters. Or you can embed a special code symbol within each spreadsheet cell when you first create the table. (Use any symbol that will not be encountered in the text. Possibilities include #, &, or *). Then you search for this symbol with your word processor and replace it with the tab character.

Another method makes use of a utility program called CON-VERTD. This utility is provided free with the IBM PC version of Microsoft Word. It can solve the space character problem for any spreadsheet-generated ASCII file.

To use CONVERTD, set up the rows and columns in the spreadsheet. Disregard formatting options such as right alignment or centering. The spreadsheet is just a temporary format. The final alignment and formatting will occur inside Ventura. Second, *write down the column widths in order.* You'll need that information later. For example: 10, 6, 5, 5, 10. When you've entered all the information, print the spreadsheet to disk to create an ASCII file. (In Lotus 1-2-3, you do this with the /PF command).

Now exit the spreadsheet and load CONVERTD from DOS. The utility will ask you for the type of input file you wish to convert. Respond with option 1, columnar text file. Next it asks for the column widths. Here's where you type in the numbers you wrote down earlier (10, 6, 5, 5, 10). Proceed with the utility until it asks you for the type of output file. Respond with option 2, delimited file.

A delimiter is any symbol or character used to separate different fields. Some mail merge programs, for instance, use commas or semicolons to separate name, address, city, and so on. Others use the return— they ask you to type each entry on a separate line. In our case, when the utility asks for the field delimiter, we will respond by hitting the Tab key.

CONVERTD will proceed to scan the spreadsheet, strip out the spaces, and insert the field delimiter— in our case, the tab character. You will be left with a straight ASCII file where each column is separated by a single tab character. And that is what Ventura requires to create impeccably formatted tabular material.

To take the use of the spreadsheet program one step further, program the left-most column to contain the tag name along with the labels. Instead of Sales, for example, you might type in:

@TABLE = Sales

Since you use the same tag name for every line of the table, use the spreadsheet's copy or macro function to automate this insertion. See the final section of this chapter for more information on inserting formatting codes directly into text files.

Lotus 1-2-3 users can consider yet another way out. Ventura Publisher can directly import Lotus *graphic* files stored in the PIC format. You may want to consider converting the spreadsheet file into a chart or graph if a visual aid would make your point more effectively than a table.

Still another option is to use a monospaced font such as Courier after bringing the table into Ventura Publisher. Since all characters— and spaces— in this font have the same width, you can be certain that the columns and rows will align in Ventura Publisher just as they did in the spreadsheet program.

♦ *Note: If you use this technique, be sure to set the desired space width for the tag to the same as the width of each character in the font. For example, with a 12-pitch monospaced font, the space width should be set to .0833 inch (1/12 inch). Use the* TYPOGRAPHIC CONTROLS *option from the paragraph menu for this setting.*

Using a Programming Language

The section at end of the chapter explains how to insert tags and Attributes directly into a file. Once you understand how the process works, you'll realize that programming languages like BASIC and Pascal can do the work of inserting the tags. This presents some novel opportunities for creating Ventura Publisher documents. There are as many possibilities here as there are programmers to create them. One example might be a program that prompts the user for certain variable information such as the price of gold or the names of the department managers and then outputs a customized Ventura Publisher document. You need only program the computer to insert the proper Ventura Publisher tags before each piece of variable data.

Creating Text With Ventura Publisher

To this point, we've discussed how to create separate files to be brought into Ventura Publisher. But you can also create and edit text during page layout. Although Ventura Publisher's text editing function was not designed to take the place of a full-function word processor, you may find it convenient for making minor edits to existing files. In addition, you can also create separate files. This saves you from the need to exit the program, call up your word processor, create the file, and then re-enter Ventura Publisher. We do not, however, recommend the use of Ventura to generate more than a page or so of text.

Since you would normally use Ventura's text editing tools during the page layout process, we have covered the topic in Chapter Six, Document Design and Layout.

Editing Text After Using Ventura Publisher

As we noted earlier, the text editing process does not end once you have created a document layout. In all probability, there will be revisions or additions to the text. This is where Ventura Publisher's approach to handling text will be appreciated.

It is totally acceptable, indeed often desirable, to edit a text file *after* it has been brought into a Ventura Publisher document. You need only apply the same techniques you used to create the text file in the first place. Add text or make corrections to any portion.

The next time you call up the text file in Ventura Publisher, all the changes made with the word processor will show up in the Ventura document. As we've said, Ventura Publisher does not store text in separate files of its own. Rather, each Ventura Publisher document (each CHP file) contains the name of the word processor file(s). As a result, your Ventura Publisher documents are never cast in stone. Any change made to a text file automatically forces a change in the Ventura Publisher document.

♦ *Warning: If you want to edit a text file after it has been loaded into Ventura Publisher, and you do not want to change the Ventura Publisher document, make a copy of the text file under a new name. Edit the new copy only.*

If you reopen a word processing file, you'll discover codes that were not present when you created the file (see Figure 3-6). These are Ventura Publisher's codes for tag names, special characters, text attributes, and other commands. Be careful not to edit or delete these codes— they control the format and appearance of the Ventura Publisher document.

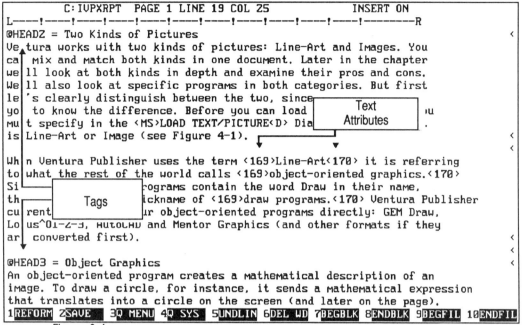

Figure 3-6
Ventura Publisher's tags and codes as they appear in your word processor.

These codes are one of the keys to Ventura's power and formatting abilities. And they are also the key to a powerful advanced technique for "preformatting" text files.

Preformatting Ventura Publisher Files

The following section outlines an advanced technique. To understand it you must understand how Ventura uses style sheets and tags. If you're new to Ventura Publisher, just skim over this section. Or skip it altogether and come back to it after you've finished Chapter Five, Working with Style Sheets, and Chapter Six, Document Design and Layout.

♦ *Note: You do not need to understand the following techniques to create sophisticated documents with Ventura Publisher.*

Even though there is no requirement to use this advanced technique, it does provide a powerful tool for preformatting files. It may seem cumbersome at first. In truth, when com-

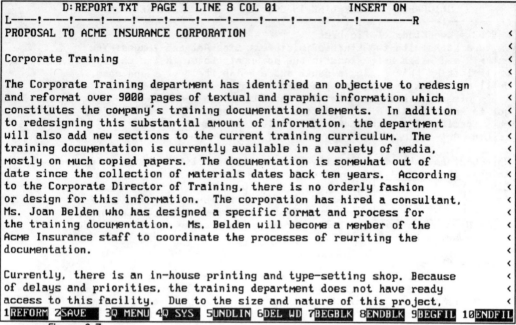

Figure 3-7
A raw text file contains no formatting information.

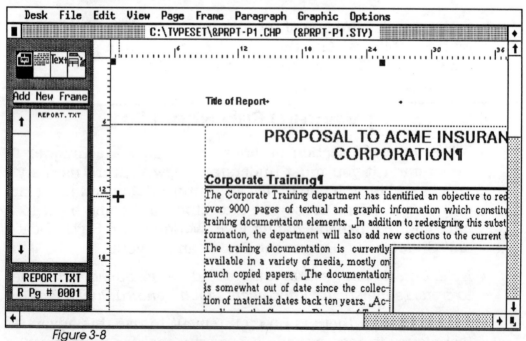

Figure 3-8
The document from Figure 3-7 after being formatted using Ventura Publisher's paragraph tagging function.

bined with a keyboard macro program like SmartKey or SuperKey, it is often the fastest way to create documents. Preformatting can save many hours of layout time. (This is especially true if you use a database manager or spreadsheet program to preformat large documents.) At the end of the section, we've given hints on when (and whether) to consider preformatting.

Let's start by quickly reviewing the standard method Ventura Publisher uses to work with text files. The process starts with "raw text." This text file contains no formatting information (see Figure 3-7). Next the file is brought into Ventura Publisher. The style sheet is applied to the file using the paragraph tagging mode. The result is a formatted document (see Figure 3-8).

When the Ventura chapter is saved, the original text file is saved as well. If we now go back to this file, we see that Ventura has inserted its tags and formatting codes into the file (see Figure 3-9).

Given this approach, it is easy to grasp how preformatting works: The author simply types the tags and codes into the text file *before* bringing it into Ventura Publisher. You can insert several types of information: (1) tag names, (2) text attributes like italics and boldface, (3) special non-keyboard characters and symbols, (4) formatting information, and (5) footnotes and indexes. We will explore all these in turn, but remember that the basic concept is always the same. You preformat a text file by typing in codes in a form Ventura can understand.

Entering Tags in Advance

Since Ventura Publisher inserts tags into the text file during layout, it makes sense that you can do the same thing *before* layout. If you know (1) the proper Ventura format and (2) the exact names of the tags, you can insert tags as you type the text file. When you load that file into Ventura Publisher, it will be automatically formatted according to the style sheet. There will be no need to use paragraph tagging mode, since the tags will already be in the file.

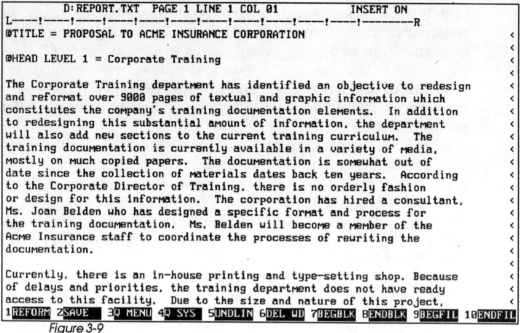

```
         D:REPORT.TXT   PAGE 1 LINE 1 COL 01         INSERT ON
L----!----!----!----!----!----!----!----!----!----!----!--------R
@TITLE = PROPOSAL TO ACME INSURANCE CORPORATION                      <
                                                                    <
@HEAD LEVEL 1 = Corporate Training                                  <
                                                                    <
The Corporate Training department has identified an objective to redesign  <
and reformat over 9000 pages of textual and graphic information which  <
constitutes the company's training documentation elements.  In addition  <
to redesigning this substantial amount of information, the department  <
will also add new sections to the current training curriculum.  The  <
training documentation is currently available in a variety of media,  <
mostly on much copied papers.  The documentation is somewhat out of  <
date since the collection of materials dates back ten years.  According  <
to the Corporate Director of Training, there is no orderly fashion  <
or design for this information.  The corporation has hired a consultant,  <
Ms. Joan Belden who has designed a specific format and process for  <
the training documentation.  Ms. Belden will become a member of the  <
Acme Insurance staff to coordinate the processes of rewriting the  <
documentation.                                                      <
                                                                    <
Currently, there is an in-house printing and type-setting shop. Because  <
of delays and priorities, the training department does not have ready  <
access to this facility.  Due to the size and nature of this project,  <
1REFORM 2SAVE   3Q MENU 4Q SYS  5UNDLIN 6DEL WD 7BEGBLK 8ENDBLK 9BEGFIL 10ENDFIL
```

Figure 3-9
The same text file after formatting it in Ventura Publisher.

Ventura Publisher's tagging code is simple to learn: Type the at-sign (@) at the left margin. (The @ sign is found above the number 2 on most keyboards.) Then type the name of the tag, followed by a space, an equal sign, and a second space.:

To use this tag name in a text file, type it immediately in front of the paragraph you want to tag. Put it on the same line. Don't forget the spaces before and after the equal sign. Here's how a headline might look in the text file:

@HEADLINE = This is the Headline

When you insert a tag into a text file, Ventura Publisher follows the format instructions for that tag *until it sees a hard return*. (Two hard returns in an ASCII file). Then it reverts to body text. It will format the following paragraphs as body text *until it sees another tag*. So don't insert tags for body text— Ventura Publisher already assumes anything without a tag is body text. But if, for example, you have three paragraphs in a row with the same tag name, you must type that tag name at the beginning of each one. Tag names will not carry over to another paragraph.

When you type a tag into a text file, it's crucial to match the style sheet tag *letter-for-letter*. You and I might realize that @HEADLINE and @HEADLINES mean the same thing, but to Ventura Publisher they are entirely different. What happens if you misspell a tag? No harm done—if Ventura Publisher doesn't recognize a tag, it formats body text. You can format it correctly later in Ventura Publisher's paragraph tagging mode.

Obviously, you can't preformat files until you have settled on the names you plan to use for tags.

Rules for Entering Tags

Put the @ sign in the left margin. If you put it any other column, Ventura will not recognize it as a tag name.

The tag name must precede the rest of the paragraph.

Spell the tag name exactly as it appears—or *will* appear—in the style sheet or Ventura will not recognize it.

Capitalization does not matter. Ventura makes no distinction between upper and lower case. However, you may want to use upper/lower case for your own tags to readily distinguish them from the ones Ventura creates on its own, which appear in upper case only.

The tag will apply to the entire paragraph. When Ventura encounters a hard return (two hard returns in an ASCII file) it will reset to body text. It will continue to format as body text until it encounters another tag name.

Using the Special PARAFILTR Tag

Normally the user must enter tag names from an existing style sheet to preformat a text file. Otherwise, Ventura Publisher will not recognize the names and will not know how to format the paragraphs. But there is one tag name that Ventura automatically recognizes. It can be used in any text file. This special tag strips out double returns.

Table 3-2
Text attributes can be
inserted into text files
using these codes:

Bold	\<B\>
Italics	\<I\>
Small caps	\<S\>
Strikethrough	\<X\>
Superscript	\<^\>
Subscript	\<V\>
Underline	\<U\>
Double underline	\<=\>
Light	\<L\>
Normal (medium)	\<M\>
Turn off effects	\<D\>
Strikethrough	\<X\>
Overscore	\<O\>

We explained above that word processing files require only one hard return between paragraphs. But as you can see in Figure 3-10, text files are difficult to read without double spacing to set paragraphs apart. This is particularly true since we do *not* want to use any indentation.

If Ventura encounters a second hard return, it will insert an extra blank line, thereby throwing off the spacing of the document. Theoretically, you could double space between paragraphs for readability, and then use the search and replace function of the word processor to strip out the extra return. However, you will find it more convenient to use Ventura Publisher's built-in PARAFILTR function.

To activate Ventura's built-in filter, which will strip out double returns, simply place this special tag name at the top left of a document:

@PARAFILTR ON =

Be sure to make it the first thing in the text file and follow the other rules for tag names. Spell it exactly as shown here. Don't forget the spaces before and after the word ON.

```
            C:SCAN2  PAGE 1 LINE 24 COL 01              INSERT ON
L----!----!----!----!----!----!----!----!----!----!----!--------R
@LIST = Camera-based scanners                                      <
@HEADZ = Flatbed Scanners                                         <
@HILITE = ^0 <MI>The most versatile type for office use is the flatbed
scanner<D> (Figure II-1). The operation is similar to that of an office
photocopier<197>the user simply places the page to be scanned face
down on a glass window or platen. A major advantage of the flatbed
scanner is that a large book or even a solid object can be scanned.
The detector and light source are underneath the glass window. The
detector moves along the length of the page, sensing one horizontal
line on the page at a time.                                        <
Some flatbed scanners have an automatic sheet feeder as an option.
This allows the user to scan a stack of pages sequentially, without
having to place each page on the platen individually.             <
@HEADZ = Sheetfed Scanners                                        <
With sheetfed scanners (Figure II-2), the process is just the opposite
to that in the flatbeds. A single page is fed into the scanner either
by hand or by an automatic sheet feeder. The detector and light source
are stationary and the page moves over them. This is very similar
to the way an office facsimile machine works<197>in fact, some manufacturers
use the same mechanisms.                                           <
@HILITE = ^0 <MI>Sheetfed scanners usually cost less than flatbed scanners,<D>
since the optics are often less complex and the sensing element can
1REFORM 2SAVE   3Q MENU 4Q SYS  5UNDLIN 6DEL WD 7BEGBLK 8ENDBLK 9BEGFIL 10ENDFIL
```

Figure 3-10
A text file without extra space between paragraphs can be difficult to read.

♦ *Note: When Ventura Publisher saves the text file again, the double returns will be gone. You must reinsert them if you wish to double space again.*

Entering Text Attributes

The basic principle used to enter tags also works for text attributes like boldface and italics. tag names use the @ sign in the left margin to signal Ventura to accept the code. Text attributes are turned on using a single letter code stored between two angle brackets. For instance, <I> turns on italics, <B> turns on bold, and so on. (On most keyboards, the angle brackets are located immediately above the comma and the period.) When Ventura Publisher sees brackets in a text file, it does not print the brackets or put them on screen. Instead, it treats the information inside as a formatting code. These formatting codes do not need to appear in the left margin. They can be anywhere in the text, as long as they are enclosed in brackets.

Ventura uses one code to turn on an effect and a second code to turn it off. Table 3-2 shows a list of the code letters and the effects they achieve.

♦ *Some of the effects in Table 3-2 may not be supported by your laser printer. If you specify an effect not available from your printer, Ventura will ignore it.*

The <D> code turns off any and all text attributes. No matter how many attributes you are using together, apply the <D> code only once at the end to turn them all off. Even if you do not type in the <D> code, Ventura automatically turns off all text attributes when it encounters a hard return. You will recall that Ventura also cancels tag names when it sees a hard return (two hard returns in an ASCII file). You can think of a hard return as a reset device that returns everything to normal.

Place the bracketed code letter next to the word(s) you wish to affect. We recommend that you not place any space between the code and the word. Thus, to italicize the phrase Xerox Ventura Publisher, you would type this:

<I>Xerox Ventura Publisher<D>

What if you want to apply more than one effect at a time? You must put all the attributes inside one set of brackets, like this:

<BI>Bold italics<D>.

If you fail to put them inside one bracket you will discover that when Ventura encounters a new coded bracket it cancels all the previous ones.

You may have noticed that some of the text attributes duplicate the ones available through word processing commands (see preceding section). Use whichever method you prefer. Enter attributes such as boldface and underline with the word processor or with the technique spelled out here. Ventura interprets them equally well and they achieve identical effects.

On the other hand, some valuable effects like small caps cannot be created with word processor commands. To insert them directly into text files you must use the bracket technique described here.

Ventura's use of angle brackets can cause one slight problem. What if you want to put brackets into the text file? If you enter them normally, Ventura will assume they enclose a formatting code. It will not print them on the screen or on the page. To make angle brackets appear on the page as themselves, you must double them up:

- Single brackets (<X>) are treated as a formatting code.

- Double brackets (<<X>>) cause the inside set to print on the page.

Entering Non-Keyboard Characters

We've shown you how to preformat text files with tag names and text attributes. You can use the same basic technique to insert special characters and symbols into text files, symbols that are not available on the normal computer keyboard.

One of desktop publishing's primary advantages is that you can create documents that look professionally typeset. There are many important characters and symbols used by typesetters that are not found on the typical personal computer keyboard. Ventura Publisher gives you access to these "non-keyboard characters." The process of inserting them is very similar to the process of inserting text attributes. To insert a non-keyboard character directly into a text file, type its decimal equivalent inside angle brackets. For instance, <197> denotes the em dash; <169> stands for open quotes.

As you are typing the text file, you'll only see the code in brackets, but when you bring the text file into Ventura Publisher that code will be translated into the proper character or symbol. That symbol will appear on the Ventura Publisher screen and on the printed page.

In addition to entering non-keyboard characters, you can also enter discretionary hyphens with <->, line breaks with <R>, and non-breaking spaces with <N>. You will have little occasion to use these three items. Discretionary hyphens have little value beyond adding an additional hyphenation op-

Table 3-3
Often-used fonts and
their number codes.

Font	Code
Courier	1
Helvetica (Swiss)	2
Times Roman (Dutch)	14
Century	20
Palatino	21
Garamond	22
Bookman	23
Lubalin	24
Souvenir	25
Zapf Chancery	29
Avant Garde	51
Optima	52
Symbol	128
Dingbats	129
Reset to original font	255

portunity for Ventura's algorithm. And most people will prefer to use the direct commands of the word processor to add line breaks and non-breaking spaces.

Entering Other Formatting Codes

The same angle brackets used to enter attributes and special symbols can also be used to put other important formatting codes directly into text files. The most important are typefaces and point sizes.

If you are a newcomer to Ventura, you will be wise to work with Fonts directly in the program until you gain an understanding of typefaces and point sizes. If you are familiar with typographical terminology, you may wish to insert formatting codes in advance. Often an author knows that he wants a certain typographical effect—a special font, for example, or a large type size. It may be easier to insert the code while typing the manuscript than to make a note to the editor.

Formatting codes are contained within angle brackets. They consist of a single capital letter followed by a number. To change fonts, for instance, you bracket the code letter F followed by the number of the font. For example, <F1> tells Ventura to switch to the Courier font and <F128> to switch to the symbol font. Table 3-3 gives a list of some important fonts and their number codes.

Place the bracket code immediately preceding the first word you wish to change. Thus, to put the word typeface into the Courier font, type <F1>typeface. Ventura will continue with a font until it encounters a hard return, a different font code, or the special code <F255>, which resets the font to the font originally found in that paragraph.

Changing point sizes works in exactly the same fashion. The code letter is P, followed by the point size you desire. To change to 14 point, type <P14>.

Like all bracket codes, typefaces and point sizes can be combined. Thus, <F51P24> will change to 24 point Avant Garde.

Other Formatting Options

Several other formatting options can be entered directly into text files, including baseline jumps (shifting letters up or down), kerning (shifting letters left), and color (specifying the color of text for color printers). These options follow the same rules as other angle bracket insertions. However, we do not recommend entering these three formatting options in advance. You will get better results if you work with them on Ventura's WYSIWYG screen where you can immediately see the results of your changes.

Footnotes and Indexes

We have already seen how to insert tag names, text attributes, non-keyboard characters, and formatting options. There is another type of information some users may want to insert directly into text files before they are brought into Ventura Publisher. These are codes for footnotes and index references.

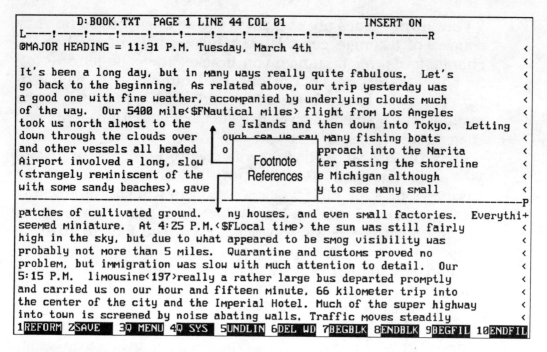

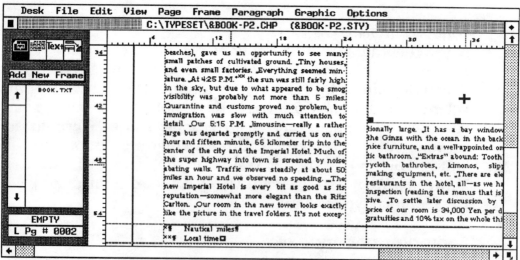

Figure 3-11
The word processor (top) and Ventura Publisher (bottom) versions of a footnote.

Both footnotes and index references can be created within Ventura Publisher. The process involves making a choice from the edit menu and then using a dialog box to type in the reference information. When Ventura saves back to the original word processing file, it places the reference information from the dialog box into angle brackets.

The angle bracket code for footnotes is $F followed by the text of the footnote. <$FSee Section 5 for further discussion> is a typical footnote code. Figure 3-11 shows the word processor version of a footnote reference in the top half and the result on the printed page in the bottom half. Notice that the bracket code immediately follows the word that is to receive the footnote symbol.

Some users may prefer to continue inserting footnotes during page layout in Ventura. However, others will prefer to ask the authors to type in the reference as they are creating the text. This is generally more convenient than saving the reference information on paper to be typed in later. By preformatting footnotes as explained here, Ventura will take care of placing the actual reference on the correct page and in the correct format.

The angle bracket code for indexes is similar to that for footnotes, but slightly more complicated. That's because Ventura's indexes can have two levels:

> Text
>> creation   123, 125-129

In this example, "Text" is a first-level, or *primary* entry and "creation" is a second-level or *secondary* entry. In a real index, a primary entry is usually followed by several secondary entries:

> Text
>> creation   123, 125-239
>> editing   115
>> files   167-172
> See also Word Processing

As with footnotes, indexes can be created after text files have been brought into Ventura Publisher. Or you can enter the Ventura codes directly into the text files in advance. The bracket code is $I followed by the primary reference and the secondary reference, which are separated by a semicolon. Thus, in a text file the example above looks like this:

<$IText;creation>. Notice that there are no spaces within the brackets.

Ventura's indexing function also accommodates "See" and "See Also" references. The bracket code for See references is $S; for See Also references $A. Thus, the bracket code for the See Also reference in the example above would look like this: <$AText;Word Processing>.

Finally, Ventura's indexing function also handles words that must be listed out of normal alphabetical order. One possible example is names that begin with "The." You would not, for instance, want to find "The Acme Company" listed under the letter "T." Instead, it belongs under the letter "A." Ventura permits you to enter a different sorting criteria. This alphabetizing information is listed inside square brackets. For example, the code <$IThe Acme Company[Acme Company]> would create a primary entry that would be printed "The Acme Company" but be alphabetized by "Acme Company." You can enter alphabetizing information for the primary entry, the secondary entry, or both.

Once it sees an index code in the text file, Ventura handles all aspects of creating, formatting, and numbering the index. You should be aware that an index entry made in the text file can be modified or deleted in Ventura Publisher. Likewise, an entry made in Ventura Publisher can be changed by returning to the word processing file. Some authors prefer to write, edit, and format in Ventura Publisher, and then return to the word processing files to do the indexing as one of the last steps.

Anchoring Frames

Ventura Publisher also gives you a way to link graphics to text within your word processor. With this technique, you can ensure that a particular graphic image will appear immediately after the reference to it in text— even before you create the graphic with, or import the image into, Ventura Publisher.

To accomplish this, make use of Ventura's anchor frame capability. You merely insert the code for frame anchor where you want it to appear in text. For example, the code <$&bar chart[v]> will cause Ventura to place the frame named "bar chart" immediately after the line of text that contains this code. You will assign the name "bar chart" to a graphic when you create the frame with Ventura Publisher.

Chapter Nine, Special Tips & Techniques, offers more detail about the frame anchor capabilities of Ventura Publisher.

Hidden Text

Use the same technique to mark text in a file as a remark that is not to be printed. Most word processors have a similar feature that allows text to show on the screen but not be printed. The hidden text feature works the same way. Text marked as hidden shows and prints in the word processor but not in Ventura. It may be useful for including editorial comments and notations that don't belong in the printed version. For example, authors might use hidden text to remind themselves which illustration they intended to use or where they want to add more information once their research is more complete.

The bracket code for hidden text is <$!>. Thus, to place the hidden remark "Use the sales chart to illustrate this point" into a word processing file you would type <$!Use the sales chart to illustrate this point>.

Macro	Expansion	Purpose
[SS x]	<$I>	Index entry
[Alt I]	<I><P> <D>	Italics
[Alt S]	<S><P><D>	Small
[Alt D]	<D>	Revert to Normal
[Alt L]	@LIST =	Bullet
[Alt C]	@COMP =	Company
[Alt N]	@NOTE =	Note
[Alt 9]	<169>	"
[Alt 0]	<170>	"
[Alt -]	<197>	—

Figure 3-12
The SmartKey macros used by the authors to enter text attributes in WordStar.

Shortcuts to Preformatting Files

At first glance, preformatting might seem like a tedious and confusing process. In fact, it can be a very powerful and work-able technique. What's more, there are several techniques that make it faster and simpler.

Using Keyboard Macros

Typing out tag names and bracket codes can slow writers down. To speed the process, use a keyboard macro program. A keyboard macro program lets you assign a string of charac-ters to one key on your keyboard. Just define keyboard shortcuts to automatically type in the Ventura Publisher codes. For example, you could define the Alt-h key to automatically type in the string:

We used SmartKey, from Software Research Technologies, in this fashion when we typed the text files for this book. Any good program will work. We happen to like SmartKey because it's simple to use and because it lets us build windows. We used a window to remind ourselves of the special keys.

Figure 3-12 shows our personal list of keyboard macros. To achieve the effects listed on the left, we simply pressed the key combinations on the right. (The symbol ss stands for the SuperShift key, another of the reasons we like SmartKey. The SuperShift key is like an extra Control or Alt key; it works when pressed together with another key.)

Like most other keyboard enhancers, SmartKey also sup-ports a pause function. We used this pause function to help us when entering attributes. As you will recall, you must enter one code to start an attribute and another to end it. The danger is that you may start an attribute and forget to stop it. You can end up italicizing an entire paragraph instead of just one word. So we set up our SmartKey macros to enter the stop code automatically. When we press Alt-I, for instance, Smart-Key inserts the Ventura Publisher bracket code to start italics (<I>). Then it waits for us to type the word or phrase. Meanwhile, it keeps blinking at us to remind us to press enter when we've finished typing the phrase. When we hit enter, SmartKey automatically enters the stop code (<D>). Thanks to

Table 3-4
Search/Replace Procedures for Special Characters

To create	Search for	Replace with
Open quotes	space "	space "
Close quotes	" space	" space
Em dash	--	—
Correct spacing	space space	space

this simple system, it's virtually impossible to forget to stop an attribute.

You'll find some type of macro program almost essential to effectively enter footnotes and indexes directly into text files. It is cumbersome and time-consuming to repeatedly type brackets and dollar signs.

Many word processors have macro facilities built-in, or you can buy separate programs like SmartKey, ProKey, SuperKey, Keyworks and others. Whichever the program and whichever the exact technique, we highly recommend the use of macros for preformatting files. One good side effect is standardization. When using multiple tags it's far too easy to forget the correct syntax. Was that supposed to be @HEAD, @HEADING, or @HEADLINE? Does the style sheet use @COLUMN1, @COLUMN ONE, or @COL1? If you misspell the tag name by even a single letter you nullify the advantage of preformatting. And if you have multiple authors you will find it critical to pass out a standardized list of tag names. Storing those names in a macro file that can be used by all is one way of enforcing compliance while boosting productivity.

Search and Replace for Special Characters

To save the trouble of entering bracket codes for nonkeyboard characters, consider having authors enter ordinary keyboard characters. At the end of the writing session, they can use the word processor's search and replace function to strip out the incorrect characters and insert bracket codes in their place. This process can be automated using a keyboard macro program.

Table 3-4 summarizes some substitutions you might want to make on a routine basis to improve the appearance of your documents. You can go further with this technique by using special symbols while typing, then replacing the symbols with bracket codes before bringing the file into Ventura.

Document Templates

Here's one more idea for speeding up preformatting: Create document templates for your word processor. The first step is to create a raw text file and bring it into Ventura Publisher. Experiment with layout and formatting until it looks perfect. Now save the chapter.

Saving the chapter automatically saves the word processing files. But now the file contains the tag names, text attributes, and formatting codes created by Ventura Publisher. To create a document template, delete the text, but leave the tags and codes intact. The next time you create a similar document, call up the blank file and type in the new text.

To make it easier for users to remember what goes where, replace the deleted text with instructions— "Type name here" or "Place part description here" for example. Users can replace these instructions with the actual text each time they use the document template. Some word processors, including Microsoft Word, have a hidden text feature that is perfect for creating template instructions. Users make the hidden text visible for hints on what to do, then turn it off before sending it to Ventura Publisher.

This technique could be particularly valuable for applications where authors produce different versions of a document following rigid specifications. Technical and military documentation, for example, often uses a highly structured approach. Once a Ventura document has been created, it can form the basis for a word processor template. This template can be given to all authors. Authors need only "fill in the blanks" to create a completely formatted document for use by Ventura Publisher.

When to Preformat Files

Start with the standard method until you've learned Ventura Publisher. Create raw text in your word processor, and do all the special formatting in Ventura Publisher. Stick with the basic approach at least until you've defined some standard tag names that you'll be using over and over again. When you first start using Ventura Publisher, you may call a tag a Headline in one style sheet, a Title in another. It will take you some time before you settle on a consistent system of names.

Once you have standard formats and tag names, consider preformatting. It offers several advantages. It saves layout time since the editor doesn't have to tag every single paragraph. If authors use keyboard macros and document templates, preformatting doesn't really take any more time while typing. And preformatting prevents mixups when one person writes the file and a second person edits and formats. It's easy for an editor to misinterpret the author's intentions. If authors insert tags and attributes themselves, there's less room for error.

Still, it is not necessary to preformat files. You may never use this approach. Depending on the preferences of you and your company, you may want to leave all formatting decisions to editors. Some editors prefer it that way. So do some writers, who feel that it slows down the creative flow if they have to pause to give any thought to tags, attributes, or formatting.

There's no need to decide right now. You can switch over at any time. The more you use Ventura Publisher, the more comfortable you'll feel inserting format codes in advance. Most people will probably end up with some kind of compromise. They'll insert some codes while creating the file and do the rest of formatting in Ventura Publisher.

That's one of the great things about Xerox Ventura Publisher—it gives you choices. In this chapter, we learned about the alternatives it provides for creating text files. In the next chapter, we'll discuss Ventura Publisher's wide range of choices for creating pictures.

Chapter Four

Creating Pictures

As we saw in the previous chapter, the Ventura Publisher approach to text is uniquely versatile. You can create text files with almost any word processing program, then load those files into a document. Ventura's approach to pictures is similar. You can create picture files with your favorite graphics program, then place those files into a document.

This chapter has one major purpose: to show you how to produce images of the highest quality for use with Ventura Publisher. To do this we will examine a variety of ways to generate pictures, including draw programs, paint programs, scanners, and screen capture utilities.

Ventura Publisher also incorporates drawing tools of its own. The built-in graphics drawing mode can create simple drawings directly just as text editing mode can create small amounts of text. But clearly, most people should use an external graphics program to create complex images. In fact, graphics drawing mode is most often used during the layout to annotate or enhance pictures brought in from other programs. For this reason, we have covered graphics drawing separately in Chapter Six, Document Design and Layout.

The Ventura Approach to Pictures

Ventura's manner of dealing with pictures will make your life easier. As with text, Ventura Publisher deals with the original file from the outside program. But there's a difference between Ventura's approach to text and graphics. Ventura Publisher changes text files by adding tag names and other codes. By contrast, Ventura *does not change or modify picture files*, no matter what changes you make to the picture after bringing it in.

Rather, Ventura uses its chapter file to store a *pointer* to the original file, along with instructions on how to display it. This approach presents a powerful capability to publishers. It allows them to revise a picture file *after* it has been used in a Ventura document. The next time you access or print that document, the updated image will automatically be included, in the correct location and in the correct size. Since Ventura Publisher documents point to picture files but do not store them, those documents are automatically updated whenever a picture file has been changed.

Consider, for example, a corporate editor responsible for producing a quarterly financial summary. Now she can include bar charts in the first draft, even if based on preliminary data. When the final quarterly results come in, the bar charts will change. The nice part is that the Ventura financial document will automatically be updated, since it merely points to the file containing those charts.

We'd like to emphasize that this allows tremendous flexibility in using artwork from other programs. You can, for example, incorporate graphs from Lotus 1-2-3 or technical drawings from AutoCAD with complete assurance that those important files will not be modified in any way. This holds true even if you use Ventura's graphics drawing mode to add to the pictures after they are brought into the document.

Two Kinds of Pictures

Ventura works with two kinds of pictures: line-art and images. You can mix and match both kinds in one document. Later in the chapter we'll look at both kinds in depth and examine their pros and cons. We'll also look at specific programs in both categories. But first let's clearly distinguish between the two, since Ventura requires you to know the difference. Before you can load a picture file, you must specify in the LOAD TEXT/PICTURE dialog box whether it is line-art or image (see Figure 4-1).

When Ventura Publisher uses the term "line-art," it is referring to what the rest of the world calls "object-oriented graphics." Since many of these programs contain the word Draw in their name, they also go by the nickname of "draw programs." Ventura Publisher currently supports eight object-oriented programs directly: GEM Draw, Lotus 1-2-3, AutoCAD, Mentor Graphics, Macintosh PICT, VideoShow, CGM, and HPGL (and other formats if they are converted first).

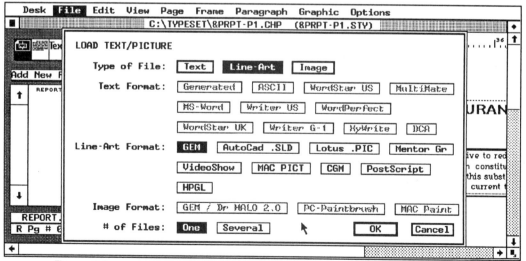

Figure 4-1
The load text/picture dialog box brings graphics into Ventura Publisher.

An object-oriented program creates a mathematical description of an image. To draw a circle, for instance, it sends a mathematical expression that translates into a circle on the screen (and later on the page). To get a bit more technical, these programs define images in geometric terms; each image is a compilation of lines, circles, squares, and other elementary objects. Hence, "object-oriented." In essence, the software redraws the picture each time it is displayed or reprinted.

Contrast this with the second type of picture: Images. Images are created by "bit-map graphics programs," also known as "pixel-oriented programs." The words *bit* and *pixel* refer to the individual dots on the computer screen. Since many of the product names contain the word "Paint," they are nicknamed "paint programs." Ventura Publisher currently supports four bit-map programs, GEM Paint, PC Paintbrush, Macintosh MacPaint, and Halo DPE (and other programs and devices if they are converted to one of these formats).

To understand bit-mapped pictures, think back to the card sections that are often part of the halftime activities at football games. Each person in the section holds a card. One side of the card is dark; the other is light. These sections can make patterns to create pictures.

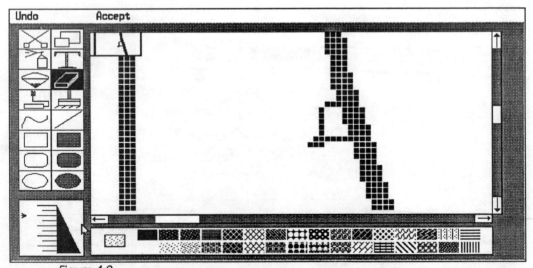

Figure 4-2
In a pixel-oriented graphics program like PC Paintbrush, images are constructed with a collection of dots, shown here in magnified mode.

Your computer screen is like a miniature card section. To create an image, a bit-map program simply tells some of the dots on the screen to turn on, and others to turn off, just the way the halftime director tells some cardholders to show the light side and others to hold up the dark side (see Figure 4-2). Hence the name "bit-map." The program creates a "map" showing which bits should be on and which should be off. To get a hard copy of this image, the program sends the same pattern of dots to the printer.

It's at print time that we see the vital difference between the two kinds of pictures. Bit-mapped programs (images) can generally only send a map of the screen. If the screen has a resolution of 72 dots per inch (dpi) then the printed image will have an effective resolution of 72 dpi, even if the printer is capable of better resolution (most laser printers can achieve 300 dpi). Figure 4-3 shows a circle created by a bit-map program.

Now look at Figure 4-4, which shows a circle created by an object-oriented program (line-art). Notice how much smoother it looks? Here's why: When the object-oriented program sends a circle to the printer, it sends the mathematical description. That description is translated into the full resolution of the printer (in this example, 300 dpi). If we were to send this same circle to a phototypesetter, it would be printed at 1200 dpi (or

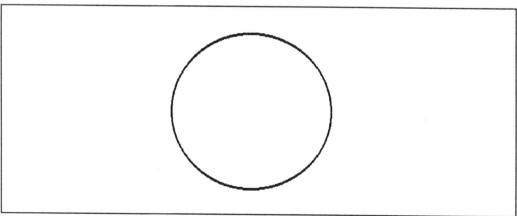

Figure 4-3
An image created with a bit-map graphics program reveals jagged curves.

higher). Consequently, object-oriented programs are not limited by the rather poor resolution of most computer screens.

Let's examine both kinds of pictures in turn and some of the specific software programs in each category.

Creating Line-Art

Charts, graphs, and other illustrations are an integral part of most corporate publications. Whether you're producing schematics for a technical manual, organizational charts for a departmental brochure, or blueprints for an engineering proposal, the art is often as important as the text.

Object-oriented programs such as GEM Draw and AutoCAD are well suited to the preparation of drawings. As noted above, the picture prints at the full resolution of the output device. And there's a second advantage to line-art from object-oriented programs: It can be changed in size without any penalty in quality.

This advantage allows you to create pictures without regard for the size they'll be on the page. For example, many people

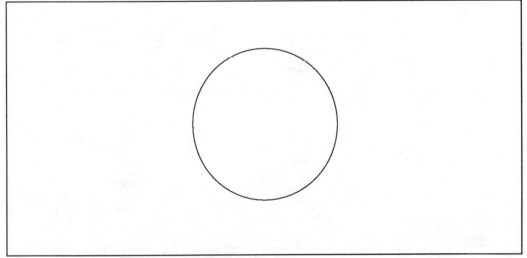

Figure 4-4
An image created with an object-oriented graphics program displays better resolution than a bit-mapped image.

produce layouts by allocating text columns and leaving holes for the pictures. Since the size of the hole depends on how much text is on each page, you need the ability to change the picture to fit. The ability to change size—called "scaling"—makes life much easier than if you had to worry about drawing the picture to fit the available space.

Perhaps the only disadvantage of object-oriented graphics programs is that they lack the flexibility of free-form paint programs. Since each image must be constructed from geometric primitives, it is more difficult to touch up a picture by adding or erasing a small portion.

Graphics Programs for Line-Art

Ventura Publisher directly accepts line-art files from the object-oriented graphics programs discussed below. It can use line-art from other programs provided it is converted to one of these formats.

GEM Draw Plus

GEM Draw Plus is an easy-to-use graphics program for the IBM PC and compatibles. Like Ventura Publisher, it is built around the GEM environment from Digital Research Inc. GEM Draw Plus incorporates a toolbox for selecting boxes, lines, circles, and freehand sketching. You point with the mouse to the desired tool, then position the cursor where you want to begin drawing. You drag the mouse to indicate the size of the object, such as the length of a line, the corners of a rectangle, or the radius of a circle. When you release the mouse button, the object is drawn on the page.

The program also features icons for fast and easy zooming to one portion of the page. With the touch of the mouse, you can move between five levels of magnification, plus a sixth view that reduces the full page to fit on screen. Use the panner icon to display different portions of the drawing by selecting the position of the screen window. Other features include on-screen rulers, a grid that can be either shown or hidden, and the ability to have multiple windows on screen at one time, each displaying a different drawing.

GEM Draw Plus can also add several different text fonts to a drawing. This is useful for annotating a diagram or filling boxes in an organizational chart.

Lotus 1-2-3

The popular Lotus 1-2-3 spreadsheet program incorporates a graphics module. This facility converts numerical data into graphs or charts. It has long been a popular feature of the program, since graphs are easier to comprehend than columns of numbers. Ventura Publisher adds to these capabilities by allowing you to integrate Lotus 1-2-3 graphs into your documents. This option will be particularly valuable to professionals who produce financial reports and summaries. They can continue to process their financial data in the spreadsheet, and then import a graphic representation for the final report.

To create a graph in Lotus, access the graph menu with the /G command. Select the desired options from the format submenu. Save the graph in a file with the .PIC extension.

♦ *Notice: Ventura Publisher can read PIC files but not WKS worksheet files.*

Words & Figures, a Lotus 1-2-3 compatible spreadsheet program from Lifetree Software Inc., offers a wider selection and better quality fonts than does 1-2-3. You may prefer to use this program to produce graphics from your spreadsheets. It can read Lotus WKS files directly.

A Tip for Working with Lotus Graphs

Touch up Lotus 1-2-3 graphs with PC Paintbrush's Chart Interpreter module. First create a PIC file in Lotus. Call up PC Paintbrush and select Merge Pic from the page menu. PC Paintbrush will read the Lotus graph onto the screen, where you can edit and enhance it. The advantage to this approach is that Paintbrush offers a wider variety of fonts, patterns, and other effects. The disadvantage is that the image will be treated as a bit-mapped graphic rather than an object graphic (PC Paintbrush and other bit-map programs are discussed below).

♦ *Warning: Normally, Lotus graphs are treated as line-art. But once a Lotus graph has been brought into PC Paintbrush it must be loaded into Ventura Publisher by specifying* IMAGE *and* PC PAINTBRUSH *in the* LOAD TEXT/PICTURE *dialog box.*

AutoCAD

AutoCAD is widely regarded as the most popular computer-aided design and drafting program on the market. It can generate sophisticated product diagrams, blueprints, and building designs. Many professional architects and designers use the program in place of manual drafting methods. AutoCAD images can be brought in to Ventura Publisher in SLD format. Alternatively, CAD pictures stored in DXF format can also be converted into GEM format using the DXFTOGEM utility supplied with Ventura Publisher.

A functional description of AutoCAD is beyond the scope of this book. However, most of the principles discussed above for other line-art apply equally to AutoCAD.

A Tip for Working with AutoCAD.

Get the orientation right in AutoCAD first, before bringing line-art into Ventura. Many users will create AutoCAD drawings in landscape mode rather than portrait mode. Landscape offers a larger view of most floorplans and other designs. But unless you want a landscape orientation within the Ventura document, you must rotate the drawing 90 degrees before leaving AutoCAD. Ventura Publisher does not perform rotation of pictures.

Mentor Graphics

Mentor Graphics manufactures a sophisticated computer-aided design system for engineering professionals. The company's software runs on Apollo workstations. Ventura Publisher supports the PicED format used by Mentor Graphics. In order to bring a Mentor Graphics image into Ventura Publisher, you must first transfer the PicED format file from the Apollo workstation to an IBM PC. Since PicED consists of ASCII characters, this is relatively easy to do using communications software.

Other Line-Art Formats

Xerox added support for several new object-oriented graphics programs when it announced version 1.1 of Ventura Publisher. These include:

- Video Show

- HPGL

- Macintosh PICT

- CGM

- Encapsulated PostScript

Video Show is a general-purpose graphics program from General Parametrics, Inc. that lets users produce a slide presentation with PC-generated graphic images. Many other graphic programs, including Harvard Presentation Graphics and Lotus Freelance Plus, can save images in this format.

HPGL refers to Hewlett-Packard's Graphics Language for plotters and other vector-oriented devices. (This is different from the PCL language that resides in the Laserjet and Laserjet Plus.) There are several CAD-type programs that can save images in HPGL format.

Macintosh PICT files are object-oriented graphics created with programs such as Apple Computer's MacDraw, Silicon Beach Software's SuperPaint, and IDD's MacDraft.

The CGM format refers to the Computer Graphics Metafile standard devised by Graphic Software Systems and others. This format is used by engineering-oriented programs such as the Concept Designer and the Concept Equation Setter from QMS.

The Encapsulated PostScript format provides a very useful method of incorporating detailed graphic images into Ventura Publisher. Images stored in this format can only be printed on a PostScript printer such as the Apple LaserWriter. Moreover, EPS format graphics cannot be displayed on screen; when you load an EPS picture into Ventura Publisher, a large X is placed on screen where the final image will appear (Figure 4-5).

Since Ventura Publisher files produced on a PostScript printer can be output on a disk file rather than the printer itself, this gives users of Ventura Publisher the opportunity to incorporate reduced-size versions of Ventura documents with the program itself. We will discuss this capability in greater detail in Chapter Nine, Special Tips & Techniques.

Tips for Working with Object-Oriented Programs

Annotate pictures in Ventura Publisher. When possible, create text such as callouts, captions, and labels with Ventura, not in the graphics program. You will get better, more uniform-quality fonts in Ventura Publisher. If you create text in the graphics program, the size may be inappropriate when you bring the picture into Ventura Publisher. For example, 8-point type in your diagram becomes 16-point type in Ventura Publisher if the picture is enlarged by a factor of two. By

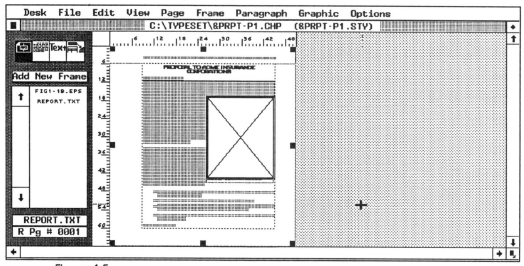

Figure 4-5
When you load a PostScript Image into Ventura Publisher, the screen displays a large X to indicate the boundary of the image.

creating the text in Ventura Publisher, you can enforce a consistent font and point size from picture to picture.

♦ *Note: One exception is rotated text, which can be useful to annotate certain graphs, vertical boxes, or extremely tight spaces. Since Ventura Publisher cannot rotate text, you must create it in the graphics program.*

Hide the labels if they are generated automatically by the graphics program and there is no way to eliminate them before bringing in the image (e.g. Lotus 1-2-3 graphs). Cover them with box text in graphics mode. Use an opaque white fill pattern so the box masks out the old label, then type in the new label using Ventura's superior fonts.

Make the image as large as practical in the graphics program so fine detail can be added. Then reduce the image to the correct size when it is brought into Ventura Publisher.

Bring in files from object-oriented programs by using the LOAD TEXT/PICTURE dialog box. Specify line-art as the type of file and then click on the name of the program to specify the line-art format (see Figure 4-1). Chapter Six, Document Design and Layout, gives complete instructions on bringing pictures into Ventura documents.

Creating Images

Line-art is created from the object-oriented programs discussed above. Images, on the other hand, are made by using bit-map programs (also called pixel-oriented programs or paint programs). This type of software offers a bit more flexibility and spontaneity. One important feature is the ability to edit the individual pixels that make up the picture. This is usually accomplished by zooming in on a portion of the image. Such detail work is important to many creative designers, who spend a great deal of time touching up a picture before it is finished.

The major disadvantage of paint programs concerns resolution. Images produced by a bit-map program are limited by the resolution of the computer display. Thus, an image created on a 72-dpi screen display will print at an effective resolution of 72 dpi, even if the printer is capable of much higher resolution.

Graphics Programs for Creating Bit-Map Images

Ventura Publisher directly accepts image files in several formats. It can use images from other sources provided they are converted.

GEM Paint

GEM Paint is a simple-to-use, pixel-oriented graphics program for the IBM PC. Like GEM Draw, it runs under the GEM environment. Also like GEM Draw, it incorporates a toolbox of graphic functions. GEM Paint has two important tools not found in GEM Draw: the eraser and the microscope. The former lets you erase parts of your picture by dragging the eraser icon over it. The microscope magnifies an area of the picture, letting you fine-tune the image by turning individual pixels on or off.

Other useful GEM Paint features include the ability to invert a picture— change white to black like a photographic negative. You can also select from a number of patterns to fill regions of the picture.

Perspective

Perspective, from Three D Graphics, allows Ventura users to incorporate very good quality, three-dimensional charts and graphs into their publication. The program can read Lotus 1-2-3 WKS files and can choose from a near unlimited variety of graph types and orientations. The program can save graphics in GEM's IMG format. Thus, to bring them into Ventura Publisher, select the GEM option under image in the LOAD TEXT/PICTURE dialog box.

PC Paintbrush

PC Paintbrush, from Z-Soft Inc., is one of the most popular graphics programs for the IBM PC. It offers a number of powerful tools and functions for creating detailed paintings. In addition to the ability to draw and fill rectangles, circles, and free-form lines, the program has several unique tools. One such tool is very useful for drawing curved lines. It lets you establish two points on the curve as well as the direction of the curve approaching either point.

In addition to supporting the original PC Paintbrush, Ventura Publisher can import images created with two enhanced versions, PC Paintbrush Plus and Publishers' Paintbrush. All three programs share the same user interface and many of the same commands. PC Paintbrush Plus offers the ability to scan an image directly from a scanner (described below). Publishers' Paintbrush offers the unique ability to edit an image at the 300 dpi resolution of a laser printer, which is much higher than a computer's display resolution. To accomplish this, you zoom in to a magnified view of a portion of the picture, essentially editing individual pixels on the laser printer.

Halo DPE

Halo DPE from Media Cybernetics, Inc., which is also marketed by IMSI as the Desktop Publishers' Graphics program, is a full-featured pixel-oriented graphics program for the IBM PC and AT. Like PC Paintbrush, it offers tools for creating lines, circles, rectangles, and shaded regions. It also has a Fat Bit Edit mode that displays an area of the screen in detail for pixel editing. Halo DPE can also control a scanner directly from within the program. Scanners supported include the Canon IX-12, the CompuScan PCS 240, the Ricoh IS-30, the Microtek MS-300A, and the IBM 3117.

Macintosh Paint Images

Ventura Publisher can import paint-type graphics created on the Apple Macintosh computer. These include images created with MacPaint, FullPaint, and several other programs. In order to incorporate a Macintosh image into Ventura Publisher, you must first convert the Macintosh file into IBM PC format. There are several methods you can use to do this.

First, a program such as MacLink from DataViz can transfer files between a Macintosh and PC using a serial cable, or "null modem." Networks such as Centram Systems' TOPS and Apple's AppleShare allow PCs and Macintoshes to share files and disk space on a network, so that transferring files is as easy as a standard operating system copy command. Finally, several companies manufacture disk drives for the Macintosh that can read and write IBM PC format. This allows you to transfer files via a media conversion process.

Tips for Bit-Map Programs

Produce bit-map pictures larger than they will appear in Ventura Publisher. You can then scale the image within Ventura Publisher using the scale picture command (see Chapter Six). Reducing the size of the image increases its apparent resolution. For example, if the screen has a resolution of 72 dots per inch the original picture will have a resolution of 72 dpi. But if you reduce that image in Ventura Publisher to 50% of its original size, it will print with an effective resolution of 144 dpi.

Annotate images in Ventura Publisher rather than in the paint program. The font quality of paint-type programs is even worse than from draw programs. If you must use the paint fonts, look for a "stroke" font such as Roman in PC Paintbrush. These fonts scale better than bit-mapped fonts. Stroke fonts can be readily identified by examining the name of the file holding the font. Stroke fonts do not contain the word "bit," which is used to identify bit-mapped fonts.

Use the screen patterns from Ventura Publisher rather than from the bit-map program if possible. Ventura Publisher's patterns are better matched to laser printer output than those from most graphics programs. Ventura Publisher's patterns will also print at the maximum resolution of your output device, unlike the bit-mapped patterns of paint programs.

Bring in files from bit-map programs by using the LOAD TEXT/PICTURE dialog box. Specify IMAGE as the type of file and then click on the name of the program to specify the image format (see Figure 4-1). Chapter Six, Document Design and Layout, gives complete instructions on bringing pictures into Ventura documents.

Creating Images with Scanners

Scanners are devices that examine pictures on paper to create an electronic description suitable for use by a computer. In essence, they look at a picture and create a bit-map image of it. This image can be brought into Ventura Publisher just like the ones created by bit-map graphics programs—but with certain advantages, as we will see.

To import a picture from a scanner, you must first convert it to one of Ventura's two bit-map formats: GEM Paint or PC Paintbrush. This conversion is accomplished by the software that accompanies the scanner. Then you bring the image into Ventura Publisher just as you would bring any other GEM Paint or PC Paintbrush picture file.

Two scanners can currently convert files to the proper formats: the Microtek MS-300A and the Dest PC Scan. In addition, by using the scanning function built into PC Paintbrush Plus or Halo DPE, you can also import images from any scanner supported by those programs, including the Canon IX-12. Finally, other scanners, such as the Datacopy model 700, can save scanned images in PC Paintbrush format, and thus are indirectly supported by Ventura Publisher.

Background on Scanners

There are two general types of scanners available today: flatbed and sheetfed. In a flatbed scanner, the paper rests face-down against a glass window, much like an office photocopier. With sheetfed scanners, pages are fed into the scanner and pass by the sensing element. In either type, the method of imaging is essentially the same. A sensing element called a charge-coupled device (CCD) creates a bit-map description of the dark and white areas on the page.

Certain scanning characteristics affect the quality of the image:

- Resolution

- Gray scale

- Brightness

- Contrast

Resolution refers to the number of dots per inch. In general, the higher the resolution, the better the quality. However, high-resolution images take up more space on the disk and usually require more time to print on a laser printer. In practice, line drawings are less sensitive to resolution than photographs. You can achieve acceptable quality for drawings by scanning with resolution as low as 100 dpi.

Gray scale is a measure of the different levels of gray (darkness) that make up an image. Line drawings require only two levels of gray—black and white. Each pixel is either on or off. Photographs, however, require somewhere between 16 and 256 levels of gray to look acceptable.

You can verify this by examining a newspaper photograph with a magnifying glass. The photo is made up of rows of dots. Although equally spaced within each row, some dots are bigger than others. In dark regions the dots are large; in light regions they're small. The number of different sizes is a measure of the photo's different gray scales.

Interestingly, a typical newspaper or magazine photo is between 85 dpi and 133 dpi. Since both scanners and laser printers are capable of resolving 300 dpi, you might think that this is enough to produce magazine-quality photos. Unfortunately, this is not the case. Today's laser printers cannot vary the size of the dots they print. Thus there is no intrinsic gray scale capability.

Today's scanners don't have intrinsic gray scale capability either. To get around this problem, manufacturers simulate the appearance of gray scale by grouping a square array of laser printer pixels into larger halftone "dots." For example, each halftone dot might consist of 16 printer pixels; four on a side (see Figure 4-6). This process, known as dithering, allows scanned photographs with 16 levels of gray. But if you use four pixels in each direction to represent one dot, then you cut the effective resolution by four— from 300 dpi to 75 dpi in the case of a laser printer.

There is always a tradeoff between effective resolution and number of gray levels. You cannot have both.

Brightness refers to the overall lightness or darkness of the scanned image. Increasing the scanner's brightness setting is like turning on a brighter light when taking a photograph. If you set the brightness too high, you may wash out some of the detail in the image. If you set it too low, you will get un-recognizable black spots.

Contrast indicates the variation in intensity— the range of difference between the darkest dark and the lightest light. Increasing or decreasing the scanner's contrast setting has

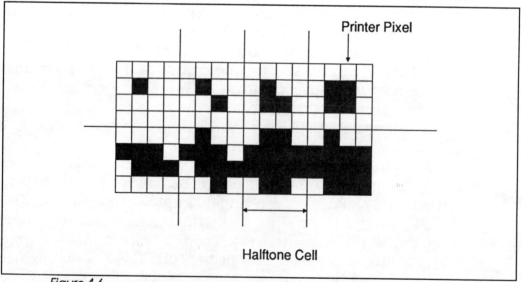

Figure 4-6
The dithering process simulates the appearance of gray levels by constructing halftone cells out of an array of printer pixels. By darkening more or fewer pixels in the array, the printer simulates bigger or smaller halftone dots.

the same effect as decreasing the contrast setting on a television set.

Scanner Products

Microtek MS-300A

The Microtek MS-300A was one of the first scanners available for desktop publishing. It is a sheetfed unit with a resolution of 300 dpi and can simulate up to 52 levels of gray. The MS-300A offers three scanning modes: line art, halftone, and mixed mode. The latter mode is very useful when you want to scan a document such as an advertisement that has both line art and photographs on it.

The Eye-Star software that accompanies the MS-300A allows you to specify a region on the page to be scanned. Thus, you need not scan an entire 8 1/2 by 11 page just to get a 1-inch square photo. You can also specify multiple windows for both line art and halftone portions of the image. Eye-Star also lets you control the brightness, contrast, and number of gray levels. A conversion module within the program lets you convert an image into either PC Paintbrush or GEM Paint format, which you must do in order to bring the image into Ventura Publisher.

PC Scan Plus

The PC Scan Plus sheetfed scanner from Dest Corp. offers a number of worthwhile features. It offers a 700 Kbyte internal memory buffer, which speeds up the image capture process. It also uses an SCSI interface to transfer image data from the scanner to the computer; this is faster than the serial communication used by some other scanners.

The PC Scan Plus comes with Dest's Publish Pac software. This program allows you to establish settings such as halftone vs. line art and brightness. It also allows you to save an image in PC Paintbrush format. Alternatively, you can drive the PC Scan Plus directly from PC Paintbrush Plus (see below), thus eliminating the need for the Publish Pac software.

Other Scanners

As we mentioned earlier, the PC Paintbrush Plus program can drive some scanners directly, thereby placing their images in a file format usable by Ventura Publisher.

PC Paintbrush Plus currently supports the Dest PC Scan Plus, the Canon IX-12, and the Panasonic scanners. As noted above, the Dest machine has its own conversion facility for putting images into the right file format, or you can use it directly through PC Paintbrush.

To bring in an image directly from PC Paintbrush Plus, select the scan option from the PC Paintbrush's Page menu (Figure 4-7). You will be presented with a menu of scanner settings (which will vary according to the available features of your scanner). You will also be able to specify a region on the page to be scanned.

PC Paintbrush Plus will then scan the image and bring it onto the screen. Once there, you can edit it with the program's graphics tools. Although you can only see the scanned image at the resolution of your display screen, *it will print at the full resolution of the scanner and printer*. If you scan the image at 300 dpi and you have a 300 dpi laser printer, you will get a 300 dpi image on the printed page. By contrast, bit-map im-

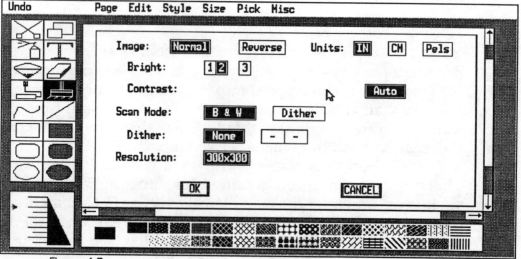

Figure 4-7
PC Paintbrush Plus can control a scanner directly.

ages from most paint programs are limited by the resolution of the computer screen, typically 72 dpi.

PC Paintbrush provides two different drivers for the Canon IX-12 scanner. One version is for the interface board supplied by Canon itself. The other version is for the JLaser Plus board. The JLaser Plus is an add-on board that installs inside a personal computer. It offers an additional two megabytes of RAM memory plus several capabilities of value to desktop publishers, including the ability to drive any laser printer based on a Canon CX engine at a full 300-dpi resolution.

If you use the JLaser Plus to drive a laser printer for Ventura Publisher, you will certainly want to use it to drive your scanner as well. In addition to saving the expense of buying another interface card, it also speeds up the imaging process considerably, since its two megabytes of memory serve as an image buffer.

Tips for Scanners

Keep these factors in mind when scanning artwork intended for Ventura Publisher.

Bringing in photographs requires experimentation. The only way you will arrive at the best parameters is to try different values for brightness, contrast, and gray scale and compare the results.

To find the best brightness and contrast settings, start with the contrast at its highest value. Leave it there while you find the appropriate level of brightness. Start at a low brightness level and gradually increase until the unwanted black areas disappear. Then, maintain this level of brightness and gradually reduce the contrast level until different regions of the image begin to blend in with one another.

Select only the portion of the page you absolutely need. While it is possible to crop an image within Ventura Publisher, you will save both scanning time and disk storage space by keeping the image data to a minimum.

To scan a small photograph into a sheetfed scanner, tape it to a piece of paper. This makes it less likely to jam and allows more precision in selecting the region to be scanned.

Print scanned images at full size if possible. Although both your graphics program and Ventura Publisher can scale an image up or down, the quality will be decreased. The halftone cell pattern created by the dithering process is optimized for the current size. If you must go up or down in size, use an integer multiple, such as 200% or 50%.

Scan line drawings at 150 dpi. Since line drawings use only two shades of gray, little is gained by increasing the scan resolution to 300 dpi. A resolution of 150 dpi provides acceptable quality and cuts down on disk space by a factor of four.

Bring in scanned images by using the LOAD TEXT/PICTURE dialog box. Specify IMAGE as the type of file and then click on the image format you are using (GEM Paint, PC Paintbrush, or Macintosh Paint format). Figure 4-8 shows a scanned image brought into Ventura Publisher from a Canon IX-12 scanner.

Screen Capture Utilities

It is often useful to incorporate a picture from a computer screen into a Ventura document:

- In software documentation to show the reader a sample screen from the program.
- To include a graphic image from a program not directly supported by Ventura Publisher.
- To annotate an existing document or graphic with descriptive labels.
- To produce reduced-scale replicas of existing documents.

Several utility programs can help you incorporate screen images into documents. We will examine three such programs here. All three create a bit-map image of the screen that can be loaded into Ventura Publisher like any other image file.

Frieze

Frieze is a support module for the PC Paintbrush graphics program. It is a memory-resident program, which means that it is accessible while you are running other programs. It can select a portion of the screen to be saved, save either portrait or landscape screen images, and reduce or enlarge the screen.

Once installed, Frieze is invoked by typing the Shift-PrtSc key on the PC keyboard. A two-line menu pops up at the top of the screen, including options for specifying the region to be saved, the size, the orientation, and the file name for the captured screen. This new file can be edited directly by PC Paintbrush, or incorporated into Ventura Publisher using LOAD TEXT/PICTURE and the PC Paintbrush image format.

♦ *Note: Frieze is installed automatically whenever you run PC Paintbrush.*

Figure 4-8
This image was captured from a Canon IX-12 scanner using PC Paintbrush Plus.

Snapshot

Snapshot is a desk accessory that accompanies the GEM
Paint program from Digital Research Inc. You can use the
program with any application that runs in the GEM environment. It cannot be accessed from programs that do not run
under GEM.

♦ *Snapshot cannot capture images from Ventura Publisher,
since it consumes too much memory. Snapshot images can be
loaded into Ventura Publisher, however.*

To install Snapshot, copy the files SNAPSHOT.ACC and SNAP-
SHOT.RSC from the GEM Paint diskette to the GEMBOOT
directory of your hard disk. Thereafter, it will be present as an
option in the Desk menu.

To invoke Snapshot, select it from the Desk menu. You will
see a dialog box with a camera icon in it. Click on the camera
icon and an item selector box will appear that prompts you for
the name of the image file you wish to create. Enter a
filename, using the extension IMG so you can later find the
image with Ventura Publisher's LOAD TEXT/PICTURE item selector. A cross hair will appear that lets you select the region of
the screen you want to capture by dragging the mouse across
the screen. When you release the mouse button, your image
will be saved to disk.

The image will be saved in GEM Paint format. You can call
up the captured screen with GEM Paint to edit or enhance it.
You can also incorporate the image directly into Ventura
Publisher using LOAD TEXT/PICTURE and the GEM image format.

HotShot

HotShot is an extremely useful program for capturing
screen images from IBM PC programs. Like Frieze, it is
memory-resident, and appears when you invoke its activation
key. HotShot incorporates two different modules: one for capturing text-based screens and another for capturing graphic
screens.

Among the unique features of this program are the ability to modify a captured text screen, edit text that is on the screen, draw lines and arrows, and add shading. The drawing tools are useful for creating organizational charts and other drawings from word processor files.

Once you have captured and saved a text screen image, convert it into PC Paintbrush format using the conversion module supplied with HotShot (or the Ventura conversion utility described below). The PC Paintbrush format file can then be brought into Ventura Publisher like any other image. Graphics screens are automatically stored in PC Paintbrush format; they can be loaded into Ventura Publisher directly.

SideKick

The popular SideKick background utility has a screen capture utility that can be used to bring text screens into Ventura. It is especially useful when combined with the Ventura TXTTOPCX conversion utility described below. Normally SideKick captures text only, but the Ventura utility permits you to bring in certain screen effects as well.

To capture a screen or a portion of a screen with SideKick active, use the import command. This function allows you to define a rectangular region on the screen by using the block begin and block end markers—just as you would with a word processing program. Once you have done this, hit the escape key to return to the SideKick window and then issue the block copy command to paste the screen contents into a new file. This file can then be saved as an ASCII file and converted to PC Paintbrush format.

Converting File Formats

Many of the programs and scanners mentioned above contain utilities that convert files to different formats. We've tried to mention them as we went along. But there are also other ways to convert pictures to formats usable by Ventura Publisher.

If you own a graphics program not directly compatible with Ventura, you may still be able to use it by converting its files to one of the formats supported by Ventura:

- Line-Art

    - GEM Draw (.GEM)
    - AutoCAD (.SLD)
    - Lotus (.PIC)
    - Mentor Graphics (.P**)
    - Video Show (.PIC)
    - Macintosh PICT (PCT)
    - Encapsulated PostScript (.EPS)
    - HPGL (.HPG)
    - CGM (.CGM)

- Image

    - GEM Paint (.IMG)
    - PC Paintbrush (.PCX)
    - Macintosh Paint (.PNT)

Many graphics programs with other file formats can convert to one of these listed above. To name just one example, Media Cybernetics Inc., makers of Halo DPE, offers a conversion program called CUTTOIMG that allows both graphics and text to be transferred to Ventura Publisher.

When converting files, consider using the file extensions noted above. Although there is nothing to prevent you from loading a file with a different extension, these are the ones Ventura Publisher looks for when you tell it which format the file is in.

Figure 4-9 offers a diagram that details how to go about converting several different graphics file formats into Ventura Publisher format.

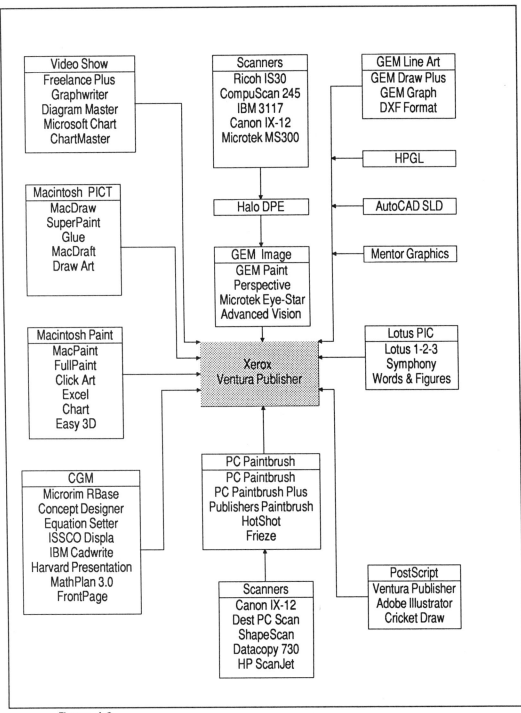

Figure 4-9
Some of the popular graphics programs that Ventura Publisher supports.

Ventura Conversion Utilities

The Ventura Utilities disk (#11) contains three conversion programs that may be of use. These programs should be invoked from the DOS prompt.

Text screen to PC Paintbrush. A text screen of 25 lines or less can be captured using a separate utility (such as Side-Kick), then converted to PC Paintbrush format using Ventura's TXTTOPCX utility. By converting to Paintbrush, you can capture reverse video, lines, and other screen effects not available if you bring the text in normally.

First capture the screen with a separate utility like SideKick or Hotshot (described above) and save it to a text file. Next, at the DOS prompt type the name of the utility followed by (1) the name of the file you wish to convert and (2) the type of display you are using. The formula is "TXTTOPCX filename /display code." The four display codes are:

- A: AT&T or Xerox 6065
- C: Enhanced Monitor (EGA)
- M: Monochrome Monitor (EGA)
- O: Color Monitor (EGA or CGA)

Thus, a user with a monochrome monitor and an EGA card would convert a text file called EXAMPLE.TXT, by typing:

TXTTOPCX EXAMPLE.TXT /M

Notice that there is a space after the file name and that the slash is a *front* slash (found below the question mark on most keyboards).

♦ *This conversion program does not work with the Hercules Graphics Card.*

AutoCAD to GEM. The DXFTOGEM utility changes AutoCAD (DXF) files to GEM Draw format (GEM). This is not strictly required, since Ventura Publisher supports AutoCAD directly. However, there may be occasions when you prefer the simplicity and ease-of-operation of GEM Draw Plus to the power and sophistication of AutoCAD. This utility permits you to bring an existing AutoCAD picture into GEM for modification. At the DOS prompt, type the name of the conversion utility followed by the name of the AutoCAD DXF file you wish to convert. The utility will create a new file with the same name but the GEM extension. Thus, to convert SAMPLE.DXF, type:

DXFTOGEM SAMPLE.DXF

The utility will create a new file called SAMPLE.GEM.

This chapter has examined several approaches to creating graphics for Ventura Publisher. There are also some powerful graphics tools within Ventura Publisher, which we explore in Chapter Six.

We have now examined text and pictures, two of the three critical building blocks that form a Ventura Publisher document. The third piece of the puzzle, style sheets, will be discussed in the following chapter.

Chapter Five

Working with Style Sheets

T his chapter is devoted to style sheets, the third part of our formula and the key to Ventura's sophistication and flexibility. Accordingly, it is one of the most important parts of this book. Once you master style sheets you'll be able to unleash the full power of the program.

By the time you finish this chapter, you'll know how to load a style sheet, how to apply it to a document, and how to change it to create a new style. Along the way, we'll become acquainted with portions of three key menus: the page menu, the frame menu and the paragraph menu.

Loading a Style Sheet

Loading a style sheet is a simple process:

Open the file menu.

Select LOAD DIFF. STYLE.

Select the style sheet you want from the list.

Click OK.

Notice in Figure 5-1 that all the style sheets shown in the item selector use the same file extension: STY. Ventura automatically assigns this extension to all style sheets. If you copy or rename using DOS, be sure to stick with the STY extension—Ventura can't apply a style sheet without it. If the item selector becomes too crowded, use the selection line to filter some of them out. Better yet, move the style sheets you don't use very often to a separate subdirectory. Treat style sheets as you would any computer file—that is, *be sure to back them up.* Every time you create a new one, make a copy on floppy disk for safekeeping.

♦ *As a general rule, you should always save your style sheet under a new name immediately after calling it in to your document. If you forget and then later save your chapter file, you will permanently modify the previous style sheet.*

To work with a style sheet, you must be able to see the results of your changes. Always load some kind of text onto the page before working with a style sheet. Even if you are only changing margins and columns, having text present makes it much easier to see the effects.

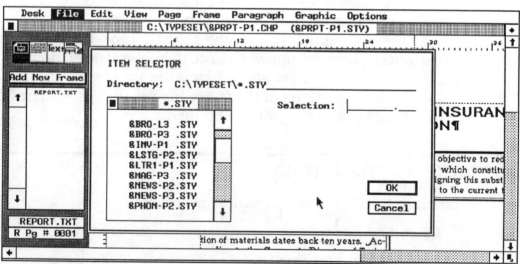

Figure 5-1
The item selector for loading a style sheet.

Applying a Style Sheet

Returning to our definition of style sheets will help us understand how to apply them. A style sheet is a collection of formatting rules. Some of the rules apply to the overall page— the margins, columns, vertical rules, etc. Others apply to the text— for instance: all Headlines will be set in 18 point Helvetica Bold; all subheads in 12 point Helvetica Bold with a 1 point rule below; and so on. These individual text formats are called tags.

When you load a style sheet, Ventura automatically applies the margins, columns, and other general format rules. To apply the rest of the format rules to the text, you must tell Ventura which tags refer to which paragraphs on the page. The only exception is body text. Ventura automatically assumes that anything not otherwise specified should be treated as body text.

You can tag text in three ways: with the mouse, with the function keys, or with the word processor.

Tagging with the Mouse

The mouse provides the simplest method of tagging. To begin, enter paragraph tagging mode by clicking on its icon in the function selector. You can also enable this function from the View menu or with the keyboard shortcut ^I.

The assignment list will change to show the tags in the current style sheet. To apply a tag, click once on the paragraph. When you click the mouse, Ventura looks for two Returns. It looks first for the the preceding Return, then for the following Return, and highlights everything in between (see Figure 5-2). This makes tagging quick and efficient. There's no need to delineate the boundaries with the mouse. Just touch any part of the paragraph and click once.

Next, click once on the name of the tag in the assignment list. The formatting rules of that tag will be applied to the highlighted paragraph, which will immediately change on screen to show the results.

To highlight more than one paragraph at a time, select the first paragraph normally. Move the mouse to the second paragraph and *hold down the shift key while clicking.* Repeat this for as many items as you wish to select at the same time. If you accidentally select an item, deselect it by clicking on it a second time *while still holding down the shift key.* Figure 5-3 shows how you might use this function to tag all the items in a list at one time.

Tagging with the Function Keys

Ventura permits you to assign tags to the 10 function keys on the left side of the standard IBM keyboard. You only need to assign the keys once—from then on, they are available whenever you use that style sheet. Once assigned, you can select a tag by pressing a function key (in place of clicking on the tag name in the assignment list). More importantly, with the function keys you can tag items while in text editing mode as well as in paragraph tagging mode.

Tagging with the function keys presents several possible advantages. First, it can eliminate the back and forth motion of the mouse, from text to assignment list and back again. Second, it permits you to edit and tag at the same time while

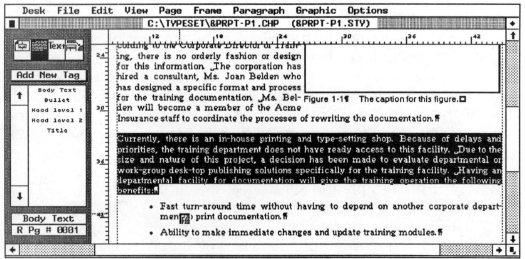

Figure 5-2
Ventura Publisher defines a paragraph as everything between two carriage returns (black area).

in text editing mode. Using this method, you can correct typos and mistakes at the same time you are tagging. Third, it permits you to compose documents directly in Ventura and tag them as you go along, without switching back and forth from text editing to paragraph tagging. And fourth, it allows you to work on a page with the sidebar hidden, since you won't need to access the assignment list. This lets you see more of the page on screen.

Assigning the Function Keys

It's up to you which tags are assigned to which function keys. Here's how it works:

Open the paragraph menu.

Select ASSIGN FUNCTION KEYS. The dialog box shown in Figure 5-4 will appear.

Type the names of the tags into the blank spaces and click OK.

Figure 5-5 shows one way to assign the function keys. Notice that the tags are in alphabetical order— the same order found on the assignment list. If you use this convention, it's

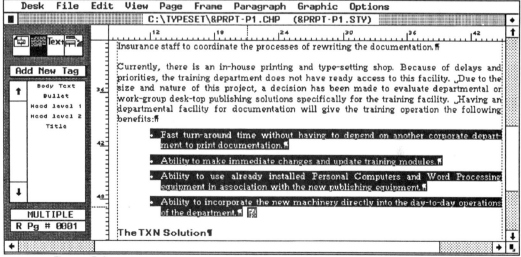

Figure 5-3
The shift-click function makes it easy to tag multiple paragraphs simultaneously.

easier to remember which tags are under which function keys— if you are in paragraph tagging mode, you can simply glance at the assignment list. The only other ways to refresh your memory are to select ASSIGN FUNCTION KEYS from the paragraph menu and review the dialog box or write your assignments down on a piece of paper.

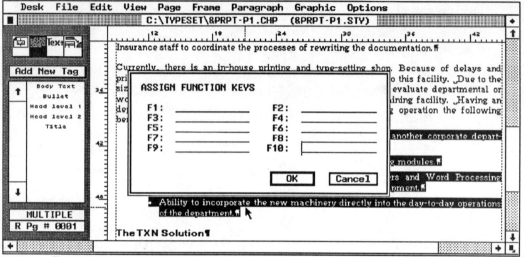

Figure 5-4
The assign function keys dialog box.

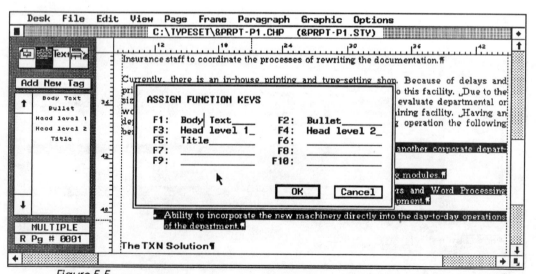

Figure 5-5
One strategy for assigning tags to function keys is to place them in alphabetical order, which is the order they appear in the assignment list.

We suggest you choose a standard way of assigning function keys and stick with it for all your style sheets. The alphabetical system is probably the most practical for most applications. But you may find certain style sheets lend themselves to different mnemonic devices. When tagging this book, for example, we used the tag names Head1, Head2, etc. for first level subheads, second level subheads, etc. It was an obvious and easy-to-remember choice to assign Head1 to F1, Head2 to F2 and so on.

Using the Function Keys

Once you've assigned tags to the function keys, you can use them when in paragraph tagging mode or in text editing mode. In paragraph tagging mode, proceed as normal to select a paragraph. But instead of using the mouse to select a tag from the assignment list, simply press the appropriate function key.

In text editing mode, simply move the text cursor anywhere in the paragraph you want to tag. There is no need to mark off the boundaries of the paragraph as you would if you were going to cut, paste, or copy it. Simply make sure the cursor is somewhere in the paragraph, then press the appropriate function key.

To tag more than one paragraph at a time, highlight everything with the mouse, then press the appropriate function key.

Tagging Paragraphs from the Word Processor

When you tag with either of the first two methods explained above, Ventura inserts the tagging information into the text files. If you prefer, you can insert these callouts in advance, thereby saving the time of paging through the document to tag each paragraph. Refer to the end of Chapter Three for detailed instructions on how to "preformat" by placing tags directly into word processing files.

Tips for Faster Tagging

These techniques can speed up the tagging process:

Use shift-click to highlight as many similar paragraphs at one time as possible, then apply the tag to all of them at once.

♦ *You can only select paragraphs on one page at a time. You cannot go to the next page and continue selecting.*

Use both hands. With the right hand, use the mouse to highlight paragraphs. With the left, press function keys to assign tags.

Page up and down through the document using the pathway illustrated in Figure 5-6. Ventura's Page Down and Page Up functions make it difficult to read a document in normal order. When you reach the bottom of the page and press Page Down, Ventura takes you to the *bottom* of the next page. To continue your reading, you must pause to use the scroll bar to get to the top of the page. Instead, consider making a quick pass through the document just to place tags. This tip applies only if you are tagging and editing in separate stages. If you are editing too, you must go through in normal order to make sense of the words.

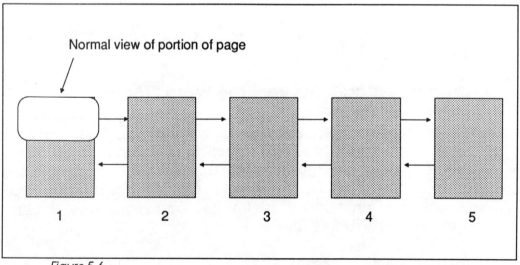

Normal view of portion of page

1   2   3   4   5

Figure 5-6
It is often easier to tag a document by paging first through the top half of each page and then through the bottom portions of the pages.

Plan carefully when naming tags. We'll have more on creating and naming tags later in the Chapter. For now, remember that the assignment list shows tags in alphabetical order. Using names like Subhead1, Subhead2, and Subhead3 would cause these tags to be listed together where they would be easy to find. Naming them Firstsub, Secondsub, and Thirdsub would scatter them around and make location difficult.

Plan carefully when assigning function keys. Some style sheets have ten or fewer tags; they present no problems. But if you have more tags than function keys, leave off the ones you'll only use once or twice, like chapter headings, titles, and headlines. Include those you will encounter frequently, like lists, tables, and subheads. Body text can also be dropped if you're short on room. Since Ventura automatically assumes that everything is body text unless you tell it otherwise, you will seldom use this tag. In fact, its only real application is to correct something you tagged by mistake. However, if there's space to include body text, we suggest you place it on F10. This is the convention followed in the style sheets included with Ventura Publisher.

Plan carefully when choosing the order of function keys. To make it easier to remember which tags belong to which function keys, use the same alphabetical order used in the assignment list. Alternatively, choose an order that makes it simple to remember.

Edit and tag in one pass if you are responsible for both tasks. You'll have to experiment to see if this method works for you. Some people prefer tagging first, then going back to edit. But you'll save time if you can manage to combine the two jobs. Use the function key assignments so you can tag paragraphs while staying in text editing mode.

Make changes to tags in the first few pages of a lengthy chapter if possible. You will find that Ventura implements the changes faster than it would on the last page of the chapter.

Changing a Style Sheet

Now we come to the crux of the matter, the techniques that will enable you to tailor Ventura Publisher to your own unique requirements.

When you create style sheets of your own— even style sheets for odd, unusual documents—you will always start with an existing style sheet. You will modify it until it matches your new specifications, and then you will save it under a new name. Consequently changing an existing style sheet and creating a new one are really the same process. If you save your changes under the same name, you permanently alter the original style sheet. If you save under a new name, you have created a new style sheet.

A Plan of Attack

Style sheets are versatile, powerful tools. If you approach them haphazardly, you are almost certain to get confused as you negotiate Ventura's multitude of options. As a result, you need a plan of attack.

A frequent complaint from beginning Ventura users is that they lose track of which features are found under which menu options. This is particularly vexing when working with a style sheet. It's not unusual to complete the job only to find you forgot to change an essential element. Fortunately, there are five steps you can take to make the process more manageable (see Figure 5-7).

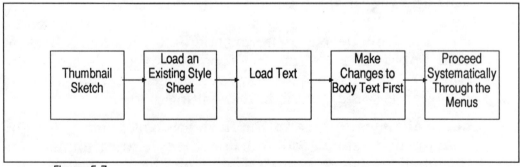

Figure 5-7
The five steps to changing a style sheet.

Step One: Make a Thumbnail Sketch

Before you start working with Ventura, it's often helpful to make a simple drawing of the new page style you want to create (or of the changes you want to make to an existing page design). Graph paper is the easiest to work with, but any blank paper will do.

Step Two: Load a Similar Existing Style Sheet

Obviously, if you are just making changes to an existing style sheet, you will load that sheet first. But even if you are setting out to create an entirely new style, start by loading the existing sheet that is closest in format. If you fail to load a sheet, you'll end up working with the last style sheet used by Ventura. It makes sense to save yourself as much work as possible by starting off with a style sheet that resembles what you want to do. The sample style sheets included with Ventura Publisher provide an excellent "launching pad." Don't worry about damaging the existing sheet. As long as you save your changes under a new name the original style sheet will remain unchanged.

Step Three: Load Text

Load a text file to see the results of changes as you make them.

Step Four: Make All Changes to the Body Text Tag First

When you create a new tag for a style sheet, the program bases this new tag on an existing tag, most often, body text. If you first make the changes you desire to body text, you will not have to repeat those changes for new tags that are later derived from body text.

Step Five: Proceed Systematically Through the Menus

To avoid overlooking key points, we suggest you go step-by-step through the three menus that contain most of the options stored in style sheets: the page menu, the frame menu, and the paragraph menu.

We suggest you start with the page menu, which you should normally need to go through only once. Next, proceed to the frame menu, which you must use once for the underlying page and once for each additional frame in the document. Finally, move on to the paragraph menu, which you must use once for each tag you add or change. In the beginning, you may have to look at each and every menu choice to discover which ones you need to change. As you improve, you'll quickly learn which ones you can skip and when.

Working with the Menus

In this section, we're going to step through the three menus you'll use when building style sheets: the page menu, the frame menu, and the paragraph menu. Not every option in these menus is recorded in a style sheet; we will ignore the ones that are not. We will spotlight key features, with special attention to trouble spots and difficult functions.

If you're familiar with Ventura Publisher, you may want to skim through this section looking for commands and options that have given you trouble. If you're new to Ventura, you may want to go step-by-step on your computer through all the features as we discuss them below. Hands-on practice is the best way to learn your way around Ventura.

The Page Menu

The page menu contains formatting options that apply to the entire document. At first glance, you might think that it would include all the options for the underlying page. But the underlying page is actually a special kind of frame and many of its options are controlled in the frame menu. Perhaps the best way to understand the page menu is to think of it as the *chapter* or *overall* menu. It controls features that apply throughout the document regardless of what else is on the pages.

Page Layout

See Figure 5-8. This menu choice does not apply to the layout of the page, as the name implies, but to the way pages are printed.

Orientation refers to whether the text will appear vertically (Portrait) or horizontally (Landscape).

Paper Type refers not to the type of paper, but to the size. The buttons B5 and A4 refer to paper sizes popular in Europe.

Although Ventura contains a half-size option, you are often better off to use larger paper sizes for small pages. Small pages are difficult to handle when being marked up and photographed for offset printing. Instead, increase the margins of the underlying page until the live area matches the dimensions of the smaller page. Or you can use the REPEATING FRAME option to place a frame the exact size of the smaller page.

If you select either the Double or Broadsheet options, Ventura will, at print time, present you with several options, depending on the capabilities of your printer. If your printer is capable of outputting only letter-sized paper, you can choose

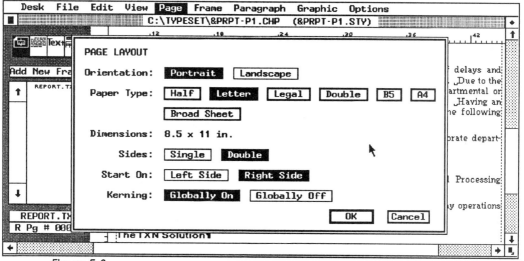

Figure 5-8
The page layout dialog box controls the physical attributes of each page in the chapter.

to shrink the page area to fit on one sheet, an option that makes proofing somewhat easier. Alternatively, Ventura will overlap several output sheets that can be pieced together to form your large page for camera-ready output. Of course, if your printer is capable of outputting 11 x 17 inch pages, you need select neither of these options; pages will come out exactly as you see them on screen.

Dimensions changes according to the paper size you choose on the line above. It allows you to confirm that you have selected the right size. If, for instance, you are interested to know the exact size of the B5 and A4, click on those choices to see the dimensions.

Sides determines whether the document is single-sided, like most business letters and memos, or double-sided like books and magazines. This is an important option, since it controls other Ventura features. For instance, if you choose single, you cannot choose FACING PAGES VIEW from the view menu (since there are no facing pages in a single-sided document). Likewise, you cannot create different headers and footers for left and right pages.

If you choose double, Ventura will automatically make "mirror" copies of such things as headers, footers, repeating frames, and margins. Suppose you place the page number on the upper left of the left-hand page and then copy this to the facing page. Ventura will automatically mirror the command. It will place the page number on the upper *right* of the right-hand page.

It is important to understand that this option refers to the *finished* form of the document. When assembling camera-ready pages for the printer, you will usually output on only one side of the paper—even though the final result will have type on both sides. The one-sided pages are printed and assembled into a double-sided document.

Start On sets the first page of the document. It is traditional in publishing to make page one a right-hand page. We suggest you stick with this convention—it is convenient to know that right-hand pages always have odd numbers.

Kerning is provided as a global override to the individual kerning options for each tag in a style sheet. Kerning will be discussed in more detail in Chapter Eight, Advanced Functions. For now, you need only realize that it is possible to suppress Ventura's kerning feature.

Widows & Orphans

See Figure 5-9. This menu choice controls the number of isolated lines that can appear at the top and bottom of a page or column.

At Top (Widow) and At Bottom (Orphan) work in precisely the same fashion. The number you select represents the minimum number of lines that must appear together. The default setting is two. If only one line appears alone at the top or bottom, Ventura will move that line to another page or column so it can remain with the rest of the paragraph. If two lines appear alone, Ventura will allow them to remain on the page. If we were to increase the setting to five, Ventura would not allow four (or less) lines to appear alone.

Eliminating isolated lines makes text easier to read. However, it also creates a problem by leaving a blank space

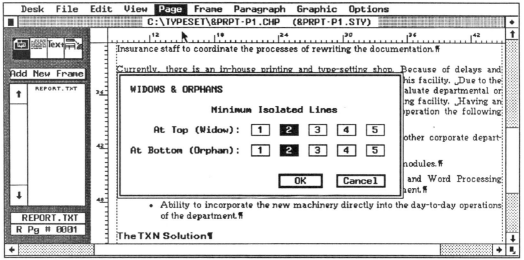

Figure 5-9
The widows & orphans dialog box lets you control the number of isolated lines at the top and bottom of a column.

where the lines would otherwise have appeared. For most purposes, select the smallest number that will make the text easy to follow, usually two. But for books, manuals, and other documents with only one column and long paragraphs, you might want to increase the settings to three.

Headers & Footers

This feature places text at the top (header) or bottom (footer) of every page, regardless of what frames may or may not be on those pages. Strictly speaking, the HEADER & FOOTERS option is not recorded in the style sheet— the settings you provide in this dialog box apply only to the Chapter you are currently working on. However, this function creates two different tags, called Z_HEADER and Z_FOOTER. The attributes that you apply to these tags *are* recorded in your style sheet, even though the content of the header and footer are not.

Formatting headers is a two-stage process in Ventura. Text and placement are defined in this menu choice. But the headers and footers created here have the attributes of body text. To change these attributes— for example to change the type size or style— you must go to the page and make the changes with the paragraph menu while in paragraph tagging mode. The paragraph menu is explained in detail later in the chapter.

Define tells Ventura precisely what you want: header, footer, left, right, etc.

Usage turns this feature on *for the entire document*. Another menu choice from the page menu turns headers and footers off for an individual page while leaving them on for the rest of the document.

Left is where you enter the text for the left side of the footer. Ventura lets you separately enter text for the left, the right, and the center of the header or footer. You can make these entries alone or in combination. Each one can be up to two lines.

Ordinarily, you will want to copy the instructions to the facing page, so left- and right-hand pages of the document will look the same. To do so, simply select COPY TO FACING PAGE. When you click on this option, you will see it turn dark briefly before becoming light again. Don't worry—your options have been properly copied.

If you do not want a mirror copy, do not choose COPY TO FACING PAGE. Instead, click on LEFT PAGE FOOTER and type in the different text.

♦ *Remember, you can't have different headers or footers on left and right pages unless you've chosen double-sided printing from the page layout dialog box.*

Frame Menu

The frame menu controls the size, appearance, and position of frames. The underlying page is a frame; so are any separate containers placed on top of it. If you remember that these frames can hold either text or pictures, you'll understand why the frame menu includes choices that relate to text (such as margins & columns) as well as those that concern pictures (such as caption setting). This menu contains the features associated with a frame as a whole. Formatting options for the individual text elements within a frame are contained in the paragraph menu.

♦ *Note: Only the attributes of the underlying page are recorded in a style sheet. Attributes of frames placed on top of the underlying page apply only to the current chapter file.*

Margins & Columns

See Figure 5-10. This choice allows the creation of up to eight columns of text. They can be of equal or varying widths.

# of columns is self-explanatory. Click on the number you want on the page.

Settings For tells Ventura which page is being described, in case you wish to have different left and right pages.

Margins sets the frame margins. We recommend you experiment with different values here. We explain below how Ventura calculates the width of the columns as you go along and displays the results at the bottom of the page. If you enter the correct margins first, you can use these calculations to check the accuracy of your results.

Frames can contain either text or pictures. In the case of text, the margins you set here will usually represent where you want the text to appear. However, Ventura also provides the capability to create additional "supplementary" margins for text using the SPACING choice from the paragraph menu.

In the case of pictures, you may often choose to do without margins so that the picture will extend to the edge of the frame. By entering margin values here, you can create a band of white space around the picture.

Widths/Gutters sets the widths of the columns and the spaces between them (the gutters). The columns are numbered from the left. When you enter values for Column 1 you are describing the left-most column on the page.

Also, observe that it is not necessary to enter the values for all the columns. All you need do is type in the measurements for the first column and the first gutter. Then tell Ventura to make all the others equal by clicking on MAKE EQUAL WIDTHS.

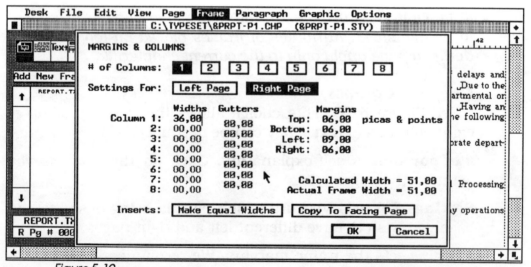

Figure 5-10
The margins & columns dialog box controls the number and width of columns in the current frame or underlying page.

Inserts contains two important functions. We have already demonstrated how to make columns equal by entering the first two values, then clicking on MAKE EQUAL WIDTHS. You can also transfer all your values to the opposite page by clicking on COPY TO FACING PAGE. Ventura will automatically make a mirror copy of the margins.

Calculated Width and Actual Frame Width enable you to see in advance if your measurements will fit into the frame. As you enter values for columns, gutters, and margins, Ventura adds them up (calculates them) and displays the results next to calculated width. Next to actual frame width Ventura shows the size of the frame you have selected.

♦ *A reminder: Calculated width = left margin + all the columns + right margin. To make use of this feature, enter the correct margin settings first. Then you can check the accuracy of the column settings.*

Vertical Rules

This choice permits the user to place rules between columns, or anywhere on the page.

Settings For tells Ventura which page you are working on.

Inter-Col. Rules creates vertical rules between columns. You specify the width of the rule. Ventura will automatically make the rule the proper length and center it in the gutter.

♦ *Warning: All the measurements in this dialog box are controlled by the units shown for rule 1 width. If it shows inches, every measurement in the dialog box will be set to inches. In almost all cases you will want to use fractional points to specify rules. If the rule 1 width shows something else, move the mouse cursor on top of the word and click until it changes to fractional points. Now every measurement in the dialog box will be in terms of fractional points.*

Ventura can create rules as small as a fraction of a point and as large as 36 points. Figure 5-11 shows a range of sizes for comparison.

Rule 1 Position and Rule 2 Position are used only if you wish to place vertical rules on the page other than between columns. One possible application would be to place vertical rules on the *outsides* of columns. However, Ventura provides no way to automatically control the length of these rules. This feature, therefore, should be used only if you want vertical rules which extend all the way from the top margin to the bottom margin.

For more precise placement, or to create rules that are not vertical, use Ventura's graphics drawing mode instead. If graphics lines are placed on a blank underlying page, they will be reproduced in the same position on every page of the document (just like the vertical rules explained here). If they are drawn onto a page that already contains text, graphics lines will show for that page only.

Although Ventura does not allow control of the length of the vertical rules, it does permit their placement from left to right. To place a vertical rule, specify its distance *from the left edge of the page* (see Figure 5-12). Do not measure from the margin or the edge of the frame (unless the edge of the frame is the same as the edge of the page). Even when placing a vertical rule into a small frame, you must always measure from the

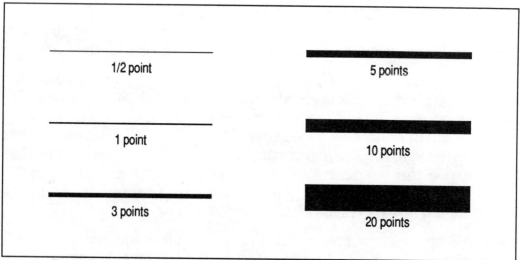

Figure 5-11
Various weights of rules.

left edge of the page that frame is on. If you have trouble deciding where to place the rule, use the Options menu to turn on the rulers.

Rule 1 Width and Rule 2 Width control separately placed rules. The values you place here have no affect on the width of inter-column rules, which are specified in the space to the right of the On and Off buttons.

Inserts permits you to copy your specifications to the opposite page. This feature works exactly as it has elsewhere.

Ruling Lines and Boxes

Ruling functions work almost identically in both the frame and paragraph menus. The techniques you learn later in the chapter for working with rules in the paragraph menu will apply equally to using rules with frames.

Paragraph Menu

The paragraph menu controls the typographic attributes of tags. Using this menu, you can create an amazing assortment of formats and effects. Each new "look" can be assigned to a

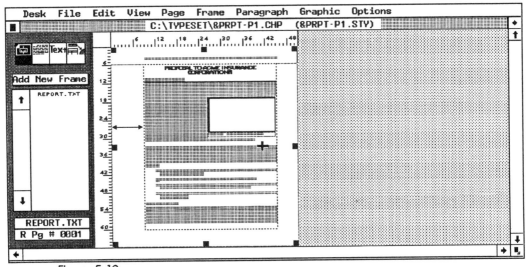

Figure 5-12
The location of a vertical rule is determined by the distance from the left-hand margin of the frame or underlying page (see arrow).

tag. (You can have up to 128 separate tags in a single style sheet.)

A tremendous amount of typographical sophistication lurks in the paragraph menu. Plan to spend considerable time learning its intricacies and mastering its options. It will be time well spent. Ventura Publisher is so powerful that many tasks can be accomplished in several ways. As a general rule, *it is usually best to do the job with a tag* even if you have other options. Once you create a properly formatted tag, you can easily and consistently reproduce your results. And tags tend to introduce fewer surprises and unexpected results.

Font

See Figure 5-13. A type*face* is a particular design. A type *font* is one specific variety of that typeface. Helvetica medium is a typeface. Helvetica 14-point bold italic is a font, one specific variety of the Helvetica typeface. The FONT option permits you to select the variety of type you wish to associate with a tag.

When you select the FONT option, a dialog box with four item selectors appears (see Figure 5-14). Available options within each of these item selectors depends on which printer is currently installed.

Face is where you specify which typeface you wish to use for this particular tag. The choices shown here will vary according to which printer you have selected. Figure 5-14 shows the typefaces available for a PostScript laser printer. Your display will differ if you are using a different printer. Likewise, if you install new fonts on your existing printer, the names of those new fonts will appear in this item selector.

(See Chapter Seven, Producing Output, for tips on how to add typefaces, sizes, and styles to your printer.)

Size controls the point size of the type. As with typeface, the numbers shown here vary according to the capabilities of your printer. If you are using a PostScript, Interpress, or DDL printer, the word "Custom" will appear in this item selector. You will then be able to enter any point size desired

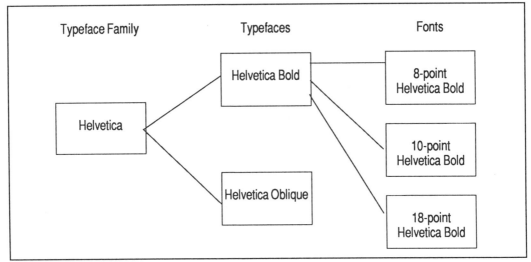

Figure 5-13
Examples of a typeface family, typeface, and font.

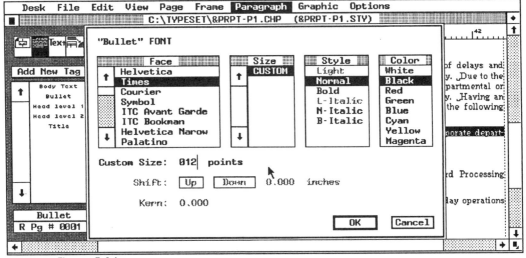

Figure 5-14
The item selector for choosing font (installed for a PostScript printer).

on the CUSTOM SIZE line below. If you are using any other printer, this item selector will show the available point sizes you can choose from.

Style enables you to control the weight (light, medium, bold) and the slope (normal or italic) of the typeface. Only the styles available for your printer will be darkened in this item selector.

Color, Shift, and Kern are advanced features covered in Chapter Eight, Advanced Functions.

♦ *Special Note: It is also possible to change the font while in text editing mode. Changing in the paragraph tagging mode results in a new font for every tag throughout the document. Changing in text editing mode changes only the words you have selected, and only at that one place in the document.*

Alignment

This menu choice governs the manner in which text lines up— whether it is centered, flush left, indented, and so on.

Alignment controls the four basic methods of setting type in a column. Figure 5-15 shows the effects of the four choices.

Hyphenation governs whether or not text for this tag will be hyphenated, and if so, with which dictionary. Ventura Publisher automatically inserts soft hyphens into text files when they are loaded. By choosing On, you are telling Ventura that it has permission to use these hyphens if needed. By choosing Off, you force Ventura to keep words undivided. In general, you will want most text hyphenated, since this improves the appearance of most documents. The exception: headlines and other large display type, which should not be hyphenated. We will discuss the use of different hyphenation dictionaries in Chapter Eight, Advanced Functions.

Overall Width determines whether the tagged text will be confined to the column or will be spaced across the entire frame. Choosing frame-wide causes a headline to be spread across the entire page, even though the rest of the text is restricted to narrow columns.

First Line affects only the first line (or lines) of a paragraph. The rest of the paragraph is unchanged. Thanks to this option, there is no need to insert tabs or spaces to indent the first line of a paragraph. Type the paragraph flush left in

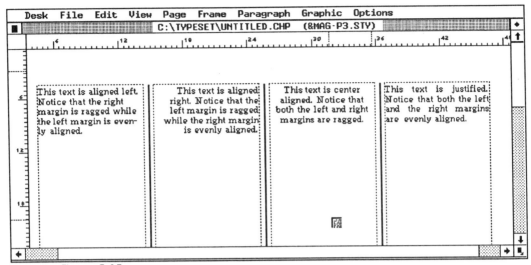

Figure 5-15
The four different choices for paragraph alignment.

your word processor, then use this option to instruct Ventura how much of an indent you want.

Choosing indent causes the first line(s) to be spaced to the right of the original margin. Choosing outdent causes it to be pushed to the left (see Figure 5-16). Neither indent nor outdent will take effect unless you enter an amount in the last line of this dialog box.

In/Outdent Width controls the amount of fixed space you will add. This amount applies to whichever choice you made in the FIRST LINE option above, whether indents or outdents. If you do not want an indent, simply make sure this amount is zero.

In/Outdent Height specifies the number of lines for which the indent or outdent will take effect. Under most circumstances, this would be 1. However, you may want to carry the indent or outdent over to two or more lines in order to produce a special typographic effect.

Relative Indent is an advanced feature covered in Chapter Eight. For most purposes it should be turned off by choosing None.

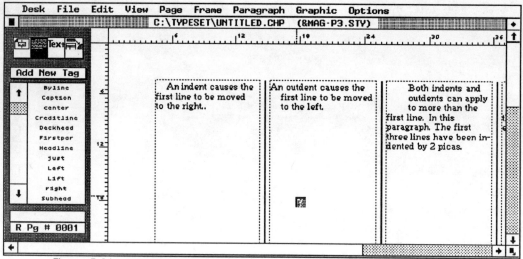

Figure 5-16
The effect of different settings for first line indent/outdent.

Spacing

See Figure 5-17. It is easy to confuse SPACING with ALIGN-MENT, the menu choice that precedes it. In general, ALIGNMENT controls the *way* in which text is placed horizontally on the page. SPACING controls the *amount*. And SPACING applies to vertical placement as well as to horizontal. In fact, the top half of the SPACING dialog box refers exclusively to vertical spacing; the bottom half exclusively to horizontal spacing.

We recommend using fractional points to measure vertical spacing. Vertical spacing has a direct relationship to type sizes, which are always specified in points. Using the same units makes it easier to create consistent, pleasing designs.

Above and Below refer to extra vertical space allotted above and/or below *the entire paragraph.* It does not affect the space between lines of a paragraph. In general, this amount should have an integer relationship with the inter-line spacing shown on the line below. If, for example, the inter-line spacing were 10 points, then 5, 10, 20, and 30 would be among the appropriate choices for above and below space.

Inter-Line refers to the spacing between lines of a paragraph. Typographers refer to it as leading. Whenever you

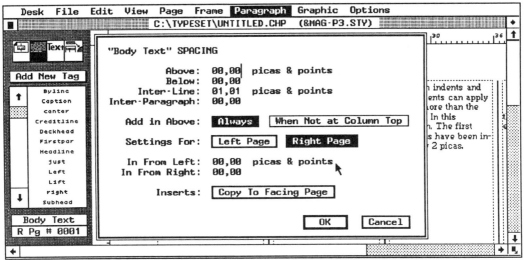

Figure 5-17
The spacing dialog box controls the amount of space allowed on all four sides of a paragraph.

choose a type size from the font menu choice, Ventura Publisher automatically selects an inter-line spacing. It automatically adds an extra 20 percent to increase readability. If you choose 10-point type, for instance, and then check the inter-line spacing, you will see that Ventura has automatically entered a spacing of about 12 points (in many cases the actual amounts will be fractionally more or less).

If you don't like the spacing chosen by Ventura, enter a new value here. Remember: inter-line spacing refers to lines *within* a paragraph.

Add in Above. Text elements like subheads need extra space above them when they are in the middle of the page. This space helps set them apart from the body text. But these same subheads don't need the space when they are the first line at the top of a column. In that case the additional white area would throw off the balance of the page. The ADD IN ABOVE option allows you to control this problem by selecting WHEN NOT AT COLUMN TOP.

Settings For applies only to the bottom half of the dialog box, which concerns itself with horizontal spacing. As with other Ventura options, facing pages can be identical or different. Different pages are created by entering separate values for the left and right pages.

In From Left and In From Right are supplementary margin settings that can be used in addition to the original margins of the frame. They have several applications. The most common is for temporary indents. Long quotations, for instance, are often set apart from the rest of the text by temporary indents on the left and the right (see Figure 5-18).

There are other cases when you want supplementary margins different from those of the frame or column. Complementary left and right pages are one example (see Figure 5-19). In this case, the frame margin is identical for each page, but the text is spaced in from left on one page and in from right on the other.

It is important to distinguish the IN FROM option from IN/OUTDENT WIDTH, which appears in the ALIGNMENT dialog box. IN/OUTDENT WIDTH affects only the first line (or first few lines). IN FROM LEFT and IN FROM RIGHT affect every line in the tag. The two options can be used together. First line indent is measured relative to the left text margin, not the frame margin. So-called hanging indents, for instance, can be created by choosing an IN FROM LEFT setting, then choosing an *equal*

The following quotation demonstrates the use of the in from left and in from right settings. This is an excerpt from the Declaration of Independence:

> **When in the course of human events, it becomes necessary for one people to dissolve the political bands that have connected them to another and to assume among the powers of the earth the separate and equal station to which the laws of nature and of nature's God entitle them, a decent respect to the opinions of mankind requires that they should declare the causes that have impelled them to the separation.**

This paragraph returns to the regular format for the document. It is tagged as body text.

Figure 5-18
The in from right and in from left settings are useful for handling quotations within text.

amount for the first line *Outdent*. The result is that the first line stays even with the rest of the text (since the IN FROM LEFT and the Outdent cancel each other) and the rest of the paragraph is indented.

Inserts applies only to the IN FROM LEFT and IN FROM RIGHT settings. Use it if you wish to create a mirror copy of your settings onto the facing page.

Breaks

See Figure 5-20. The BREAKS dialog box determines what happens before and after the selected paragraph. You can instruct Ventura to start a tag on a new line, a new column, or a new page, or to leave it on the same line as the previous tag. Breaks is an extremely versatile and useful menu choice with many advanced applications. It provides a high degree of control over the placement of text elements. We will cover advanced uses such as tables and autonumbered section headings in Chapter Eight.

Page Break sends tags to a new page. Selecting BEFORE means that the tag will always start on a new page. This might be appropriate, for example, for chapter or section

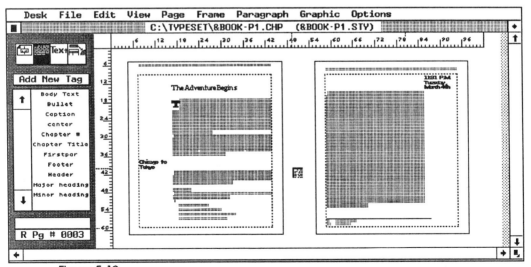

Figure 5-19
In complementary pages the margins for the left and right pages are mirror images.

headings in a book or manual. Selecting AFTER means that the next tag, whatever it might be, will be forced onto the next page. Selecting BEFORE & AFTER will isolate the tag on a page by itself. BEFORE/UNTIL LEFT and BEFORE/UNTIL RIGHT refer to page spreads in a double-sided document. If you select BREAK ON BEFORE/UNTIL LEFT, Ventura will force a page break, and if necessary, a blank page in order to get to the next left-hand (even-numbered) page. BREAK/UNTIL RIGHT ensures that text will break until the next right-hand page is encountered. These options are useful in certain technical manuals or books that require the first page of each section to begin on either the right or the left.

Column operates in the same fashion. Most tags will use the No option here. Selecting BEFORE will cause a tag to start at the top of a new column. Selecting AFTER will send the next tag to the top of a new column, no matter how much space is left below. And selecting BEFORE & AFTER will cause the tag to stand alone in a column.

Line Break works in the same fashion as the previous two options. Most tags will include some kind of line break. BEFORE causes the tag to start on a new line, no matter what

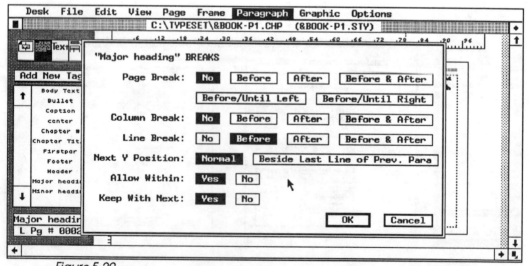

Figure 5-20
The breaks dialog box determines how a paragraph may be broken from one line, column, and page to the next.

preceded it. Choosing AFTER means that a tag can start on the same line as the previous one, but that the next item must begin on a new line. This choice is useful for the last column in a table format, as shown in Figure 5-21. Choosing BEFORE & AFTER means that a tag must always be separated by a line above and below. And choosing No means that the tag can reside on the same line with other tags. This option is useful for the middle columns in a table.

The line break option does not affect lines *within* a paragraph. It concerns itself only with line breaks that occur *between* paragraphs (before and after paragraphs). If you choose the no line break option, words within the paragraph will still wrap to the next line when they reach the right margin. There will not, however, be any line break between this tag and those before and after.

You should also be aware that the line break choice of one tag can override that of another. If you choose no line break, but your tag still resides on a separate line, check the tag that precedes it. It is quite likely that this tag contains an After or a Before & After line break.

Next Y Position refers to the vertical position of the tag. It applies only if you have *not* specified a line break before the

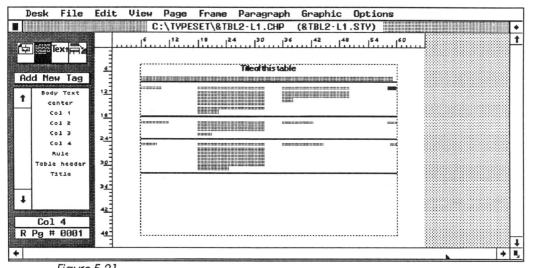

Figure 5-21
In this table, the middle columns use Line Break: No to permit other text to be vertically aligned, while the rightmost column uses Line Break: After.

tag. If you choose a line break before, then the vertical position is automatically determined—the tag will start on the next line down. But if you do not specify a line break before, you have two options. NORMAL will place the beginning of the tag at the same spot vertically as the *first* line of the previous tag. BESIDE LAST LINE OF PREV. PARAGRAPH will place it next to the *last* line. Figure 5-22 shows the difference this would mean in a tabular application.

Allow Within allows you to force all of a paragraph to stay on the same page. Choosing YES allows a break to appear within the paragraph. If it occurs near the bottom of the page, part of the paragraph may be sent to the next page. Choosing NO does not permit any breaks within the paragraph and forces the entire paragraph to stay on the same page. If there is not enough room, it will be sent to the next page.

Keep With Next is useful to prevent headings and subheadings from becoming separated from the text they refer to. If a subhead occurs at the bottom of a page, it is possible that it could be isolated, while the following paragraph is sent to the next column or page. This reduces readability. To avoid this possibility, choose Yes for headings. Most other tags should use NO, since forcing tags to stay on the same page greatly reduces Ventura's ability to produce balanced, pleasing pages.

Tabs, Special Effects, and Typographic Controls

These three advanced features are covered in Chapter Eight.

Ruling Lines Above, Below, and Around

See Figure 5-23. The three ruling lines menu choices are identical in function except for the position of the line—whether it is above, below, or around the tag.

There are several limitations to the use of these ruling lines. Lines above and below can appear either separately or together. You cannot, however, combine lines around with lines above or below. You can have up to three lines of varying

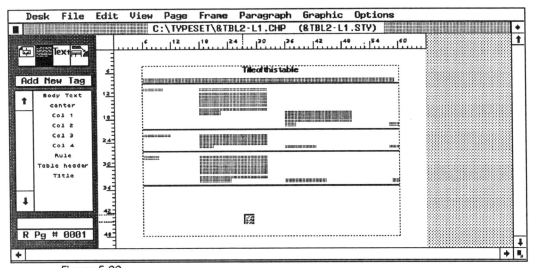

Figure 5-22
In this table, next Y position has been set to beside last line of previous paragraph for the third column.

widths, up to a total of 36 points. (You can also add lines anywhere on the page with graphics drawing mode). Although you can vary the widths, all the rules must be the same pattern and color. Lines around will not extend past page boundaries.

It is important to distinguish between the lines created here and those created with graphics drawing. Ruling lines from the paragraph menu are associated with a tag. If the tag is moved or changed, the ruling lines change with it. Every tag with the same name will have identical ruling lines. If, for example, you alter the ruling line to make it thicker, that one single change will affect every instance of that tag throughout the document, whether it is one page or one hundred.

Graphics lines, on the other hand, remain in their original position in the frame when you move other elements around. If you place them on a blank underlying page, they will show up in the same position on every page. If you place them on a page that contains text or pictures, they will appear only at that one place in the document.

Width determines where the line appears in relation to the tag. Choosing none turns off the ruling line feature, even if there are specifications entered into the rest of the dialog box. Choosing text will cause the line to appear only below the text, even if the text does not extend all the way across the column or page. Choosing margin will create lines that stop at the edges of the text margin. Choosing column creates lines that extend to the column boundaries. Choosing frame creates lines to the margins of the frame. And choosing custom lets you select a special position for the line. Figure 5-24 illustrates the effect produced by each of the width options.

♦ *Note: The ruling lines function in the frame menu works identically to those found here in the paragraph menu, except that you can only choose None or frame for the width. The other choices are grayed out to indicate that they are not available.*

Color controls the color of the line. The same color is assigned to any and all lines you create in this dialog box. Black will be the normal choice for rules. The other colors refer to color printing options as covered in Chapter Seven, Producing Output. White will create an invisible line under normal circumstances. However, if you create a white line within a frame that has been filled with black, the white lines will appear.

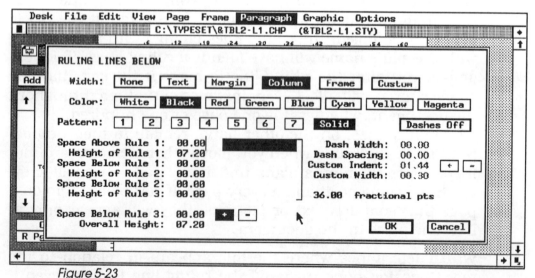

Figure 5-23
The ruling line dialog box is essentially the same for lines above, below, or around a paragraph or frame.

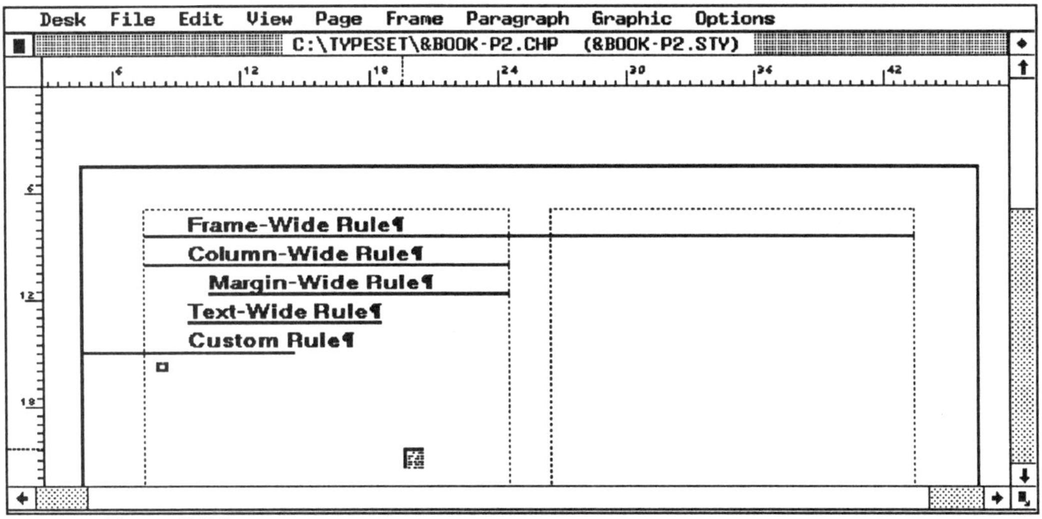

Desk   File   Edit   View   Page   Frame   Paragraph   Graphic   Options

■ C:\TYPESET\&BOOK-P2.CHP   (&BOOK-P2.STY)

> **Frame-Wide Rule¶**
> **Column-Wide Rule¶**
> **Margin-Wide Rule¶**
> **Text-Wide Rule¶**
> **Custom Rule¶**

Figure 5-24
The four possible placements for a ruling line below a paragraph.

Pattern permits you to vary the appearance and shading of the lines. The same pattern is assigned to any and all lines. Your choice is displayed in the lower half of the dialog box. However, nothing appears until you enter the height of rule. Then a representation is shown in the correct height and pattern.

Dashes Off turns dashed lines on or off for patterned rules.

Dash Width and Dash Spacing allow you to control the size of the dashes and the white space in between them. The numbers shown here are measured in whatever units are shown at the lower right corner of the dialog box just above the OK Button.

Custom Indent and Custom Width allow you to specify a nonstandard position for the rule. Indent specifies how far from the left margin the rule should be indented. Notice that by choosing a negative indent you can force the rule to the left of the margin, as demonstrated in Figure 5-24. Width specifies how wide the rule should be.

Space Above Rule 1 allows you to allot extra space between the rule and the top edge of the frame.

Height of Rule 1 specifies the thickness of the rule. Although you can enter any units, we recommend that you use point sizes. To change the units displayed, click anywhere on the units shown just above the OK Button. The units shown here control all the numbers in the dialog box.

When you change to fractional points, you will see the number 36.00 displayed. This refers to the space encompassed by the large bracket. You can have any combination of rules and spaces up to a maximum of 36 points.

Space Below Rule 1 affects the white space allotted between rules.

Space Below Rule 3 can be misleading. The number you enter here can indeed apply to the space below the third rule. But it might better be called "Space Below *Last* Rule" or "Space Below *Lowest* Rule" or even "Space Below *All* Rules." The plus and minus Buttons shown here can be used for some interesting advanced applications. Most tags should use the plus, to indicate positive space. If you choose the minus sign, you indicate negative space, in which case the amount you specify will be *subtracted* from the normal line spacing. Instead of adding extra space below, you will reduce the space below. You can use this feature, for example, to cause a wide black rule to overlap white letters, creating a reverse type effect, as explained in Chapter Nine.

Overall Height shows the total of all rules and all spaces. If the addition seems inaccurate, click OK to force Ventura to recalculate and then return to the dialog box.

Style Sheet Maintenance

Adding a New Tag

In most ways, adding a new tag is virtually identical to changing an existing one. That's because you don't start from scratch. Instead, Ventura copies the attributes from another tag to the new name. From there, you make changes until the new tag fits your specs. You can copy attributes from any existing tag, so it naturally makes sense to select the one that most closely resembles the new tag.

Here's how it works:

Select a paragraph that is already tagged.

Click on the add new tag button in the sidebar.

The dialog box shown in Figure 5-25 will appear. (Since you started by selecting a paragraph, Ventura assumes this is the existing tag you wish to copy as a starting point for your new one. You can change your mind simply by typing in the name of a different existing tag here.) Type in the name of the new tag and click OK. You will now see the new tag name on the assignment list.

At this point, the new tag is identical to the old one. To make it match the new specifications, go down the paragraph menu to change its format.

Removing and Renaming Tags

Removing and renaming tags are straightforward operations available by selecting the appropriate choice from the paragraph menu. When you remove a tag, Ventura will normally convert all paragraphs with this tag to body text. If you want to convert them to something else, type in the tag name here.

Saving a New Style Sheet

To avoid altering a style sheet you want to save, you must choose the SAVE AS NEW STYLE option from the file menu and give the changed version a new name. As we mentioned earlier in this chapter, do this immediately after loading a style sheet.

Final Tips About Style Sheets

Keep these tips in mind as you create style sheets on your own:

Standardized procedures are our recommendation whenever feasible, as you've no doubt noticed by now. We think it's the best way to gain control over Ventura's vast array of features. Style sheets and tag names are another area that can benefit from a standard approach.

If possible, try to agree in advance on a core group of tag names, and use these names in every style sheet. This can make style sheets more versatile and valuable. If you have standard tag names, you can store libraries of different style sheets. You can completely change the look of a document just by loading a new sheet. *If the tag names are identical, the tag attributes from the new sheet will instantly be applied throughout the document.* If the names are different, you will have to go through the document page by page to reassign the new tags.

This single tip can save you hours of time, especially if you work with long documents. To get you started with a system of your own, Table 5-1 below shows the tag names we used for this book. We designed them to be self-descriptive and general enough to apply to many different kinds of documents. Perhaps they can serve as starting point for standard names of your own.

Headers and Footers are created in two stages. First, type in the text and where you want it to appear using the HEADERS & FOOTERS choice from the page menu. Then, to change the

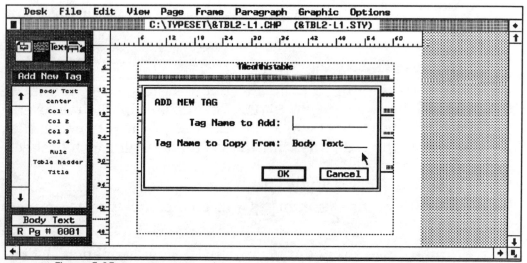

Figure 5-25
The add new tag dialog box.

appearance of the text, treat the header or footer like any other paragraph. Click on the paragraph to select it, and choose the appropriate option from the paragraph menu to make the changes you want.

Create an empty style sheet called EMPTY.STY that holds only body text. You can then use this as a starting point for creating a completely different style sheet. You won't have to worry about tags appearing in your style sheet that are unused.

With the conclusion of this chapter, we have shown how to build all three elements of the Ventura Formula. Now it's time to bring them all together. In the next chapter we outline an easy, efficient way to lay out documents with Ventura Publisher.

Table 5-1
Tags Used to Produce This Book

Body Text	Body Text
CHAP #	Chapter Number
CHAP TITLE	Title of Each Chapter
FIRST PAR	First Paragraph of Each Chapter
HEAD2	Major Headings
HEAD3	Minor Headings
HEAD4	Sub Headings
HEAD5	Run-in Heads
HEAD5_TEXT	Text Following A Run-in Head
INSTRUCT	Instructions to the Reader
LIST	Bulleted Lists
NOTE	Notes, Tips, Warnings
PROMPT	Computer-Generated Text
SEGUE	Last Paragraph of Chapter

Chapter Six

Document Design and Layout

O nce you've created text, pictures, and a style sheet, you're ready to assemble these ingredients into a document. This chapter will outline simple, efficient layout techniques. With certain modifications, they apply to any kind of document. When you finish this chapter, you'll know how to bring in and work with text and pictures, how and when to add frames, and how to save what you've done.

A Game Plan for Laying Out Pages

To avoid getting bogged down in Ventura's power and options, you need a game plan. This plan of attack will keep you on course and streamline the layout process.

This chapter explains a layout method for simple documents. By *simple*, we are referring to a straightforward design that does not change much from page to page. In simple documents, *most of the text appears on the underlying page* in the same basic format. Most books are simple documents, even though they may contain hundreds of pages.

Figure 6-1
In a simple document (left), articles follow one after the other on the underlying
page. In a complex document (right), multiple articles are combined on the same

By contrast, *complex* documents vary widely from page to
page and contain multiple articles and pictures. In complex
documents, *much of the text appears in separate frames* that
lie on top of the underlying page. The document has several
different text formats. A brochure with a complicated design
would be considered a complex document even if it only contained a few pages. Newsletters and magazines usually fall
into the complex category as well. Figure 6-1 shows the difference between simple and complex documents. Complex
documents require a few adjustments to the layout process.
Chapter Eight, Advanced Functions, gives suggestions. But
read this chapter first, since the game plan for complex documents is merely a modification of the basic techniques shown
here.

Assuming that text, pictures, and style sheet are prepared
and ready to go, the best order for working on a simple document is (1) load the style sheet, (2) work with the text and (3)
work with the pictures. Table 6-1 gives a slightly more
detailed version of the recommended game plan:

Table 6-1
Laying Out A Simple Document

Load the style sheet

Work with the text
Load the text file(s) onto the underlying page
Tag the text
Edit the text

Work with the pictures
Create a frame
Load the picture
Edit the picture
Caption the picture
Repeat for other pictures until finished

Save

One more tip before we start: It's easier to work with a document if you turn the following features on before you start. They help you visualize the page more accurately.

Feature	What it Does
Show Tabs & Returns	Visible marks in the text denoting tabs, return, line breaks, index marks, and end of file
Show Rulers	Puts rulers on the top and left edges of the page
Show Generated Tags	Displays in the assignment list the name of tags created by Ventura Publisher
Show Column Guides	Displays dashed lines to denote the boundaries of the columns
Column Snap On	Forces frames to align to column edges
Line Snap On	Forces frames to align vertically with the line spacing of body text
Text to Greek	Set to 6. Speeds display in reduced view by showing small text as blocks instead of actual characters

Loading the Style Sheet

Begin the layout process by loading in the correct style sheet, as explained in the previous chapter. In theory, it is best to have the style sheet completed before starting to layout the page. In practice, you are almost certain to change the style sheet the first few times you use it, usually to add a new tag for an unexpected contingency. Although you can recreate most formatting effects using Ventura's text editing tools, we recommend creating new tags in most cases. Although this may take more time initially, the next time you encounter a similar condition you will have a ready-made tag.

Whenever you make changes, pause to consider if you want those changes to be reflected in the original style sheet, or if you want to create a new one. If you want to preserve the original style sheet intact, remember to use the SAVE AS NEW STYLE option from the file menu as soon as you bring in the style sheet.

♦ *Warning: If you save the chapter before saving as a different style sheet, you will permanently alter the original style sheet.*

Working with Text

With the proper style sheet in place, you can proceed to load, place, tag, and edit the text.

Loading Text

Load text files by choosing the LOAD TEXT/PICTURE option from the file menu. Select the type of file you will be loading from the dialog box and then choose the file you want from the item selector. There will be a brief pause when you load the file while Ventura brings it into memory and hyphenates it. Once hyphenated, the file name will be visible on the assignment list in frame setting mode.

To load more than one file at a time, select SEVERAL from the line labeled # OF FILES. Each time you select a file name, Ventura will load and hyphenate that file, then redisplay the dialog box so you can select another one. When you are through selecting files, click on CANCEL to return to the workspace.

Tips for Loading Text

Load all the files at one time to save time and make the layout process more efficient.

Don't load unnecessary files. Each file takes up memory, whether or not it is actually put to use in the document. The less memory, the fewer pages you can process at one time. If you load a file and later decide not to use it, remove it from the assignment list by choosing REMOVE TEXT/FILE from the edit menu.

Don't use the USENGL2.HY2 alternate hyphenation algorithm unless absolutely necessary. It is about four times slower than the default algorithm. See Chapter Eight for complete details on hyphenation.

To keep the original text file intact, assign a new name to the text file. After the file has been loaded and placed on the page, select the frame or underlying page containing the text file. Choose FILE TYPE/RENAME from the edit menu. Enter the new name. When the chapter is saved, Ventura will create a new text file, leaving the original unchanged. This tip may be useful in technical documentation applications where editors are required to keep an unchanged copy of the original manuscript. If you write over the original file by mistake, you can still retrieve the backup copy made by Ventura. This file has the same file name as the original, except that the first letter of the extension has been changed to a dollar sign ($).

Placing Text

If you load only one text file, it may automatically appear on the workspace. This will occur if you are in frame setting mode and select a frame *before* you load the file. If you did not have an active frame, the file name will appear on the assignment list when you switch to frame setting mode. To place the file, enable frame setting and click once anywhere inside the frame (or underlying page). Then click on the name of the file in the assignment list. The file will be loaded into the frame.

Ventura Publisher has two modes for placing text. This is one of the keys to its flexibility. You have the speed and efficiency of batch mode for long documents *and* the accuracy and flexibility of interactive mode for design-intensive publications. The key point to remember:

♦ *When text is placed on the underlying page, Ventura creates new pages to accommodate the entire file. When text is placed in separate frames, Ventura fills the frame and then stops.*

Here's how it works: If you place the file onto the underlying page, the entire file will be loaded in. Ventura will automatically create as many new pages as needed. But if you place the file into a separate frame on top of the underlying page, *Ventura will only place as much of the file as will fit into the frame.* To continue placing this file, go to the new frame (or underlying page) where you want the rest of the text to appear and repeat the process: click on the frame and then click on the name of the file in the assignment list. Ventura will proceed to fill this new frame with the remaining text. You can continue this process as many times as necessary until the text file has been completely placed.

You will be pleased to know that Ventura does not require you to place an entire file at one time. You can stop in the middle and begin another task, such as placing a different file in another frame. Whenever you are ready to put more of the first file somewhere else, Ventura continues where it left off. This feature greatly speeds up the layout of complex documents like newsletters. You can start several articles in different frames on page 1. When you are finished, move to page 2 and continue any or all of them onto that page. Then move to page 3 and so on. Whenever you are ready to place more of a file, simply click on the frame and then click on the file name.

More good news: once you specify a "path" for the text, Ventura remembers this path and will dynamically adjust the text. For instance, suppose you place a text file into frames on pages 1, 3, 4, 5, and 8. As you make changes to the text, Ventura will flow text back and forth as necessary between these frames.

♦ *Caution: Ventura will not flow text backwards. You cannot, for example continue an article from page 8 to page 2.*

Placing More Than One File on the Underlying Page

Placing multiple files takes a special technique to avoid writing one on top of the other. If you simply click on a second file name in the assignment list, Ventura will assume that you want to replace the first file. In fact, this is a shortcut method of removing a file from a frame: Select the frame and click on the name of a new file. The old file will be erased from the frame and replaced with the new one.

But what if you want to place two text files one after the other on the same underlying page? Two techniques will help you avoid this problem. The first is to combine all the files into one *before you load them into Ventura*. This can be done using DOS or (better yet) using the word processor. Obviously, neither of these methods will work properly if the two text files are from different word processors. In that case, you may want to use the conversion technique outlined in Chapter Three to convert all the files to the same format.

Combining text files is the most efficient way to handle batch-oriented tasks like books and manuals. It can even be used for newsletters and magazines. You may also find that putting text into a single file will save on memory versus loading the equivalent amount of text in several files. Memory

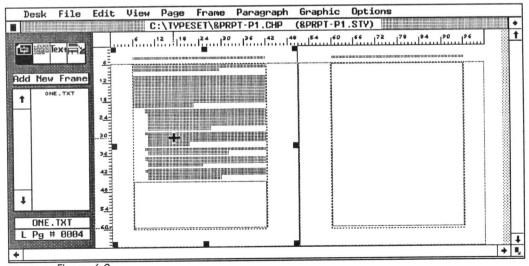

Figure 6-2
In order to layout a second text file immediately following the end of the first file, add a small frame at the bottom of the underlying page.

limitations can be an important consideration when formatting documents with multiple frames and graphics.

If you cannot combine the text files, you have a second alternative: Ventura's insert page feature. Place the first file, then press End to go to the end of the file. Select IN-SERT/REMOVE PAGE from the page menu and add a page *after* the last page. Now go to this new blank page, and select the second file from the assignment list. The second file will begin on the blank page, and Ventura will automatically create as many new underlying pages as necessary to place the entire file. You can repeat this process for additional files.

This is a neat and simple procedure provided the first file ends exactly at the bottom of a page. If not, you will have some blank space between the end of the first file and the bottom of the page. To fill this blank space, you must use a slightly different procedure to place the second file.

Let's assume that you have a single-column layout and two text files, ONE.TXT and TWO.TXT. ONE.TXT ends halfway down page 5. To fill the other half of page 5, add a frame, as shown in Figure 6-2. As you can see, this frame is *not* the same width as the underlying page. Since new frames are by default created without any margins, create the new frame with the

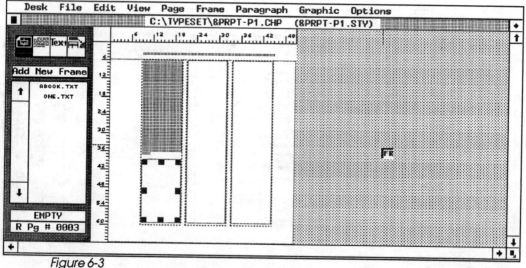

Figure 6-3
To place multiple text files in a multiple-column page, create frames that are as wide as the column.

same width as the *margins* of the underlying page. (To help with placement, select SHOW COLUMN GUIDES from the options menu and turn COLUMN and LINE SNAP on.) End the new frame exactly at the bottom margin of the underlying page. With the new frame still selected, select the second file from the assignment list. The new frame will be filled with the first portion of TWO.TXT.

What about the rest of TWO.TXT? Now that the blank space on page 5 has been filled, you can follow the procedures described above to place the rest of the file. Use the INSERT/REMOVE PAGE function to create a blank page 6. Go to this new page, select it and click on TWO.TXT in the assignment list. The remainder of the TWO.TXT file will be placed starting on page 6. Ventura will create as many more underlying pages as needed to completely place the file.

The method described above works well for single-column material. For multiple-column layouts, the procedure depends on whether you have column balance on or off. With column balance off, create a new frame for each column or portion of a column left blank after the first file has been completely placed (see Figure 6-3). Each of these frames must be the exact width of the column margins. Flow text from the second file into each of the frames in turn. Only after all the columns on the page have been filled should you insert a blank page and place the remainder of the file.

With column balance on, create a new frame that is the same width as the text margin of the underlying page. Assign the same number of columns and the same gutter widths to this frame as in the underlying page. Then proceed as above.

Inserting a Text file Into the Middle of Existing Pages

On occasion, you may need to put a separate file into the middle of a text file that has already been placed. This may occur if you accidentally load files in the wrong order, if you collate contributions from multiple authors, or if you make revisions that are too long to type with Ventura's built-in text editor.

You have three options for adding text in the middle. The first is to create a new frame on top of the underlying page. This is a viable alternative if you are adding a page or less of text. It is a good way to handle small boxes and sidebars. A second, similar approach is to create box text, using Ventura Publisher's graphics tools. This is especially true if you want to separate the new text with a ruling box around, or give it a different graphic treatment, such as a different type style or a gray screen.

But for longer additions to the underlying page, use the same method used to add a new text file at the end of a document. As before, you will select INSERT/REMOVE PAGE from the page menu. Place a blank page where you want the new text file to begin. Go to the blank page and select the new file from the assignment list. The new file will be "sandwiched" into the old one. Ventura will create additional underlying pages as necessary until all of the new file has been brought into the document. The remainder of the old file will be pushed aside to make room.

Once again, this technique has its limitations if the insertion point is not conveniently located at a page break. If not, you will have to duplicate the procedures described above. First you will add a frame to fill up the blank space. Then you will fill this frame with a portion of the new file. Finally, you will insert a page, go to that blank page, and select the new file. The remainder of the new file will be placed on new underlying pages.

What happens if the new file ends so as to create a blank space on a page? As you will recall, the new file is sandwiched in the middle of the old one. To solve this problem, fill the blank space on the page with a frame. Select this new frame and click on the name of the *old* file. Text from the old file will flow into the frame, and the remaining pages will be properly adjusted. In effect, you are dragging text from the next page and using it to fill up the blank space.

Tips for Placing Text

End of file markers are useful for confirming that you have placed all of the available file and there is no more remaining. End of file markers are small squares that appear immediately after the last character in a file. However, end of file markers appear only if you select SHOW TABS & RETURNS from the options menu. Always select this option before working with text.

Save the chapter as soon as you finish placing all the text. As in all computer applications, it's smart to save every 20 minutes or so in case of computer or power line malfunctions. It's also wise to save at logical breaking points. In this case, saving now will guarantee that if problems occur with the rest of the layout, you can return to this point, with all files loaded and in their correct order.

Use reduced view when you first place a text file in a frame or underlying page. This will let you see how much of the page is filled or how much space remains on the last page. It will also speed the text flow process, assuming you have set text to greek to 6 or higher. Once text has been flowed, return to normal view.

Tagging Text

The next step in the layout process is to tag the text. If you prefer to edit and tag in separate steps, we recommend tagging first. It seems to be easier to spot mistakes when text is in its proper format. However, if you are responsible for both editing and tagging, you may want to experiment with doing both in a single pass through the document.

Editing Text

Ventura Publisher provides a built-in text editor that is ideal for making minor corrections. It can also double as a word processor, especially on computers equipped with an 80286 or 80386 processor. With some computers based on the 8088 or 8086 processors, fast typists may discover that the computer cannot keep up with their fingers, especially in multi-column layouts or complex formats.

To edit text, begin by activating text editing mode. Then position the mouse cursor at the insertion point and click once. The flashing text cursor will appear and you can begin typing. The Backspace key erases characters behind the cursor. The Del key erases characters in front of the cursor.

Copying, Cutting, and Pasting

Copying, cutting, and pasting are accomplished by highlighting the text, then selecting a function from the Edit menu. As you become more familiar with the program, you will find that it saves time to use the keyboard shortcuts (listed for your convenience on the menu): Shift-Del for copy, Del for cut and Ins for paste. Highlight the text, then press the appropriate key.

You can highlight text in two ways. For most applications, place the mouse cursor at the beginning, and drag the cursor to the end of the selection. This method is the fastest and the easiest for larger pieces of text. For small edits where placement is difficult, use the shift-click method. Click once to place the text cursor at the beginning of the selection. Move the mouse cursor to the end, and click again *while holding down the shift key.* The text between the two clicks will be highlighted. This second method allows more accurate positioning. It is best for selecting, for example, a single letter. It is also useful to shorten or lengthen a selection. Let's say you accidentally grab two extra words while making a selection. Place the mouse cursor at the correct end point and click while holding down the shift key to shorten the selection.

You may recall that paragraph tagging mode permits you to select multiple paragraphs. These paragraphs do not need to be located next to each other. In text editing mode, however, you can only select one contiguous range of text at a time. And you cannot cross page boundaries, even in facing pages view.

Any material you cut or copy is stored in memory and will remain there until you cut or copy something else. This means that you can cut or copy anything from a word to a sentence to a paragraph and repeatedly paste it elsewhere in the document. It also means that you *cannot* cut several items once and then paste them somewhere else. Only the last item cut will remain in memory. The others will be lost.

The cut function removes the selection from the page and places it in temporary memory. The copy function works in exactly the same manner, except that the selection is not removed from the page. To place a selection anywhere in the document, move the mouse cursor to the insertion point and press Ins (or select PASTE from the edit menu).

Ventura maintains three separate temporary memories, one for frames, one for graphics, and one for text. Cutting or copying a frame or a drawing will not erase or affect text on the clipboard. The text even remains in place when you close the chapter and open a new one, so you can copy or move short text sections from one chapter to another. And there is no need to worry about the original file format of the text. Ventura permits you, for example, to move a section from a Word-Star file into the middle of a MultiMate file.

Changing Text Attributes

Ventura Publisher retains many of the attributes set within the word processor, such as boldface and underline. Nevertheless, there will be many cases when you want to add attributes within Ventura.

To change attributes, highlight the text, then select the attributes from the assignment list. When combining attributes— boldface and italics, for instance— you must select them one at a time. Text attributes are not toggle-type commands— selecting them a second time will not turn them off again. To clear attributes, select NORMAL from the top of the assignment list. Be aware, however, that NORMAL clears all attributes, not just the last one selected. If you select boldface and italics, then decide you want boldface only, you must clear out both attributes by selecting normal, and then select boldface again.

The fourth item on the assignment list is SMALL. This stands for small caps, a very useful effect that is not available on

standard word processing systems. The best way to understand small caps is to see them side-by-side with normal caps
and lowercase letters:

NORMAL CAPS   SMALL CAPS   lowercase

Small caps are an excellent way to set a word or phrase
apart from the rest of the text. It has the effect of making the
word noticeable without being obtrusive. Small caps also
come in handy for logos and headlines, either by themselves
or in combination with normal capitals.

♦ *Before selecting small caps, be sure to capitalize all letters in
the word. Any lowercase letters will appear in a smaller font.*

In addition to the standard attributes, the assignment list
can control capitalization. Those Ventura users who must edit
and integrate contributions from various authors will ap-
preciate these built-in functions. By selecting one of the three
choices at the bottom of the assignment list, you can quickly
and easily make headlines and section titles conform to the
capitalization standards you have set forth. It is almost always faster to let Ventura handle the capitalization changes
than to correct the letters one-by-one with the text editor.

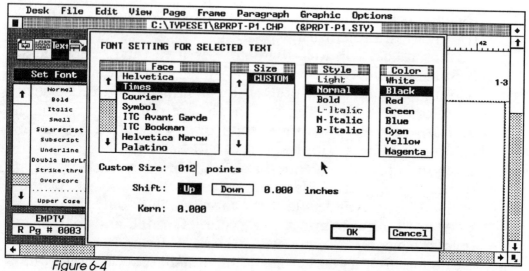

Figure 6-4
The set font button in text editing mode allows you to make font changes to a
small portion of text.

Changing Fonts

Ventura's text editing mode also lets you change the font for any section of text. Select the set font button in the sidebar to see the font dialog box (see Figure 6-4). This box is identical to the one that appears in the paragraph menu and it works in exactly the same fashion. However, the paragraph menu is unavailable in text editing mode.

As you can see, you can choose BOLDFACE or ITALIC from either the dialog box or from the assignment list. You can use either method to select these attributes; the effect is the same.

As a general rule, change the font in text editing mode when you only wish to change a few words at a single place in the document, and when you wish to have a different font "buried" inside a paragraph. If you are changing an entire paragraph, you will be wise to create a separate tag, especially if you will be duplicating this effect anywhere else.

♦ *Caution: When you change the font with text editing mode, the paragraph retains its original line spacing. If you increase the size of the font, it may be too big, overlapping with the lines above and below. One way to minimize this effect is to carefully position the new text using the Shift function found in the font dialog box. Use the enlarged view for maximum accuracy. Shift the new text up or down a half point or so at a time until it fits into the space. Shifting affects only the selected words, not the rest of the paragraph.*

Editing Tabs, Returns, Attributes, and Marks

To make editing easier and more accurate, be sure to choose SHOW TABS AND RETURNS from the options menu. Tabs in the text will be displayed as forward arrow characters (→); returns as paragraph symbols (¶) and line breaks as backwards arrows (↵). Index entries and frame anchor entries will show as the degree symbol (°).

♦ *Note: A Return starts a new line and tells Ventura to treat the next item as a separate paragraph. A line break starts a new line, but the new line is treated as part of the preceding paragraph.*

Tabs, returns, and line breaks can be edited just like text. They can be cut, copied, and pasted, in conjunction with text or by themselves. Simply highlight the symbols as you would any ordinary character and edit it using the edit menu or the keyboard shortcuts.

Here's something that's easy to overlook: Both attributes (like boldface and italics) and marks (footnotes and indexes) can also be edited. At first that might seem impossible, since the codes that turn these features on and off are not always visible on the Ventura screen, even when you select SHOW TABS AND RETURNS.

The key to finding attributes and marks is the current selection box at the bottom of the sidebar. The box is used for different purposes in different modes. In text editing mode, it remains blank *until you move the text cursor onto an attribute or mark*. Then the box displays the term "Attr. Setting."

Try this example. Move to a paragraph of body text and highlight a word. Change it to boldface. Move the text cursor to the first letter in that word. The current selection box will be blank. Now press the left arrow key once. Result: the current selection box will now display the words "attr. setting" (see Figure 6-5). In a similar fashion, you can locate other in-

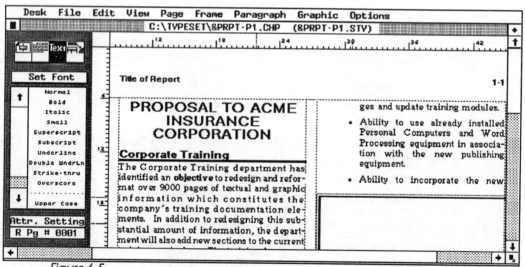

Figure 6-5
When the text cursor reaches a word in which the font settings have been changed, the current selection box shows the term attr. setting.

visible codes within the text, whether they are marks or attributes.

Inserting Symbols and Typesetting Characters

Professional-looking pages require a number of characters and symbols not available on the standard IBM PC keyboard. These special characters are quite important—without them, your pages will have an amateurish look. For example, the PC keyboard only shows one set of quote marks ("). True typeset material uses two separate sets of marks, open quotes (") for the beginning and close quotes (") for the end.

There are many other important symbols and characters that don't appear on the keyboard. In a few cases, Ventura Publisher provides access to these symbols within a dialog box. For example, when creating footnotes (described later in this chapter) Ventura lets you choose from a variety of symbols. But most non-keyboard characters are not available through a dialog box. To put them into your documents, use the extended character set.

The Extended Character Set

The extended character set is a group of characters that can be printed even though they do not appear on the keyboard. Ventura has keyboard shortcuts for the most important extended characters. For example, pressing ^] (Control-Right Bracket) places an em dash in the text. Pressing ^ Shift C creates the copyright symbol (©). Refer to Table 6-2 for a list of extended characters available from the keyboard via shortcuts. While first learning Ventura, you may want to photocopy this chart and keep it next to the computer.

You can enter other extended characters even if they don't have a keyboard shortcut. You may recall from Chapter Three that extended characters can be placed into a word processing file by typing the decimal equivalent into brackets. Those same decimal equivalents enable you to enter extended characters while in Ventura Publisher.

All characters—including those on the keyboard—have a decimal code. To access a non-keyboard character while in

Table 6-2
Commonly-Used Non-Keyboard Characters

Character	Symbol	Code	Shortcut
open quote	"	169	Ctrl-Shift [
close quote	"	170	Ctrl-Shift]
em dash	—	197	Ctrl]
en dash	–	196	Ctrl [
copyright	©	189	Ctrl-Shift C
registered	®	190	Ctrl-Shift R
trademark	™	191	Ctrl-Shift 2
bullet	•	195	
cents symbol	¢	155	
pounds symbol	£	156	
yen symbol	¥	157	
franc symbol	ƒ	159	
section sign	§	185	
paragraph	¶	188	
ellipsis	...	193	
degree symbol	°	198	

text editing mode, hold down the Alt key and enter the decimal equivalent on the numeric keypad. Table 6-2 gives the name, symbol, decimal equivalent and keyboard shortcut (if available) of several important non-keyboard characters.

For example, to place an ellipsis in the text, move the text cursor to the correct spot in the sentence. Hold down the Alt key while typing 193 on the numeric keypad (don't try to use the numbers above the keyboard). The ellipsis will appear on the screen as soon as you release the Alt key.

Table 6-2 shows only the most commonly used examples. The Ventura Publisher manual provides a complete listing of all extended characters in Appendix E.

♦ *You can use the decimal equivalent to insert different characters and symbols for bullets and footnotes. The dialog boxes for these options give several choices. If you do not like any of the symbols shown, choose an alternative and enter its decimal equivalent into the space provided in the dialog box.*

Inserting Non-Keyboard Characters Directly into Word Processing Files

You can also insert the extended character set directly into the word processing files before those files are brought into Ventura. In brief, the technique involves enclosing the decimal equivalent inside angle brackets (the same decimal equivalent explained above). Thus, Alt 197 produces the em dash character in Ventura and <197> produces the em dash when typed into a word processing file (after the file is brought into Ventura). See Chapter Three.

Inserting Footnotes

Ventura Publisher permits you to place footnote references while in text editing mode.

To create a footnote, position the text cursor after the word you wish to reference. Select INSERT FOOTNOTE from the edit menu. The footnote symbol will appear after the word. Now move to the bottom of the page, where you will see the same

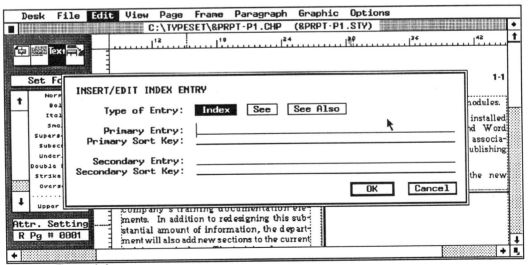

Figure 6-6
The dialog box for calling out an index entry.

symbol followed by the words TEXT OF FOOTNOTE. Erase these words and type in the correct phrase.

♦ *Although the insert footnote option is located on the edit menu, this feature will not work unless you have first turned foot-notes on using the footnote settings from the page menu. You insert footnotes from the edit menu; you control the ap-pearance and format of those footnotes from the page menu.*

Inserting Index Marks

Indexing is a three-step process in Ventura. First you mark the topics you want to index, and enter the information you want the index to contain. When the document is ready to print you perform the second step, extracting the index infor-mation along with page numbers and placing it into a separate file. Finally, you format this separate file to match the rest of the document, and print it.

The first part of the indexing process is similar to footnoting. Place the text cursor immediately before the word, phrase, or section you wish to index. Now choose INSERT/EDIT INDEX from the edit menu. Ventura will place an invisible mark in the text and display a dialog box where you can record the information that will appear in the index (see Figure 6-6).

The index mark and the indexing information are stored in the text file. However, they are "invisible" and have no effect until you perform Ventura's separate index generation func-tion using the MULTI-CHAPTER option from the options menu. This function extracts all the index entries, puts them in al-phabetical order, and lists them along with the page on which they appear into a separate file.

The INSERT/EDIT INDEX dialog box is where you type in the reference information that appears in the index. Using it takes some practice. It may be helpful to first review a typical two-level index. Such an index contains major headings, representing broad categories, and subheadings, representing specific instances. For example, here is a major heading with four subheadings:

Frames

Adding	135, 137
Deleting	138
Loading art	14, 147-153
Loading text	13, 141-144

Let's review how to create the first entry in this category. Under TYPE OF ENTRY, select INDEX. Then move to the PRIMARY ENTRY line. This represents the major heading. Here you would type in "frames." Ignore PRIMARY SORT KEY and move to SECONDARY ENTRY. Here you would enter the subhead— in this case, "Adding."

You will not need to use the sort keys for most index references. When sorting and creating the index file, Ventura uses the words typed on the entry line *unless you put something different on the sort key line.* The sort key is only for words which must be sorted differently from their spelling. You might, for example, want an index entry to read The Wilcox Company, but be sorted under "W" (for Wilcox), not under "T" (for The). In that case you would type The Wilcox Company on the entry line, and then type Wilcox Company on the sort line. The same holds true for numbers. For instance, you might place 20th Century on the entry line and Twentieth Century on the sort line.

♦ *If you want your index to show starting and ending pages (for example, 147-153), you must place an identical index entry on each page. When Ventura encounters consecutive entries, it ignores those in the middle and lists only the starting and ending pages.*

See and See Also Entries

By choosing See (or See Also) as the type of entry, you change the operation of the dialog box slightly. Normally the primary line becomes a major heading, and the secondary line becomes a subheading with a page number.

When you choose See (or See Also), the PRIMARY ENTRY still becomes a major heading. But SECONDARY ENTRY is not given a page number. Instead, the words See (or See Also) are placed in front of the subheading. Here's how it might look:

Containers

       See Frames

Frames

       Adding   135, 137
       Deleting   138
       Loading pictures into   14, 147-153
       Loading text into   13, 141-144
       See Also Graphics

Tips on Indexing

To index an item under several different names, use the IN-SERT/EDIT INDEX option as many times as needed. This will insert index marks one after another into the text file.

Always place the index mark in front of the item you are indexing. Proper indexing procedures call for the index to list the page on which the material begins. If you insert the mark after a long phrase or section you could end up with im-proper page numbering.

Try placing index marks in a separate pass through the document. We feel indexing is too complex to do simul-

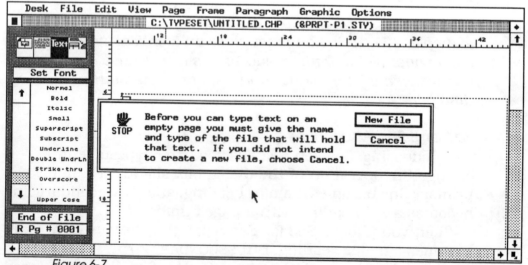

Figure 6-7
This warning appears if you try to type new text on an empty underlying page.

taneously with layout and editing. Instead, we suggest saving it until the end, and then moving through the entire document at one time. You are likely to be more consistent in your categorization if you do it all at once.

You can place index marks in a header or footer. This is a convenient way to ensure that Ventura will reference an entire range of pages for an index entry. For example, if you want to cite an entire section devoted to Australia, and the word Australia appears in your headers or footers, simply place an index mark on each page header or footer in the section. This method is most useful in conjunction with Ventura's live headers feature (see Chapter Eight).

Ventura's functions are helpful but they are not the last word in automated indexing. Be aware of their limitations. First, a Ventura index can only be two levels deep (major heading and subheading). Certain applications may demand three or four levels, which must be compiled manually. Second, Ventura provides no way to list the main headings you have already set up. To avoid forgetting what has gone before, you might want to use index cards to write down each main heading as you create it. Or, generate a trial index and use it to spot duplications and errors.

Creating Text Files with Ventura

The best use for Ventura's text functions is to modify text brought in from outside files. However, Ventura Publisher can also create text files on its own.

If you type on an underlying page (or a frame) *that already contains text*, the words will be placed into the existing text file. If you bring in a WordPerfect file, for example, and then type in three new pages of text, those three pages will be incorporated into the WordPerfect file, and saved back in WordPerfect format when the chapter is saved.

But if the underlying page is *blank* when you begin typing, a dialog box will appear asking you if you wish to create a new file (see Figure 6-7). You will have an opportunity to name the file and to specify the format in which it should be saved. You can choose ASCII or any of the other word processing formats supported by Ventura. The words you type will automatically be saved to a separate text file when you save the chapter.

A slightly different procedure occurs if you type on a blank frame (as opposed to a blank underlying page). In that case, Ventura places the text you type into its caption file. The caption file, which is stored in ASCII format, contains all the captions for all the frames in the document. Text typed into a blank frame is treated as a caption.

You may later save this text as a separate file, rather than having it in the midst of the caption file. To create a separate file, choose the FILE TYPE/RENAME option from the file menu. When the dialog box appears, enter the name and file format you wish to use. When you save the chapter, the text will now be saved to a separate file.

Controlling Page and Column Breaks

Part of the editing process—usually the last part—is to make sure all the pages break where you want them to.

Don't bother to change page breaks in Ventura until you have (1) tagged everything in the document, (2) edited the text,

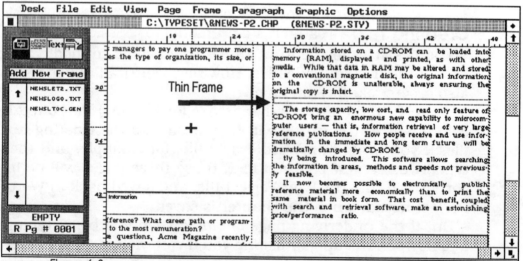

Figure 6-8
A small frame can help adjust the placement of text on the page.

and (3) inserted all the pictures. As a final step, review each page to make sure it breaks properly.

If you've set up the style sheet properly, you should have very little to do. If you find that many of your columns and pages don't end where you want them to, you may want to restructure some of your tags. Pay special attention to the KEEP WITH NEXT choice in the BREAKS option of the paragraph menu. You should also consider readjusting the WIDOWS & ORPHANS option from the page menu.

Despite these precautions, you may occasionally find a page or column that ends awkwardly. Several options are available to adjust the situation. First, you can simply add a bit of white space by creating a very small new frame (see Figure 6-8). Second, you can adjust the size of any pictures on the page. Third, you can edit the text. This is often a good choice, since you can sometimes gain or lose a line just by adding or deleting a few words from a paragraph.

But in those cases where you want to force a page or column to end, we suggest creating a special tag. This tag will have exactly the same attributes as normal body text *except* that it will have a page break after. While in paragraph tagging mode, add a new tag. Call it Body Break and copy its attributes from body text. Now go to the BREAKS option in the paragraph menu and select AFTER from the page break line. Now you can break any page by applying the Body Break tag to the last paragraph you want.

Use the same technique if the last paragraph is other than body text—for example, Bullet Break, List Break, etc. Obviously, you can also create a special tag to force column breaks as well.

Although creating a tag takes a few more seconds the first time through, it will pay off as you reuse this style sheet over and over again.

Tips for Editing Text

Assign the Body Break tag to a function key so you can control the appearance and end point of pages without leaving text editing mode.

When editing long documents don't try to enter all non-keyboard symbols and characters in Ventura's text editing mode. Instead, use your word processor's search and replace function to insert the decimal equivalent directly into the text file before it is brought into Ventura. This method is faster and offers less chance for error. A human editor is more likely to overlook a quote mark or a hyphen that a computer's search and replace function.

Don't be alarmed if a sentence disappears during editing. The sentence has not vanished— it has simply been moved. You'll find it by going to the preceding page (if you're at the top) or the following page (if you're at the bottom). Ventura reformats every time you add or delete text. Your changes may invoke automatic widow and orphan control, causing Ventura to push a section of text from one page to another.

Don't forget about the shift-click method for highlighting text. It's the best method for certain applications. If you have trouble getting just what you want by dragging the cursor, click on the beginning, then shift-click at the end. You can also use shift-click to expand (or shorten) a selection that has already been highlighted. Move the mouse cursor to the new end point and click *while holding down the shift key*. The highlighting will now be extended (or shortened) to the new end point.

Make use of temporary memory to speed editing. Ventura has three temporary memories, one for frames, one for graphics, and one for text. Use the copy function to put commonly used frames, pictures, or phrases into temporary memory where they can be reused to save retyping or redrawing.

Working with Pictures

Once you have the text loaded, placed, tagged, and edited, you're ready to add pictures to your document. The most efficient method involves these five steps: (1) load the pictures,

(2) add a frame for the first picture, (3) place the picture, (4) edit the picture, and (5) caption the picture. Repeat steps 2 through 5 for each picture.

Loading Pictures

Loading pictures is a straightforward process. It works in the same fashion and uses the same dialog box as loading text files. Select the format you want to use. Select the file name from the item selector or type it in. If you will be using more than one picture, you can load them all at one time. If you load a picture by mistake you can remove it from the assignment list by using REMOVE TEXT/FILE from the edit menu.

Adding Frames

Before you can place a picture on the page, you need a frame, a container to provide boundaries. While in frame setting mode, select the add new frame button from the sidebar. Position the cursor where you want the upper left corner of the frame. Drag the cursor to the lower right corner and release. The new frame will appear, and text will flow around it.

♦ *If the text does not flow around the frame, go to the frame menu and select* SIZING & SCALING. *Turn* FLOW TEXT AROUND *on.*

Cutting, Copying, and Pasting Frames

Frames can be cut, copied, and pasted just like text, using the Edit menu or the keyboard shortcuts. Copying or cutting puts the selected frame *and all its attributes and text* into temporary memory where it will remain until something else is cut or copied. The contents of the frame's temporary memory do not affect what is held in text temporary memory, even if the frame contains text.

♦ *Note: When you cut or copy a frame that holds a text file, Ventura Publisher places the frame and the name of the text file into temporary memory. When you later paste this frame in another place, Ventura Publisher will reflow the text, as if it were doing so for the first time. Thus, if you have made changes to the text file before pasting the frame, Ventura Publisher will update the contents of the frame accordingly.*

Fine-Tuning Size and Position

Several methods help fine tune the size and position of frames. To resize a frame, place the cursor on top of the small black handles that appear along the edges of the selected frame. *Press and hold* the mouse button. The cursor will change to a pointing finger (if it does not, you were not exactly on top of the handle). While still holding down, move the edge of the frame to its new position. Selecting a handle in a corner enables you to change both the horizontal and the vertical dimension (as you did when originally stretching the frame into position). Choosing a handle in the middle will move only one dimension at a time (see Figure 6-9). This is handy if, for example, you have the right width and don't want to risk changing it, but you need to adjust the height.

For more accurate measurements, change to enlarged view and use the hairline rules on the ruler. These hairlines move as the cursor moves. Use them to set the beginning and ending points of the frame. To make measurement easier, you can

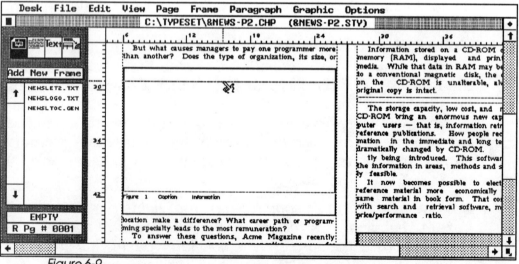

Figure 6-9
Dragging on one of the middle frame handles constrains sizing to one dimension only.

also reset the zero point of the ruler. By default, the ruler measures from the edge of the page.

For easier measuring, change the zero point to the edge of the margin. One way is to select SET RULER from the Options menu. Enter the new zero points in the dialog box. You can also set the zero points by moving the mouse cursor to the 0,0 box at the upper left corner of the ruler. Press and hold the mouse button and drag the cross-hairs down onto the screen. Place them where you want them, then release the mouse button. The zero points will reset to the mouse position.

For absolutely precise positioning, use the SIZING & SCALING option from the frame menu (see Figure 6-10). The top two lines in the dialog box specify the exact position of the frame; the next two lines specify the exact size.

In the UPPER LEFT X line, place the distance you want the frame from the *left* margin. In the UPPER LEFT Y line, enter the distance you want the frame from the *top* margin. Then adjust the size with the WIDTH and HEIGHT lines.

Adjusting Frame Margins for Pictures

If you do nothing else at this stage, the picture placed inside the frame will extend from margin to margin. In many cases

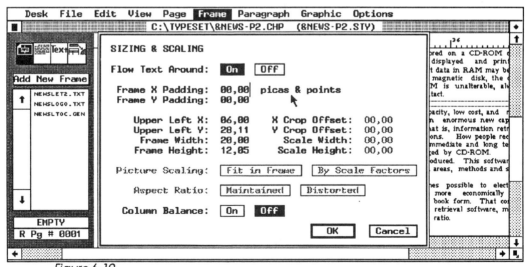

Figure 6-10
The sizing & scaling dialog box controls the size and shape of graphics placed in a frame.

you will want extra white space around the picture— especially if you have a ruling line associated with it. Use the MARGINS & COLUMNS option from the frame menu to insert this extra space.

Frame Padding

Although text will flow *around* the frame at this stage, it will butt flush against the top and bottom of the frame. To get some "breathing room" use SIZING & SCALING from the frame menu (refer back to Figure 6-9). FRAME X PADDING places buffer space in the horizontal dimension (on the top and bottom of the frame). FRAME Y PADDING places buffer space vertically (along the sides).

Where you need padding depends on the layout of your pages. As a general rule, add white space that has an integer relationship with the line spacing of body text. For instance, if you are using 10 point type with 12 point spacing, you would want to add 12 or 24 points of frame padding.

Adding Ruling Lines

Whether or not to add a ruling line around a picture depends on the type of art as well as personal taste. In general, use ruling lines when there is a lot of open space in the picture. Certain pictures, such as graphs and charts, already have rules or borders; you need not box those types. Photographs can usually do without a box around. In any case, choose only a single, very thin rule for most applications. Thick rules and multiple lines draw attention to themselves and away from the picture.

To add a box around the picture, make sure the frame holding the picture is selected. Now choose RULING LINE AROUND from the frame menu and enter the size and pattern of rule you want. When you return to the page you will find that Ventura has drawn the rule around the frame.

Tips for Adding and Positioning Frames

To create a frame template for applications such as newsletters, place a frame on the underlying page. Then fill it with a text file to get a better idea how your margins and columns will look. Once everything looks right, choose REMOVE TEXT/FILE from the Edit menu to get rid of the text and create a blank frame. Now you can cut or copy the frame to temporary memory, and repaste it as many times as necessary.

To move a frame a small distance on the page place the cursor anywhere inside the selected frame. *Press and hold* the mouse button. The cursor will change to a four-way arrow. While still holding down, drag the frame to its new position. You cannot use this method to move to another page.

To move a frame to another page use CUT and PASTE from the edit menu. Cut the frame from the old location and paste it into the new one.

To position a frame partially off the page specify a negative value for the X or Y value in the dialog box. This is not possible to accomplish using the mouse. This has limited value for laser printers, since most models cannot print close to the edge of the page, but it may have application with some phototypesetters for producing bleed pictures.

Placing Pictures

Place picture files just as you would place text files: Select the frame, then click on the name of the picture file in the assignment list. If you place the wrong picture into the frame, you can remove it by using REMOVE TEXT/FILE from the Edit menu.

Editing Pictures

You can "edit" pictures in three ways: by changing scale, by cropping, and by using Ventura's built-in graphics functions. These editing tools affect the way pictures look on the screen

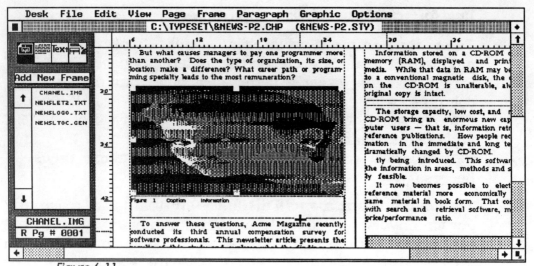

Figure 6-11
The Aspect Ratio: Distorted option lets you stretch an image in one direction or the other.

and on the printed page, but they do not affect the original graphics file, which remains untouched.

Scaling Pictures

Look back at the SIZING & SCALING dialog box shown in Figure 6-10. The top half controls the size of the frame. The bottom half controls the picture inside that frame.

The scaling function magnifies a picture. Both line art and images can use the FIT IN FRAME option, which enlarges the image until it fills the margins (or the entire frame if you did not set margins). If ASPECT RATIO: DISTORTED is selected, FIT IN FRAME may distort the picture by stretching it out of shape (see Figure 6-11). Use this option when accurate dimensions don't matter (as with cartoons) or when the shape of the original picture is close to the shape of the frame (as with a square picture and a square frame).

But often—as with technical drawings, for example—you cannot afford to distort the relationships. In such cases, use ASPECT RATIO: MAINTAINED. Ventura will enlarge the picture as large as possible without changing the ratio of horizontal to vertical. Although this option guarantees that the aspect ratio will remain the same, it may leave extra white space around the picture.

You can also scale pictures by a set amount. The dialog box shows the current dimensions of the frame and Scale dimensions. To enlarge an image, enter new Scale dimensions. If you are using ASPECT RATIO: DISTORTED you can enlarge the X (horizontal) and Y (vertical) dimensions or both. If you are using ASPECT RATIO: MAINTAINED, Ventura will only allow you to change the X value. The Y value will adjust itself as necessary to maintain the aspect ratio.

For line art, enter a scale factor for either the X or the Y dimension. When line art is brought into Ventura, it is automatically enlarged or reduced to fit the frame. When you specify new scale dimensions for line art, Ventura applies them to the original size when first brought in.

If you make the picture larger than the frame, only a portion will show. Ventura will show as much as it can, starting at the upper left corner. To show the portion you want, use the cropping feature explained below.

Tip for Scaling Pictures

When scaling bit-mapped images keep an integer (whole number) relationship between the original and final size. This will produce the cleanest images and reduce the possibility that Moire patterns and other "noise" will degrade your image. For example, note the original scale dimensions and enter new ones that are 2.0 times as big, not 1.73 times.

Scanned images should be printed at the original size if possible (or at least at an integer multiple of the original size). To make an image the same size as the original, select ASPECT RATIO: MAINTAINED, then select BY SCALE FACTORS. The act of switching from FIT IN FRAME to BY SCALE FACTORS while the aspect ratio is maintained gives you an image exactly the same size as the original.

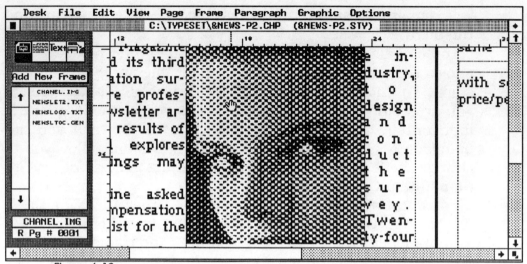

Desk File Edit View Page Frame Paragraph Graphic Options

C:\TYPESET\&NEWS-P2.CHP (&NEWS-P2.STY)

Figure 6-12
You can crop an image within a frame by holding the Alt key as you drag the
mouse with the hand icon visible.

Cropping Pictures

Scaling is one way to "edit" a picture. Cropping is a second
method. Scaling changes the size of a picture. Cropping changes which part of the picture shows inside the frame.

Start with a picture larger than the frame (if it's not, enlarge
as explained above). This picture will be displayed with its
upper left corner in the upper left corner of the frame. The
portions that won't fit are pushed off to the right and/or
below. Entering amounts for the X and Y cropping has the effect of bringing these invisible portions into view. A positive X
amount moves the picture to the left; a negative X moves it to
the right. A positive or negative Y amount brings it up or
down, respectively.

Images, but not line art, can be cropped in a second, easier-
to-use fashion.

Select the frame.

Place the cursor in the middle of the picture.

**Press and hold the mouse button *while
simultaneously holding down the Alt key.* A
small hand will appear in place of the cursor (see
Figure 6-12).**

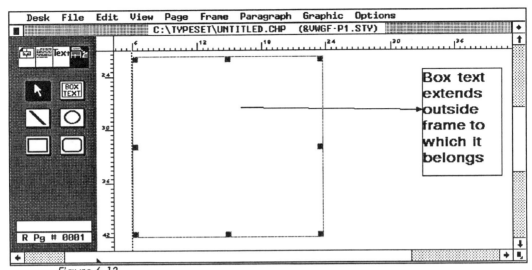

Figure 6-13
Ventura graphic elements can reside outside the frame to which they are attached.

Move the cursor until the image is repositioned satisfactorily.

Using Graphics Drawing Mode to Enhance Pictures

Ventura's built-in graphics capabilities provide an excellent way to enhance and modify pictures brought in from outside programs:

- Add simple lines to complete a drawing.

- Block out unwanted portions using graphics shapes filled with opaque white.

- Shade portions for emphasis using graphics shapes filled with transparent patterns.

- Annotate drawings using boxed text and arrows.

- Create shadow effects for headlines and banners.

All of Ventura's drawing functions work in the same basic fashion:

Select the tool you want from the sidebar.

Position the cursor where you want the graphic to start and press and hold the mouse button.

Stretch the graphic to the correct size and release the mouse button.

The graphic remains selected and you can change the lines and fill patterns from the graphics menu. Graphic tools can have a variety of different line thicknesses and patterns. And all but the line option can also be filled with various patterns. Ventura's patterns can either be transparent or opaque. Opaque patterns hide anything that is behind them. Transparent patterns still show, but anything "underneath" them (like text, for instance), will show through.

Ventura's graphics functions are particularly useful since the lines, arrows, shapes, and patterns you draw *do not have to be within the boundaries of the frame.* As you can see in Figure 6-13, box text and arrows (or any other graphic) can extend outside the frame. *All graphics are tied to the frame that was selected when they were created.* If you move the frame, the graphics move along with it, even if they extend past the boundaries of that frame.

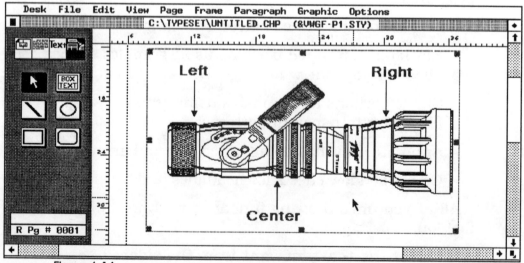

Figure 6-14
Ventura's graphics drawing function can be used to add annotations to an existing graphic.

Box Text

Ventura's box text option provides a method of annotating drawings. It does, however, have certain limitations. To use it most efficiently, follow this procedure:

First, decide in advance what to say for each annotation to gauge the approximate size of the box. Then create a box text big enough for the largest annotation. Do not type in the words yet. Copy the first box repeatedly until you have a box text for every annotation. Move the boxes into position around the drawing.

Now switch to text editing mode and type in the annotations. Change to a different font if you wish. Next, switch back to graphics drawing to take off the lines around the boxes. Use SELECT ALL to change the attributes of all the boxes at once.

Choose SELECT ALL from the graphics menu. All the boxes will be highlighted.

Select line attributes and choose a thickness of NONE.

Choose FILL ATTRIBUTES from the graphics menu.

Select TRANSPARENT and WHITE.

Finally, choose the line drawing tool and draw arrows from the text to the picture (see Figure 6-14).

♦ *Tip: Put in arrows after typing the text and removing the line. Until then, you don't know exactly where to position the beginning of the arrow.*

Theoretically, you could annotate pictures using separate frames and Ventura's standard text editing mode. Box text, however, gives you more freedom to place the annotations anywhere on the page. More important, it ties them to the picture. Anytime the picture is moved, the annotations move with it.

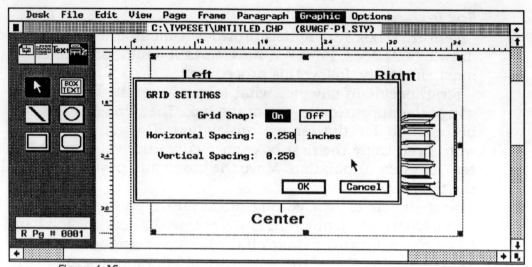

Figure 6-15
The grid setting dialog box controls the snap-to spacing for Ventura's graphic elements.

Tips for Graphic Drawing

Keep annotations as short as possible to avoid cluttering up the drawing.

Use the shift-click method to select more than one graphic at a time, just as you use it to select multiple paragraphs in paragraph tagging mode. Likewise, you can de-select a graphic (and leave all the others selected) by shift-clicking on it a second time.

To select all the graphics associated with a frame, use SELECT ALL from the graphics menu, or use the keyboard shortcut Ctrl-Q.

Pay extra attention to the frame which is selected when you create a graphic. If you don't pay attention, you could find the graphic linked to the wrong frame, with disastrous results. Remember: *it doesn't matter where you're drawing, it only matters which frame is selected when you start.* For example, if the underlying page is selected when you start drawing, the graphic will be repeated on every single page of the document.

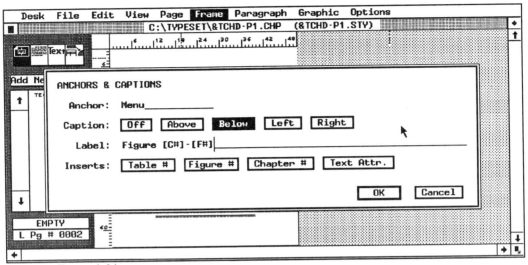

Figure 6-16
The anchors & captions dialog box lets you generate labels that are attached to frames.

To check which graphics are associated with a frame, click on the frame in frame setting mode, then use Ctrl-Q (select all).

If you have trouble getting box text to print out, set the fill attribute for the box to transparent. If you must cover up what is underneath the box text, create a graphic rectangle underneath the box text which has its fill pattern set to solid white.

Graphics that appear on every page of the document are an excellent way to create crop and registration marks for printing. Simply select the underlying page before drawing and the marks will be reproduced on every underlying page.

For more accurate placement of box text and other graphics, use the GRID SETTINGS option from the graphics menu. This option creates an invisible snap-to grid. It performs the same function for graphics that column and line snap performs for frames. The dialog box (see Figure 6-15) gives you the opportunity to choose the size of the grid. To improve the appearance of the picture, choose horizontal and vertical spacing that has an integer relationship to the size of the frame. Choose small increments to give you maximum flexibility. For example, increments of 3 picas (1/2 inch) might be a good choice for a picture 24 picas (4 inches) square.

Use an external graphics program for complex drawings and diagrams. Standalone programs have more functions and options than available in Ventura Publisher. You may also find that this speeds up the performance of Ventura Publisher.

Adding Captions

Ventura's captioning functions are powerful, but complex. You may want to spend some extra time with this section to master the ins and outs. It's probably easiest to think of captioning as a two-stage process: (1) attaching the caption to the picture and (2) enhancing the caption.

Attaching the Caption

Attaching the caption occurs with the ANCHORS & CAPTION SETTINGS option from the frame menu. At this stage you will determine the position of the caption and create a label. This label is only a portion of the entire caption. Later, during the enhancing stage, you can add more text and change the appearance.

To begin, select the frame that contains the picture you want to caption. Now select ANCHORS & CAPTION SETTING. The dialog box shown in Figure 6-16 will appear. Decide where you want the caption to appear and select the correct position from the top line.

Now move to the second line and type in the label you want to appear. This label can be up to one line long. (If you want additional text in the caption, you will add it during the enhancing stage.)

♦ *Warning: Anything you type here can be edited only by returning to this dialog box. (By contrast, text you add during the enhancing phase can be edited in text editing mode). For this reason, it is generally best to keep this label as short as possible.*

Take a look at any caption from this book. The label portion is the phrase "Figure X-Y," where X represents the number of the chapter and Y represents the number of the figure. For instance, the seventh figure in chapter four would be labeled Figure 4-7. *The rest of the caption was added during the enhancing phase.*

Let's review how that label was created. The word *Figure* followed by a space was typed into the dialog box. The number of the chapter was inserted by clicking once on the CHAPTER # button in the third line of the dialog box. This caused the code [C#] to be placed on the same line. Next a hyphen was typed. Then the number of the figure was inserted by clicking on the FIGURE # button. This caused the code [F#] to be inserted onto the line.

Note that we could have simply typed "Figure 4-7" onto the line. If we had done that, however, we would have had to go back and change the caption if the picture was later moved to another chapter, or if the order of the pictures was changed. By inserting the codes for chapter and figure numbers, Ventura automatically did all the numbering for us. If we had later decided to add another picture to the chapter in front of this one, Ventura would automatically have renumbered it to read Figure 4-8. Likewise, if we had moved it to become the first picture in chapter five, Ventura would have called it Figure 5-1, without any intervention on our part.

Note also that the only function of the four buttons at the bottom of the dialog box is to *save you the trouble of typing in the code.* There is no mystery to these three inserts; you do not have to use them if you prefer to type in the code directly; they are merely a convenience. These codes create numbers only. Any words, spaces or symbols you want in the label must be typed into the dialog box. In the example above, the hyphen between 4 and 7 was typed in. It was not created automatically by Ventura. The text attr. button performs the same function in the dialog box as the set font button performs in text editing mode.

Finally, you should be aware that the table counter and the figure counter work independently. This allows you to

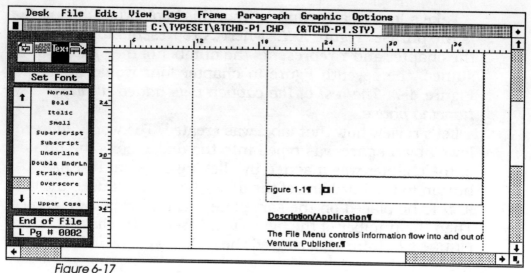

Figure 6-17
To enter a caption for a new frame, place the text cursor in front of the end-of-file
indicator (square) in the caption area.

separately number two different kinds of pictures in each
chapter. For instance, if we added a table to chapter four after
Figure 4-7, the table would be labeled "Table 4-1." Obviously,
you can label these pictures anything you want. You could
just as easily call them Illustration 4-7 and Chart 4-1, if you
prefer. Likewise, you do not have to include the number of the
chapter in the label.

Enhancing the Caption

By attaching the caption with the dialog box, you have un-
wittingly done two things: First, you have created a small caption frame that butts up against the original one.

♦ *Important: This caption frame is permanently bound to the
original frame. Move or delete the original frame and you
automatically move or delete the caption frame (and everything in it.)*

Second, when you created the label you also created a new
tag in the assignment list. If you used the FIGURE # button this
tag will be called Z_LABEL FIG. If you used the TABLE # button it
will be called Z_LABEL TBL. A few words about these new
"generated" tags: First, the letter Z has no significance. It was

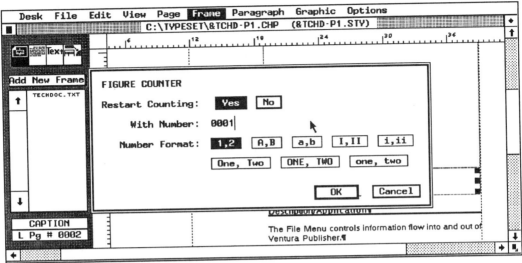

Figure 6-18
You can alter the numbering sequence for figures by calling up the figure counter dialog box.

chosen simply to guarantee that these tags would always appear at the bottom of the alphabetical assignment list. Second, you cannot change their names. Third, you cannot tag the label with anything else—in other words, you can't decide to relabel it as a Headline.

But you *can* treat these tags just like any others when it comes to altering their attributes. When first created, these tags automatically take on the characteristics of body text. To make them look different, use the paragraph menu as you would with any other tag.

So much for changing the appearance of the label. But what if you want to add text to the caption? Simply go to the caption frame, enlarge it, and type in the additional words.

Here's how it works: Make sure you are still in frame setting mode. Select the caption frame and stretch it until it is at least twice as large. Now switch to text editing mode and select SHOW TABS AND RETURNS from the options menu. You will see the end of file marker displayed in the caption frame on the line underneath the label (see Figure 6-17). Simply position the text cursor right in front of the end of file marker and start typing. If you run out of room, stretch the caption frame as far as needed to accommodate the extra text.

The text you type in this way will be stored in the caption file for this chapter, along with the label you created earlier. And, like the label, this text will be assigned its own tag, with the name Z_CAPTION. As with the Z_LABEL tags, you can change the attributes of this tag, therefore changing the appearance of all the captions throughout the document.

All the other rules of tags apply to Z tags. In the examples discussed above, the Z_LABEL and Z_CAPTION tags appear on separate lines. If you prefer, they can appear on the same line. Refer to Chapter Eight, Advanced Functions, for tips on how to use Ventura's relative indent and breaks options to make two different tags appear on the same line.

So far we've discussed how to enhance the caption by altering the tags and by adding text. You also have the option of changing the number Ventura inserts into the label. Unless you tell it otherwise, Ventura will start numbering from the number one and use an Arabic numeral.

To change the number, select the FIGURE COUNTER from the frame menu (or TABLE COUNTER if you are working with a table). The dialog box shown in Figure 6-18 will appear. If you are printing the parts of a long document separately, use WITH NUMBER to set the correct starting number. If you do not change this number, Ventura will assume you wish to start with number one.

The bottom half of the dialog box permits you to choose the format of the numbers. You can choose arabic or roman numerals or you can have Ventura spell out the numbers. You can also choose letters instead of numbers to sequence figures or tables, with full control over capitalization.

Tips for Working with Captions

If you have many captions, set and label them using the ANCHORS & CAPTIONS option from the frame menu, but type them in using a word processor. Load the CAP file as you would any other text file. Remember to work in ASCII (non-document) mode in your word processor. Ventura expects its caption file, which always has the extension CAP, to be in straight ASCII and cannot accommodate other formats.

♦ *Caution: Be careful not to delete any paragraph returns in the CAP file. Ventura keeps track of its captions by counting them. If you delete a return, you'll throw off the numbering, and captions will appear in the wrong frames.*

Use copy and paste to create multiple graphics with the same caption label. First create an empty frame. Then access ANCHORS & CAPTION SETTINGS to position the caption and specify a repeating label. Enlarge the size of the caption frame to accommodate the longest caption. Next, select COPY FRAME from the edit menu. This places both the empty frame, and its adjacent caption, into temporary memory. Then just use the Ins key to paste a copy of this frame onto a later page. Ventura will not only include the caption frame, it will even update the label with the figure or table number.

Check the caption file separately with a spelling and/or grammar checker, just as you would check any other file. Don't forget to use ASCII format.

You cannot edit the label in text editing mode as you can the rest of the caption. To change the label, use the CAPTION

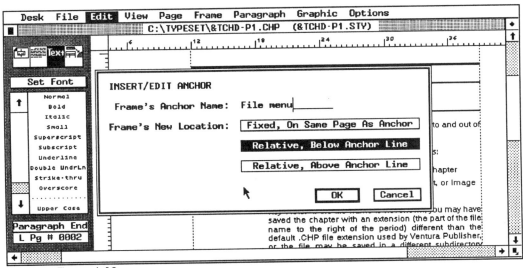

Figure 6-19
The insert/edit anchor dialog box lets you call out a particular frame that should be placed in proximity to the current text position.

SETTING option from the frame menu to return to the original
dialog box.

Don't get overly frustrated by the process of getting captions to look the way you want. Remember that you are
creating tags that can be reused over and over again. Once
you have fine-tuned the format and the appearance, you can
reuse these settings in other documents that access the
same style sheet.

Anchoring Frames

Ventura provides a method for ensuring that frames appear
on the same page as the text that refers to it. This feature does
not have perfect judgment; it doesn't do away with the need to
check each page. You will still have to reposition some of the
frames manually. But it can speed the layout process.

Normally, editors wait until all text changes have been made
so they can place pictures as close as possible to the text
reference. If they place pictures too early, changes to the
chapter may cause the text to move while the pictures stay
put. By inserting a frame anchor, you insure that the frame
will move along with the text.

Perhaps the most difficult thing about anchors is that they
involve three separate options from three separate menus. It's
a three-step process: (1) insert an anchor into the text, (2) tie
a frame to that anchor, and (3) reformat the chapter (to reposition anchored frames).

To insert the anchor mark, place the cursor where the
anchor should appear. The most obvious spot is at the beginning or end of the text reference. (In this book, for example, we
use phrases like "See Figure 6-5.") With the cursor at the right
spot, select INSERT/EDIT ANCHOR from the edit menu (See
Figure 6-19). The resulting dialog box will ask for the frame's
"anchor name." Choose this name with care and write it down.
You must reuse it later when you tie a frame to the anchor,
and you must get it exactly right. The most obvious choice is
to name the anchor the same way you labeled the caption.
Thus, if the caption reads "Fig. 5," then Fig. 5 is the logical
name for the frame anchor.

However, using numbers runs the risk that things will change. Using automatic figure and table counters (covered in a later chapter) may change the number of the figure. Fig. 5 for example, may become Fig. 7. The frame anchor will remain intact, however, as long as the names match, even if the names are inconsistent with the final numbering when the chapter is printed. To avoid this inconsistency, you may prefer to use anchor names that describe the picture or repeat the first few letters of the caption. Use any naming scheme you like as long as you are consistent.

Now tell Ventura where the frame should appear. If you want all illustrations in the same location on each page, choose FIXED, ON SAME PAGE AS ANCHOR. For frames above or below the text reference, choose RELATIVE, BELOW ANCHOR LINE or RELATIVE, ABOVE ANCHOR LINE.

So much for the text anchor. It has no value, however, until you tie it to a specific frame. That is done in frame setting mode. First, select the frame. Then choose ANCHORS & CAPTIONS from the frame menu. The first line of the dialog box says "Anchor." This is asking for the anchor name. Enter the same name used before.

After the first two steps, frame anchoring does not take affect until you select RE-ANCHOR FRAMES from the page menu. Then Ventura moves all the frames in a chapter to the same page as the anchor.

This feature is merely a starting point. It may cause frames to extend past the margins or to overlap each other. It will also fail to move frames if the user forgets to insert a text mark or to match the anchor names exactly. After using RE-ANCHOR FRAMES, you must check each page and manually adjust those frames that are improperly positioned. Do not select RE-ANCHOR FRAMES again or you will undo the changes.

Saving the Chapter

Your document is finished. You've loaded the style sheet, worked with the text, and worked with the pictures. You've paged through the document one last time to make sure everything looks right. Your final step, then, is to save the work you've done.

We've placed this step last, but in reality, you should stop to save what you've done several times during the layout process. As with any computer application, it's smart to periodically backup in the event of a power outage, head crash, or other disaster.

To save the chapter, simply choose SAVE from the file menu. The first time you perform this action, Ventura will ask for the name you want to use. Give some thought to the name of the chapter, especially if it will be part of a longer publication with other chapters.

These codes are more than a convenience. Used carefully, they provide a way to filter out unnecessary files using Ventura's item selector. For example, because we always used the VP code for this book, examining a subdirectory for VP*.* files would let us see every single file created for the book. Filtering with VP6*.* let us restrict things to Chapter Six only.

When you use the save function, Ventura creates and saves a chapter file. This chapter file contains pointers to all the other files used to construct the document, and tells Ventura where all these elements belong. After saving the chapter file, it saves all the other files associated with the chapter (style sheet, text, caption, and picture files).

To work on this document from now on, simply choose OPEN CHAPTER from the file menu. Ventura will automatically open and load not only the chapter file, but every other file needed to construct that document.

Now that your document is laid out and saved to disk, you are ready to print. For tips and techniques to make printing easier, turn to the next chapter.

Chapter Seven

Producing Output

The work described in previous chapters has been done on screen—text editing, graphics creation, style sheet design, and page layout. In this chapter we get to the bottom line of desktop publishing: the printed page. No matter how nice a document appears on screen, it is the paper output that readers receive and react to.

Ventura Publisher can print anything from one page to thousands of pages. It can use any of dozens of output devices. This chapter will help you get a handle on all this power and show you how to produce better printed pages. It explores several important topics, including:

- Printing options
- Using the print functions
- Printing more than one chapter at a time
- Using more than one printer
- Preparing laser-printed pages for offset printing

Throughout this chapter, we use the term *printing* to mean sending a document from Ventura Publisher to an output device. We use the term *lithography* to refer to the process of duplicating original pages on an offset press. Thus, when we speak of a printer, we are referring to a piece of hardware that outputs pages from Ventura Publisher. When we mention a lithographer, on the other hand, we are speaking of the person who supervises the offset printing operations.

Printing Options

Ventura Publisher has a wide range of printing options. It supports dot-matrix printers, ink jet printers, laser printers, and phototypesetters (via page description languages).

Which output device is best for you? As we'll see below, you can easily configure Ventura Publisher to work with more than one printer, so you can use the one that's most appropriate for the task at hand. When it comes to buying a printer, you'll have to carefully analyze your budget and your needs.

Dot-matrix printers are the least expensive alternative. Ventura Publisher supports the IBM Proprinter and the Epson MX-80, FX-80, and RX-80, plus any other brand capable of emulating one of these devices.

♦ *Warning: Some inexpensive laser printers advertise Epson compatibility. Ventura Publisher can drive these machines in Epson emulation mode, but the output will be at dot-matrix resolution (120 x 140), not at the 300 dpi maximum resolution of the laser printer.*

Frankly, we can't recommend dot-matrix printers for business applications. Although it is surprising how far Ventura Publisher can push the limits of these inexpensive devices, the final output simply is not up to professional standards. The whole point of desktop publishing, after all, is to create top-notch pages.

Nor is a dot-matrix printer a good option as a proofing device. Theoretically you might produce dot-matrix pages for proofreading, then transmit them (via phone or disk) to a laser printer or phototypesetter for final output. But printing a page on a dot-matrix printer is so slow that it is almost certain to create a production bottleneck if you produce more than a page or two per day.

If for some reason you must use a dot-matrix printer with Ventura Publisher, we recommend use of a print spooler (software) or print buffer (hardware) to permit you to continue using the computer for other tasks during the many minutes it will take to print each page.

The Xerox 4020 color ink jet printer produces text and graphics in up to eight colors at up to 240 dpi. This resolution makes it unacceptable as camera-ready art for most professional-quality publishing applications. However, the 4020 could serve as a useful output device for producing color originals for many types of in-house documents, including business charts, maps, and presentation materials. It might also be useful as a proofing device for documents produced via color offset lithography.

♦ *Note: Color separations for offset printing can (and should be) produced on a higher-resolution laser printer using the technique explained later in the chapter.*

The Hewlett-Packard Laserjet has both pros and cons. One the plus side, it is supported by many software packages—an important consideration if you use the computer and printer for other tasks. We highly recommend you use the Laserjet Plus or Series II rather than the original Laserjet, which prints pictures at only 75 dpi and cannot use the downloaded fonts included with Ventura Publisher. The Laserjet Plus will print graphics at 150 dpi or 300 dpi. However, it comes up short in the area of graphics and typesizes when compared with printers equipped with a page description language (see below). The newer Laserjet Series II printer from Hewlett-Packard is fully compatible with the Laserjet Plus and thus works well with Ventura Publisher.

The Xerox 4045 laser printer is roughly equivalent to the HP Laserjet Plus in typestyles, point sizes, and graphics capabilities. It does, however, offer a unique advantage: a built-in convenience photocopier suitable for light-duty applications. The 4045 Model 50 features 1.5 megabytes of memory, which allows graphics to be printed at a full 300 dpi.

The JLaser board from Tall Tree Systems offers certain advantages. The board plugs directly into your computer. It can drive several different laser printers, including some models that are not otherwise compatible with Ventura Publisher. Because the JLaser board contains 2 megabytes of RAM, printing is faster than with many other laser printers. That RAM can also be used for other tasks. It can act as extended memory for other programs, or as an image buffer for a scanner. In the area of typestyles and sizes, however, the JLaser does not yet match the flexibility offered by a page description language. However, third-party fonts available for the Hewlett-Packard Laserjet Plus can be output on JLaser printers using Ventura Publisher.

The Cordata Laser Printer, like the JLaser, uses a board that resides inside the computer to drive the printer. It thus produces pages faster than similar printers whose controller is inside the printer itself. It can access the same fonts as the JLaser board.

The AST TurboLaser is an 8-page-per-minute model that can produce pages very quickly. Unlike the other printers, it is based on a laser printer engine manufactured by Ricoh. This engine is heavier-duty than the Canon-based printers and can handle more pages in the paper tray.

Printers with page description languages offer the most flexibility. Although slower than some other printers, they can produce more typesizes and more graphic effects. The Apple LaserWriter and LaserWriter Plus are currently the most widely used printers in this category. The following section gives more details on the important topic of page description languages and what they mean to the Ventura Publisher user.

Phototypesetters. Most people associate desktop publishing with laser printers. But thanks to the power of page description languages (see below), Ventura Publisher users can also send their documents to phototypesetters. There are typesetting service bureaus around the country that can accept documents via disk or modem. These documents are printed on a phototypesetter equipped with a page description language, and the resulting high-quality pages are shipped back to the client. This option is particularly useful since Ventura lets you use inexpensive laser printers to create paper copies for proofreading. When everything is perfect, the document is sent to the typesetter for the final version. You will find more information on using more than one printing device later in the chapter.

Alternatively, certain third-party manufacturers have developed typesetter drivers for other models of typesetters that do not use a page description language. For example, Edco Services Inc. offers a Ventura driver for the Linotype 202 typesetter. This model cannot output pictures, however.

Page Description Languages

A page description language is a software program that controls how an output device puts text and graphics on a page. These languages endow a laser printer (or other output device) with more power and flexibility.

In addition, page description languages are *device independent*. A single page description driver can send pages to any compatible printer. Without a page description language, each separate printer requires a separate driver.

Ventura Publisher supports two page description languages: PostScript and Interpress. Although each has its unique strengths and weaknesses, PostScript is currently in the widest use. PostScript is not only supported by numerous laser printers, but also by phototypesetters.

If your budget permits, we recommend a laser printer with a page description language. In many cases, page description languages are available as add-on upgrades to ordinary laser printers. These upgrades are available from the original manufacturers and from third-party vendors.

Printing a Single Chapter

To print a single chapter, use the TO PRINT option from the file menu. Printing more than one chapter and changing to a different printer are described separately below.

The PRINT dialog box controls single-chapter printing (see Figure 7-1). It allows you to print all the pages in the chapter, a selected range of pages, or only the "current" page— the page you were on when you entered the dialog box. You can also elect to print only the left-hand or right-hand pages. This makes it easy for you to perform double-sided printing. First print the right-hand pages, then invert and reinsert the output pages into your laser printer in order to get double-sided pages.

♦ *Note: Use this technique only if you are producing a small number of final copies of your publication. If you are producing*

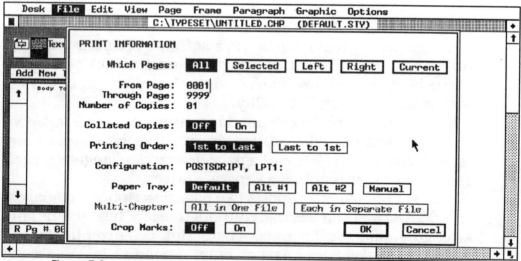

Figure 7-1
The print dialog box.

final output on an offset press, your lithographer will require single-sided original pages.

If you print more than one copy, you may choose between collated or uncollated. For example, suppose you want to print five copies of a 20-page chapter. If you choose COLLATED COPIES OFF, Ventura will print five copies of page 1, five copies of page 2, and so on. If you choose COLLATED COPIES ON, Ventura will print pages 1-20, then start over and print 1-20 again, and so on until it has produced five copies of the chapter. COLLATED COPIES OFF greatly speeds print time.

If your printer stacks pages face down in the output tray, choose 1ST TO LAST printing order. If it stacks pages face up, choose LAST TO 1ST. This strategy avoids the need to reshuffle the pages after printing to put them in proper reading sequence.

The CONFIGURATION line is for information only. It displays the name of the printer (or disk file) you have specified using SET PRINTER INFO from the options menu (see below). The MULTI-CHAPTER line does not operate when printing only one chapter.

The paper tray option applies only if your printer has more than one printer tray available. If your printer has a manual-feed option, you may select the manual button to bypass the paper tray.

Multi-Chapter Operations

Printing more than one chapter at a time is a two-step process. First, you create a *publication*. A publication is a list of the chapters to be printed, in the correct order. Once you have a publication, you can use it to (1) print all the chapters at once, (2) create a table of contents, (3) create an index, and (4) archive the publication (make a backup copy).

Creating a Publication

All multi-chapter operations occur from the MULTI-CHAPTER dialog box (see Figure 7-2). Building a publication is as simple as telling Ventura Publisher which chapters to include in which order. It's important to realize that a publication does not alter or move chapters in any way. It is simply a list that tells the program which chapters to work on. This list is stored in a file with the extension PUB.

To create a new publication, select NEW from the secondary menu at the right of the dialog box. Add chapters by selecting ADD CHAPTER from the secondary menu. An item selector will appear. Click on the name of the chapter you wish to include.

Continue this process to add as many chapters as necessary. To delete a chapter added by mistake, click on the chapter name and use REMOVE CHAPTER. Drag with the mouse to move chapters up or down the list to change the order in which they will be printed.

♦ *Warning: The* OPEN *command can be confusing. Normally it allows you to reopen a publication that already exists. But if you click on the name of a chapter before choosing* OPEN, *it will display the names of the files associated with that chapter. You must select* CLOSE *to return to the original display.*

Once the list of chapters is in the right order, save it using SAVE AS.... The PUB extension will be added automatically.

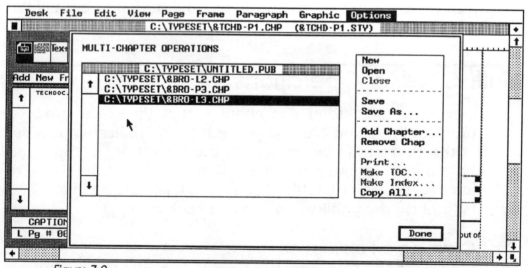

Figure 7-2
The multi-chapter dialog box lets you bind several documents into a large publication.

♦ *Note: You must save a publication before you can do anything with it. The publication must also be open before you can print, build indexes, or archive. Use the* OPEN *option to reopen a publication created previously.*

Printing the Publication

To print a publication, open it (or build it) and make sure the list shows all the chapters in the correct order. If you have a table of contents and an index, be sure to put them in their proper sequence. Now select PRINT from the secondary menu. The PRINT dialog box we have seen before will appear (refer back to Figure 7-1). Use the dialog box just as you did to print a single chapter.

♦ *Note: The* MULTI-CHAPTER *line in the dialog box does not operate unless you are printing to a disk file, as described later in the chapter.*

When you click OK, Ventura Publisher will print each of the chapters in order. It's as if you have created a large "macro" file. This macro file opens each chapter in turn, prints it, closes it, and then gets the next one.

Ventura Publisher's multi-chapter printing operation does not number pages consecutively across chapter boundaries. Unless you tell it otherwise, each chapter will start again from page 1. To number pages consecutively, you must use the CHAPTER COUNTER and PAGE COUNTER options from the page menu while in each chapter.

Here's how to achieve consecutive numbering: Load chapter one. Press END to go to the end of the file. Note the page number. For the purposes of example, let's say it's a 15-page chapter. Now load chapter two. Use CHAPTER COUNTER to reset the chapter number at 2. Use PAGE COUNTER to reset chapter two's numbering to start at 16—one more than the last page in chapter one.

Continue this process for each and every chapter. Do not print until you've completed them all. If you add or delete a page in any chapter, you must renumber all the chapters that follow. You must take these numbering steps *before* you create a table of contents or an index to get correct page numbers.

♦ *Note: Publishers of books and manuals often want each chapter to start on a right-hand page. This sometimes requires the insertion of a blank left-hand page between a chapter and the one that precedes it. Be sure to create this blank page (using the insert/remove page feature from the page menu) and count its number. A blank left-hand page is required if the preceding chapter ends on a right-hand page.*

♦ *Caution: When setting up PAGE LAYOUT in the page menu, the user must specify whether to start on right hand pages or left hand pages. If you want chapters to begin on either page, you must create two style sheets. They will be identical except for the left hand/right hand page layout specification. Before printing each chapter, you must determine whether it is to begin on a left page or a right page, then load the correct style sheet.*

Creating a Table of Contents

Once you've created a publication, you can use it to build a table of contents (TOC). Ventura will scan the chapters for the

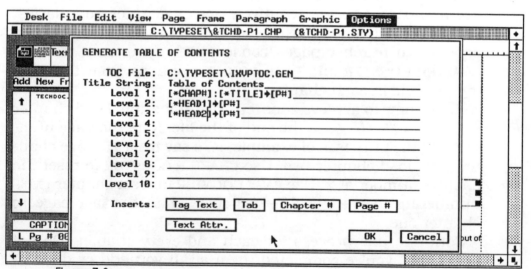

Figure 7-3
You create a table of contents by specifying which tags should be included in each level of the contents.

tag names you specify. It will list the text and the correct page number in a separate file. This file can then be printed separately like any other Ventura document.

The easiest way to understand this is to follow an example. Here's how we built the TOC for this book. First we created a publication. In our case, it was called IXVP.PUB. With this publication open, we selected MAKE TOC from the secondary menu, which brought up the dialog box shown in Figure 7-3.

As you can see, Ventura Publisher permits up to 10 levels. In practice you'll rarely want to use more than three or four. We used three levels. We started by telling Ventura what to print on the first level. If you look at Figure 7-3, you'll see that we instructed it to print the number and name of each chapter, followed by page number. On the second level we asked for the first major heading and the page number. And on the third level we placed the minor headings and their page numbers.

Given these instructions, Ventura searched through all the chapters and extracted the information necessary to create the Table of Contents. Turn to the Table of Contents in the front of the book to see the results.

That's the basic concept. Now for the details. We started by entering a name for the TOC on the TITLE STRING line. We chose "Table of Contents," but we could have used "Contents" or any other appropriate title.

Next, we told Ventura which tag names to look for. We did this using the INSERTS buttons at the bottom of the dialog box. To enter the tag name for chapter numbers in Level 1, we placed the text cursor on the line and clicked on TAG TEXT. Ventura placed this code on the line:

[*tag name]

We erased "tag name" and substituted the actual spelling of the tag we wanted Ventura to search for—in this case, CHAP#. The end result was a code that read:

[*CHAP#]

♦ *Using the* INSERTS *buttons is a convenience only. We also could have typed this code in directly.*

On Level 2 we used three INSERTS Buttons. First we selected TAG TEXT again and substituted the tag name HEAD1. Next we clicked on TAB to insert a tab character. If you refer to the Table of Contents at the front of the book, you'll see that we used this tab stop to put the page numbers at the right hand side of the page. Finally, we used PAGE # to instruct Ventura to find and save the page number where it found each instance of the HEAD1 tag name. Clicking on PAGE # caused Ventura to insert the code [P#] onto the line.

Because we use consecutive numbers in this book, we did not make use of the CHAPTER # Button. If we had wanted our page numbers to include the chapter number (as in 1-1, 2-1, 3-1, etc.), we would have entered the chapter number code and the page number code separated by a hyphen or en dash: [C#]–[P#].

Table 7-1
Elements of an Index

Line	Controls	Default	Result of default setting
Before #s	the character that will appear before the page number in the index	⇒ (tab character)	The tab character allows you to set a tab stop to control the position of the number on the page
For Each #	which numbers are extracted from each chapter and placed into the index file	[C#]-[P#] - [C#]-[P#]	Chapter and page numbers separated by a dash (for example, 7-12)
Between #s	the punctuation placed between numbers when an index entry appears on more than one page	, (comma space)	A comma and a space between each number (for example, 7-12, 8-3, 9-19)
After #s	the punctuation that appears after each number	nothing	No punctuation after the numbers
See	what text is used to refer readers to a cross reference	See	Duplicate See Copy
See Also	what text is used to refer readers to an additional reference	See Also	Text See also Word Processing

Formatting the TOC file

When you use MAKE TOC as described above, the result is a separate file. Ventura will automatically use the name of the publication to create a name for the TOC file. To do so, it changes the last six letters, substituting the letters TOC.GEN. In our case, the name of the publication was IXVP.PUB, so Ventura generated a TOC file called IXVPTOC.GEN.

We formatted this "raw" file by loading it into a new chapter we called VPTOC.CHP. To make it easier on us, we created a new style sheet specifically for the Table of Contents. If we had wanted, however, we could have included the tags for the Contents page in our standard style sheet. Once Ventura has created the TOC file it can be modified and printed like any other text file with one exception.

That exception concerns tag names. When Ventura builds the TOC file, it automatically generates tag names, one for the title (Z_TOC TITLE) and one for the rest of the text (Z_TOC). As with all tags generated by Ventura, the names cannot be changed.

♦ *Warning: Generated tags do not appear on the assignment list unless you so request using the SET PREFERENCES dialog box.*

Creating an Index

Creating an index is similar to the process of building a TOC. To build a table of contents Ventura searches for tag names and tells you what page they're on. To create an index, it searches for index marks.

These index marks are inserted into each chapter using IN-SERT/EDIT INDEX... from the Edit menu (see Chapter Six). Assuming these marks already exist, you can create an index file by opening a publication and choosing MAKE INDEX... from the secondary menu. The GENERATE INDEX dialog box will appear (see Figure 7-4).

This dialog box controls what Ventura will place into the index file. As with the TOC file, you will create a new chapter, load in the file, then format and print it as you would print any other document.

Let's step through each line of the dialog box to understand how it works. INDEX FILE displays the name of the file Ventura will create. Ventura names this file by substituting IDX.GEN for the last six letters of the publication name. For instance, our publication was called IXVP.PUB. Ventura named our index file IXVPIDX.GEN.

TITLE STRING allows you to type in the name you wish to appear at the top of the first page of the index. Enter any appropriate title, such as "Index" or "Index of Contents."

There's one crucial difference between a TOC and an index file. After Ventura creates an index file, it sorts it alphabetically. The LETTER HEADINGS line inserts separate letters before each category: An "A" before the A category, a B ahead of the B category and so on. Turn to the index in this book for an example.

The next six lines in the dialog box contain default settings placed there by Ventura Publisher. Alter these lines only if you wish something different. Table 7-1 explains each line.

We modified these default settings for this book. Since it is numbered consecutively and does not include chapter numbers, we eliminated the chapter number code and the dash ([C#]-) from the FOR EACH # line. You can modify any or all of

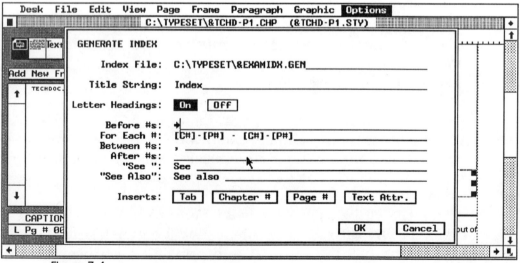

Figure 7-4
The dialog box for creating an index.

the default settings by moving the text cursor to the line and typing in the new setting.

Archiving a Publication

Once you create a publication, you can use it to copy and backup your Ventura documents. See Chapter Eight, Advanced Functions, for details on this and other file management techniques.

Using More Than One Printer

One of Ventura's most valuable features is its ability to change the output device. You can choose at print time between dot matrix printers, laser printers, phototypesetters, or disk files. There are several situations where this could prove useful:

Using a typesetting service. High-quality documents such as magazines, advertisements, and brochures require the superior resolution of phototypesetters. You might, therefore, print the document on a laser printer for proofreading, then send it to a typesetting service bureau for final output.

Speeding production. If you have more than one brand of printer in your office, you might use the fastest one to produce working copies, and another to produce final copies of higher quality. For example, a JLaser printer can produce extremely fast copies of a lengthy report, but it lacks the font and graphic capabilities of a PostScript printer.

Electronic distribution. You may decide to distribute copies of Ventura Publisher documents on diskette or via a data communications network, rather than paper. In this case, each recipient might have access to different output devices than the one you used to create the document.

There are two steps to using more than one printer at a time. The first takes place when you install Ventura Publisher, the second before you print a document.

Installing More Than One Printer

If you plan to use more than one printer, you must first install the driver for each one. The Ventura installation program lets you specify each one you want to include. It also lets you specify the communications port for each printer. Thus, it is possible to have more than one printer connected at a time. You might, for instance, install one printer to the parallel port and a second printer to the serial port. Conversely, you can use only one port and switch cables when you switch printers.

If you start with one printer and later want access to a second machine, use the installation program to add it.

Switching Printers

If you do not specify otherwise, Ventura Publisher will use the default printer driver. This is generally the first one you installed. To change to a new printer driver, use SET PRINTER INFO... from the options menu. You must take two steps. First, tell Ventura which printer you want. Second, load the proper width table for that printer.

The first line of the dialog box (see Figure 7-5) will show any and all printer drivers you selected when you installed Ven-

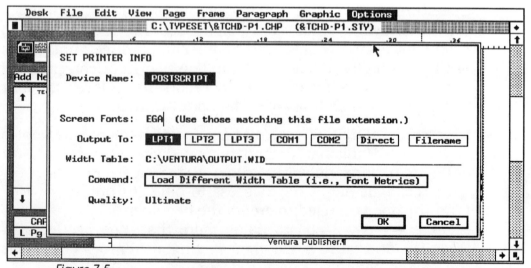

Figure 7-5
The set printer info dialog box specifies both the output device and the width table used in your document.

tura Publisher. The default driver will be darkened. To choose another driver, simply select it with the mouse.

♦ *Note: If you are using a PostScript printer and want to use a different PostScript machine, there is no need to switch printer drivers. The PostScript driver can be used without modification with any PostScript-compatible device. This same rule holds true for other page description languages.*

When you install a printer driver, you also tell Ventura which communications port to use. The program remembers this information. When you switch printer drivers, Ventura will switch to the correct port, as shown on the OUTPUT TO line. If you've changed the setup, click on the new port and Ventura will remember from now on.

♦ *Note: The option* DIRECT *applies only to output devices such as the JLaser printer which use a direct connection, and not a serial or parallel port.*

If you select FILENAME, Ventura will direct the output to a disk file, as explained below.

So far switching printers is a simple process. But there is one more step you must take to guarantee high quality output: Use the correct width table.

Width Tables

To understand width tables (also called WID files and font metrics), it's necessary to understand how Ventura Publisher works with the screen. One of Ventura's most important features is its WYSIWYG display. What you see on the screen is an accurate representation of the printed page.

Yet Ventura Publisher sometimes uses the same screen fonts for different printers. To make sure those screen fonts match the printed fonts, Ventura uses *width tables*. These tables store the space each character takes on the printed page. When Ventura displays a character on screen, it first consults the width table. This tells it how much space to allot. It also consults the identical width table when printing. In this fashion, the lines and paragraphs on the screen match those on the printed page.

As long as you are using only one printer, the width table is handled automatically. During installation, Ventura Publisher copies the width table for the first printer to a default file called OUTPUT.WID. Ventura will always use this default width table *unless you tell it otherwise*. And that's just the point— *if you switch printers, you must switch width tables*.

♦ *Important: The contents of OUTPUT.WID changes depending on which printer you installed first. If you installed a Xerox 4045 first, it contains the width table for that printer. If you installed a PostScript printer first, then OUTPUT.WID contains the PostScript widths.*

Changing Width Tables

The FONT METRICS line shows which width table is currently in use. To change width tables, select LOAD DIFFERENT WIDTH TABLE. An item selector will appear (see Figure 7-6). Choose the width table that matches the new printer. The names of the WID files clearly identify which printer they support.

There's a way to make sure that the width table matches the printer. Simply check the last line of the dialog box, labeled

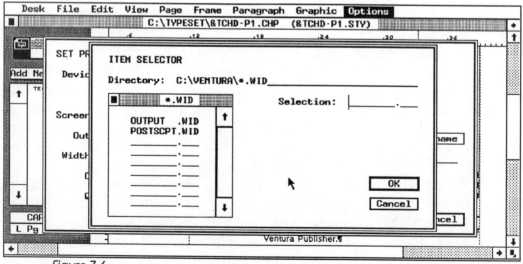

Figure 7-6
The item selector used for loading a width table.

QUALITY. If it reads "Ultimate," then the table matches the printer. If it reads "Draft," then you have loaded the wrong width table.

However, there are occasions when you will want to deliberately load the wrong width table, so one printer can imitate another.

Imitating Another Printer

On occasion, you may want to imitate another output device. For example, you may want a laser printer to imitate the final output from a phototypesetter. You can proofread the laser printed pages, then send the document to the phototypesetter when everything is perfect.

Consider the case of a magazine publisher who wants to create proof pages on his Xerox 4045, then send to a Post-Script typesetter to create camera-ready art. If he does this without making any modifications, he'll be in for an unpleasant surprise. The pages may look perfect when they come out of the 4045, but those same pages will have flaws when returned from the typesetter.

The reason for the problem goes back to width tables again. Every printer uses slightly different character widths, even for the same typestyle in the same size. The differences aren't great, but they add up. It only takes a difference of a character or two to push a word down to another line. It only takes an extra line or two to throw off the formatting of an entire page, and, therefore, the formatting of the entire document.

Fortunately, Ventura Publisher provides a simple solution. To make one printer imitate another, simply load a different width table. To make the Xerox 4045 imitate a PostScript device, load the PostScript width table. It's that simple. True, the resulting 4045 output won't look terrific—the printer will be using the wrong spacings. But the important thing is that lines will end where they are supposed to end and pages will break where they are supposed to break.

♦ *Note: It is not necessary to imitate one PostScript device with another. The pages created from a PostScript laser printer will be identical to those created by a PostScript typesetter. Only the resolution will differ, with the typesetter providing much higher resolution than the laser printer. The same is true of other page description languages.*

If you will not often be imitating another printer, simply load the different width table whenever you need it. But those who'll be doing this routinely can take a shortcut. Reinstall Ventura Publisher, and install the final output device first. For example, the magazine publisher mentioned above should install the PostScript driver first. This guarantees that the Post-Script width files will become the default. They will be saved to the OUTPUT.WID file. As you recall, Ventura Publisher always uses OUTPUT.WID unless you tell it otherwise.

Because the PostScript tables are stored in the default OUT-PUT.WID file, the publisher can choose the Xerox 4045 as the device and know that it will automatically use the PostScript widths. He can confirm this by checking the QUALITY line to verify that it shows "Draft." To print a document with the proper 4045 character widths, he need only use the SET PRINTER INFO dialog box to install the 4045 width tables.

♦ *Note: The width table you choose is recorded in the style sheet. If you change width tables to something other than the default OUTPUT.WID, the style sheet will now look for that new width table whenever it is loaded. You do not have to change tables again unless you use a new style sheet.*

Fonts

There are two types of fonts used within Ventura Publisher: screen fonts and output fonts. When you originally installed Ventura, you automatically installed a set of screen fonts for your display and output fonts for your printer.

In general, your computer display has much lower resolution than your output device. Accordingly, the fonts used on screen can never match precisely the bit-for-bit pattern produced in your printer. Fortunately, they don't have to— it is the printed page, not the computer display that your readers will receive. Thus, Ventura Publisher will always adjust the space between words on screen as necessary to assure that each line and paragraph ends at the correct location.

There is a nearly unlimited number of output fonts that can be used with Ventura Publisher. In addition to the fonts that come with each printer, many printers can use downloaded fonts. These fonts come on disk, either with or without matching screen fonts. They may be provided by the original manufacturer, by outside companies, or both. Ventura Publisher provides a core set of basic fonts for most printers, so you need not purchase standard fonts such as Dutch or Swiss.

If the font manufacturer has provided screen fonts along with the output fonts, you may be able to use them on your display. The exact steps depend on the format of those screen fonts.

If the fonts are in Ventura Publisher format *and* in EGA resolution, you need only copy these screen fonts to the \VENTURA directory of your hard disk. Make sure they have the extension EGA.

If the screen fonts are in Ventura format but *not* in EGA resolution (for instance, the Adobe Macintosh fonts available on PC format disks), take these three steps:

Copy them to the /VENTURA **directory.**

Rename with an extension other than EGA (for instance, PSF for PostScript fonts).

Install these fonts by typing the new extension onto the screen fonts line of the SET PRINTER INFO **dialog box.**

If the screen fonts are *not* in Ventura format but they *are* in Adobe Macintosh format, convert them using the ABFTOFNT converter on the utility disk. Then follow the instructions above for non-EGA fonts.

In the absence of special screen fonts, Ventura will use the closest matching "generic" screen font to represent the new output fonts.

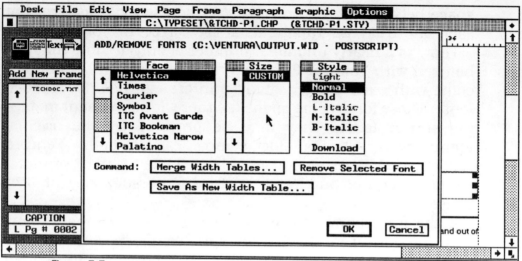

Figure 7-7
The add/remove fonts dialog box for a PostScript printer.

Downloading Fonts

Ventura Publisher can automatically download fonts to the laser printers it supports. These fonts are downloaded from the hard disk to the laser printer whenever Ventura Publisher needs them. However, before you can use a downloaded font, you must first include its width table. You accomplish this through the ADD/REMOVE FONTS option from the options menu (see Figure 7-7). The dialog box allows you to merge the fonts from another WID file into your current WID file. Normally, the third-party font supplier will provide you with Ventura WID files for their fonts. (The standard fonts that come with Ventura Publisher already have width tables.)

If you wish, you can preserve your original width table by saving the new WID file under a different name. You can also remove selected fonts from a width table by highlighting the face, size, and style and then clicking on REMOVE SELECTED FONT.

♦ *Note: If you have a PostScript printer, you need not specify a point size since every possible point size accompanies a typeface when you install or remove it.*

The last item in the style item selector will show the word "Download" or "Resident." Resident means that the font is currently installed in your printer. Download means Ventura Publisher must look for the font on the hard disk and then download it to your laser printer. Although this process is done automatically, you may want to fool Ventura Publisher into thinking that all your fonts are resident in your printer by clicking on the word download in the style item selector for each font. If you do this, you must make sure to manually download each desired font using the software provided by your font supplier. You must do this before running Ventura Publisher. The advantage to this procedure is that it can speed up printing considerably since Ventura Publisher need not download fonts each time they are required.

Printing to a Disk File

Ventura includes a handy print to disk option. Refer back to Figure 7-5 and the SET PRINTER INFO dialog box. To print to a disk file, select FILENAME from the OUTPUT TO line. Later, when you print, Ventura Publisher will give you the opportunity to specify the name and location of the file. If you are printing more than one chapter, it will also let you specify if you want each chapter in a separate file or all the chapters in one big file.

The resulting disk file can be sent (via modem, network, or floppy disk) to another location for printing. It can be printed directly using the DOS COPY command (copy the file to the printer port instead of to another disk). Or it can be spooled, using the DOS print spooling utility or a commercial utility. Print spooling permits printing to go on in the background, thereby freeing the computer for other activities.

However, these disk files can become very large. All the fonts that have been downloaded are sent to the file. This creates huge files with the Laserjet Plus. If you frequently print to disk, consider making all the fonts appear to be resident to Ventura. You do this by loading the fonts in advance using the utilities supplied with the printer. Don't turn off the printer or you will have to reload the fonts. Then you tell Ventura that the fonts are resident using ADD/REMOVE FONTS from the options menu. The print file will be much smaller and the print time much faster.

♦ *Warning: If you are sending the disk file to another location, be sure to specify the correct printer and width file before printing to disk. For the best quality, these specifications should match the printer setup at the other location.*

♦ *Note: If you spool a Ventura Publisher print file to your printer using the DOS PRINT command, you may need to invoke the /B command to warn your printer that nontextual commands reside within the file. See the DOS manual.*

If you are using a PostScript printer, you can print a one-page document to disk and then later use that document within another Ventura chapter. Load the print file using the LOAD TEXT/PICTURE command and specify PostScript as the line art format. You can then crop or scale this figure as you would any other graphic. The PostScript page does not appear on the screen (an X shows the spot) but it does appear on the printed page.

Binding Pages

Many Ventura Publisher documents will be used as camera-ready art for offset printing. (We offer guidelines for offset printing below.) In this case, the lithographer handles the issue of binding the output. But some Ventura users will distribute laser-printed originals or photocopies of Ventura Publisher pages. In that instance, it's up to the user to take care of binding.

Three-hole punching is the simplest, easiest way to bind pages. It is appropriate for certain manuals and reports, particularly if they are subject to frequent revision. It's simple to snap out just one section and replace it with a new one. Pay special attention to the inside margin to allow enough room for the holes. We recommend leaving an extra 3 picas (half inch). In other words, if you normally leave 3 picas, leave 6 instead. Although a three-hole punch is adequate for small jobs, those who do more than a few dozen pages should consider buying prepunched paper. It is available from most suppliers at prices only slightly higher than ordinary paper.

♦ *Disadvantage: Three-ring bindings have a distinct "school-book" connotation. Although practical, they do not convey a slick, professional image.*

Comb or spiral binding is appropriate for short manuals and other applications where the user will want to lay the book flat. The Ibico binding system, for example, consists of a paper punch and an insertion tool for the plastic combs that hold the pages together. Spiral bindings of more than about 100 pages are often inconvenient to use. As with three-hole punching, leave an extra 3 picas (half inch) on the inside margin.

♦ *Disadvantage: Spiral binding has the same "inexpensive" connotations associated with three-ring binders.*

Velobinding does not steal as much space as spiral and three-ring binding. It is more secure than either, with less chance of losing pages. And, Velobind offers a more professional look. We feel many desktop publishers undermine their efforts by using amateurish bindings to hold together their documents.

♦ *Disadvantage: Velobound documents cannot easily lie flat when opened.*

Guidelines for Offset Printing

Some users will distribute laser-printed pages of their Ventura Publisher documents. But many others will use those pages as camera-ready art. The pages will be taken to a lithographer, where they will be used to create printing plates. The tips and techniques outlined below will help you improve the quality of pages intended for offset printing.

Creating Windows for Photos

As we saw in Chapter Four, Ventura Publisher allows you to bring pictures directly into the document. But you may sometimes prefer to leave "windows" (spaces) in the document where photographs can be inserted using traditional methods. There are several reasons to consider this approach:

- To incorporate high-quality halftones.

- To incorporate color artwork.

- To allow space for artwork that will be photographically enhanced.

- To allow space for artwork that is not yet completed or that will be supplied by another party.

- To allow space for an oversize picture such as a poster or blueprint that will be reduced in your document.

In general, neither laser printers nor scanners are quite capable of reproducing high quality photographs, as explained in Chapter Four. The quality may be acceptable for in-house publications or certain tabloid newspapers. But for professional books, magazines, brochures, and advertisements, you will probably want to handle photographs in the traditional manner.

Here's how to prepare the Ventura pages to receive those photos: First, decide which photographs you plan to use, and where they belong in the text (approximately). Next, create an empty frame to accommodate the photograph. When choosing the size and shape of the frame, keep the subject of the photo in mind. If you are using a shot of Wilt Chamberlin, for example, do not make the frame wider than it is tall. If you are using a photo of a dachshund, do not make the frame taller than it is wide. Add a caption to the frame, as you would with any other pictures.

Keep in mind that you don't need to use the entire contents of the photo; you may "crop" it by selecting new top, left, right, and bottom edges. In this case, make sure that the shape (aspect ratio) of the frame matches that of the cropped image area.

You may want to add a ruling box around the empty frame. This gives positioning information to the lithographer. Alternatively, consider setting the frame background to black, so the frame will print as a solid black rectangle. Depending on the prepress process used by your lithographer, black windows may make it easier to insert photographs. (Consult your lithographer to see if this is required.)

Next, draw lines on the border of the photo to indicate the cropping region (the portion you want to save). Finally, compute the percentage of enlargement or reduction necessary to make the cropped photo fit the empty frame. To do this, divide the width of the cropped photo by the width of the frame and multiply by 100%. Write this number on the back of the photo with a felt pen so the lithographer will know how much to enlarge or reduce the picture.

Proof Photos

You may want to consider a second approach for photographs. Use a scanner to digitize the photos, then place them into the Ventura document. These low-quality digitized images serve only as proofing copies; the actual photos will be reshot by the lithographer as explained above. The advantage is that you see a complete "mockup" of every page before sending it off. What's more, it's easier for the lithographer to avoid mixing up photos when he or she can refer to actual low-resolution sample pages.

Scan photographs as discussed in Chapter Four. Use the scanner's software to crop the photo. Create frames just as if you were going to make blank windows for the photos. But now you will fill those frames with the digitized photos using the LOAD TEXT/PICTURE dialog box. After loading the photo, select SIZING & SCALING from the page menu and select FIT IN FRAME. If the shape of the frame corresponds to the shape of the cropped photo, the photo will fill the frame without significant distortion. Note: We don't recommend using FIT IN FRAME or fractional scale factors when you are dealing with scanned images that will actually be used as final camera-ready artwork. Use the technique described here only for proofing purposes.

♦ *Note: Use this technique only for scanned images used for proofing purposes. Scanned images used for final camera-ready copy should be original size if possible.*

Tips for Photos

When sizing photos, pay attention to the relative sizes of objects in nearby pictures. If you have a picture of a building next to a picture of a thumbtack, for instance, do not enlarge the thumbtack so that it looks bigger than the building.

If you routinely used standard sized windows for   photos, consider using the advanced tag technique described in Chapter Nine. This technique is faster than placing frames for creating blank spaces.

Color Separations

You do not need a color monitor or a color printer to create color pages. Ventura Publisher's style sheets provide a power-

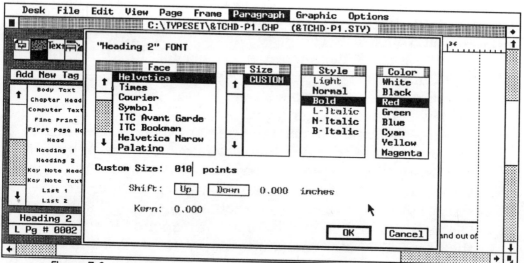

Figure 7-8
You can specify an alternate color using the font dialog box.

ful and convenient method for creating separations. With these separations, a lithographer can create color pages.

Let's briefly review how color is applied to printed pages. To keep things simple, we'll use a two-color example: An advertisement with black body text and a red headline. (The same basic concepts apply to four-color printing.)

To create this color effect, the lithographer sends the pages through the press twice: once for the black text, once for the red headline. It's obvious, therefore, that the lithographer will need two versions of the document. One will contain only the words printed in black. The other will be blank except for the headline to be printed in red.

To create two versions of the document in Ventura Publisher, we will use three different style sheets. These three style sheets will be identical in every way except for the color of certain tags. Color is specified in the FONT dialog box (see Figure 7-8).

Think of the first version as the "composite" style sheet. We'll call it COMP.STY. It exists so you can see how everything looks together. All the tags in COMP.STY have a color of black in the FONT dialog box. Since black is the default option, you don't have to do anything different to achieve this.

The second version of the style sheet, BLACK.STY will show only the black text. All the tags will still specify black *except for the headline tag.* The headline tag will be set to white. As a result, the text of the headline will still be in the document, but it will disappear (white text on a white background cannot be seen). Before you do anything else, save this version of the style sheet under its new name. This will prevent you from inadvertently modifying COMP.STY. Now print the chapter to obtain a version of the document with everything in its proper place minus the headline.

The red version of the style sheet, RED.STY will use the same approach in reverse. Change the headline tag back to black to make it visible again. Now go through all the other tags in the document and change them from black to white. This will make all the other words invisible except for the headline. Before you do anything else, save the red version of the style sheet under its new name. Now print out the chapter again. This time you'll get a version of the document that shows only the headline.

Building three style sheets takes extra effort the first time around. From then on, however, creating two-color separations is quick and simple. Create the document with COMP.STY. When it looks right, load BLACK.STY and print. Now load RED.STY and print again. You're done.

If have a color monitor, you can take the whole thing one step further. Create COMP.STY just as explained above, but specify a color of red for the headline tag. Now the headline will display in color on the monitor. This may make it easier to visualize the effects of your color choices. (Incidentally, if you use COMP.STY to output to a laser printer, the headlines will print in black.)

Four-color work uses the same basic principles. Instead of two style sheets, you will need five: one composite for the entire document, and one each for black, cyan, magenta, and yellow.

♦ *Note: Some printers, such as the Laserjet Plus, cannot print white text and therefore cannot create color separations.*

Working With Your Lithographer

Check with your lithographer before you take in laser printed pages for reproduction. She may be able to suggest steps you can take to improve the quality of the finished product. The exact recommendations will depend on the equipment she owns and the way she prefers to work. Some of the possibilities include:

- Using special paper in the laser printer.

- Over- or underexposing the negatives to "fill in the dots" and make letters appear more dense.

- Photoreducing the final pages by 10 or 20 percent to make the low resolution less apparent.

With the conclusion of this chapter, we have now covered the basics required to produce a Ventura Publisher document. These essentials are all you need to know to build straightforward, everyday applications.

For those of you who want to go further, who want to achieve true high-performance desktop publishing, we offer two more chapters. These final chapters explore the advanced functions and special techniques that turn Ventura Publisher into a desktop publishing powerhouse.

Chapter Eight

Advanced Functions

The previous seven chapters have presented a comprehensive discussion of Ventura Publisher's basic features. In this chapter, we move on to its advanced functions. Novice desktop publishers will probably not make use of these features in the beginning. But nearly everyone will eventually encounter publications that can benefit from this added power and functionality. We will study four categories:

- Typographic Functions
- Numbering Functions
- Unusual and Difficult Formats
- File Management Functions

Typographic Functions

Although Ventura Publisher doesn't have the sophistication of a dedicated phototypesetting machine, power users will discover an array of built-in typographical features that can improve the look of pages.

Special Effects

The SPECIAL EFFECTS option from the paragraph menu provides two useful features (see Figure 8-1). To use either of these, first select the paragraph you want to change, then click on SPECIAL EFFECTS.

♦ *Note: Once you create a special effect, you must return to this same dialog box to remove it.*

Big first characters, also known as dropped caps, are useful for setting off the first paragraph in a chapter (as we have done), article, or section. Selecting this option from the SPECIAL EFFECTS dialog box will allow you to set font properties (see Figure 8-2). This box provides the opportunity to specify the typeface, size, and style. You can also specify the number of lines that the character will extend downward into the paragraph.

Choose normal to set the top of the big first character flush with the top of the first line of text. Choose custom to place it

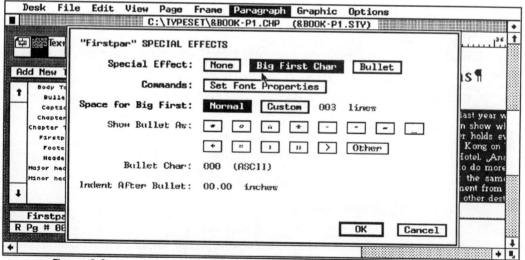

Figure 8-1
The special effects dialog box controls the size and position of large initial capital letters.

on the baseline of the lowest line. For instance, if you specify three lines, a custom big first character will rest on the baseline of the third line down.

Use text editing mode and the set font button to shift the character up or down if necessary. Experimentation will enable you to get the effect you want.

Bullets are an excellent way to set off a list. Selecting this option from SPECIAL EFFECTS also brings up a second dialog box. Use this second box to select the symbol to appear in front of the text. If you don't like any of the ones you see, you can select any of the extended characters by typing in its decimal code on the line labeled BULLET CHAR. You can also get additional bullets by using the set font button to change to a different font with a different character set, such as Symbol or Dingbats.

• *Be sure to enter an indent amount in the second dialog box or the bullet will overlap the text. We recommend a one em indentation. (An em space is equal to the point size of the type. If you are using 10 point type, for example, a 10 point indentation would be appropriate.)*

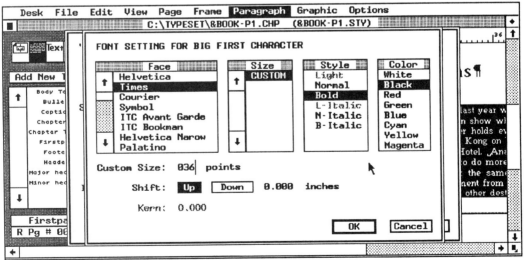

Figure 8-2
The font properties dialog box appears when you click set font properties from the special effects dialog box.

Reverse Type

Reverse type is an effective technique that is available with some (but not all) laser printers. It is accomplished by selecting a color of "white" from the font dialog box, then putting this white text onto a black background.

The easiest way to get a black background is to create a frame or a graphic drawing and choose a black fill pattern. Ventura will automatically change the font to white if the user selects a black background for a frame.

But frames and graphics have to be drawn one by one. We recommend instead a second method. Although it takes longer the first time around, it results in a tag that can be used over and over again.

The theory is simple: make the white text overlap a wide black rule. To create this effect, start in paragraph tagging mode. Add a new tag and call it Reverse (or something similar). Change the font characteristics until the text looks the way you want. Select white for the color.

Now create a black ruling line above for this tag. Select a width at least 4 points bigger than the type size.

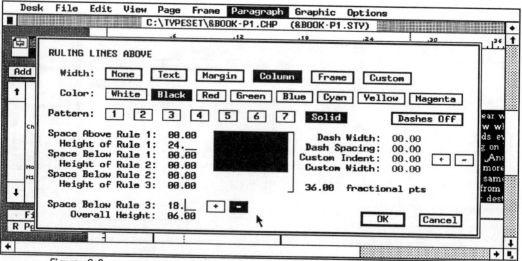

Figure 8-3
The ruling line settings required to create a Reverse text tag.

These steps will give you everything you want except the overlap. The key to forcing the text to overlap the rule is found in the RULING LINES dialog box (see Figure 8-3). Notice SPACE BELOW RULE 3 at the bottom left. As you may recall from an earlier chapter, this number actually represents the space below the last ruling line (not just the third line). If we enter a positive number here, Ventura adds space below the rule. But if we enter a negative number, by clicking on the minus sign, Ventura will *subtract* space. If we subtract enough space, the text will move up to overlap the rule.

How much space should you enter here? A simple formula centers the text inside the rule:

(height of the text + height of the rule) ÷ 2 = space.

To center 12 point text inside a 24 point rule, enter 18 points of negative space because (12 + 24) ÷ 2 = 18. Here's how that example actually looks:

Sample Reverse Type

♦ *Note: We have described white text on a black rule. The same technique can be used to put black text onto a gray rule.*

Other Type Effects

Other type effects can be created using the graphics drawings tools to lay a screen of white dots on top of large black type. Normally, when you select a fill pattern, the printer creates an arrangement of tiny black dots. Placing a box with a fill pattern over text creates a grey background with black letters.

If you select white for the color of the fill pattern, you have in essence created a pattern of white dots on the white paper. Normally that's invisible. But if you put that pattern on top of large black type, the white dots become visible on the type. The result is patterned type. Only the very largest type sizes of 24 points and up are big enough to show this effectively.

In a similar fashion, you can create a box with a series of closely spaced parallel lines. If you change the line color to white and move the box over some black type, the white lines become visible where they intersect with the type. The result is an interesting type effect often seen in logos from companies like IBM and Ventura Software.

Vertical Spacing

Most users will content themselves with Ventura's default vertical spacing. However, you have many options for overriding Ventura's choices.

Individual characters can be shifted up or down by selecting superscript (or subscript) from the assignment list while in text editing mode. For more precise placement, use SHIFT from the font dialog box. Enter the amount you want the character(s) to move up or down. Use enlarged view to fine-tune the results.

Line spacing is set by Ventura, which automatically adds approximately 20 percent extra spacing. If you select 10 point type, Ventura automatically chooses 12 point inter-line spacing. This is not a bad formula for type up to 12 points. For larger type sizes, Ventura's formulas create spacing that is too "open" for most purposes. You can override the default settings using the SPACING option from the paragraph menu. Enter the new spacing on the line labeled INTER-LINE.

♦ *Note: If you change to a larger font, the inter-line spacing will be increased by the same percentage. For example, changing from 10 point to 18 point, an 80% increase, will cause a corresponding 80% increase in the line spacing, whether you are using the default setting or settings of your own. If this isn't the spacing you want, change it after changing the font.*

Paragraph spacing can also be altered by the user, although it is more complex than line spacing. paragraph spacing is controlled in the SPACING dialog box.

The first step is to understand how Ventura handles paragraph spacing on its own. To determine the space between paragraphs, Ventura starts with the line spacing and adds any extra space the user has requested (as described below).

Begin by assuming that we have two different tags on the page. These tags do not have any extra space specified above or below. To decide how much space to leave between these two paragraphs, Ventura uses the line spacing for the first tag. If tag One has 12 point line spacing and tag Two has 16 points, Ventura inserts 12 points.

Next, Ventura looks to see if the user has requested extra space, whether below the first paragraph or above the second. Ventura adds *the greater* of the two to the line spacing. If tag One has 24 points below and tag Two has 32 points above, Ventura will add 32 additional points to the space between the paragraphs.

When computing the space between paragraphs, Ventura also includes any space caused by ruling lines. For example, a tag that has a 1-point ruling line below with 2 points above the rule and 3 points below the rule will have a total of 6 additional points added to the space described in the previous paragraph (1 + 2 + 3 = 6).

Finally, Ventura adds any inter-paragraph space requested by the user, *but only if the two tags have an identical inter-paragraph spacing.* If the two tags have the same inter-paragraph spacing, Ventura adds this space to all the others above. If the inter-paragraph spacing is different, as usually happens with two different tags, the inter-paragraph spacing is ignored.

So vertical spacing between paragraphs is a matter of addition and comparison. Ventura adds up:

- The line space from the first tag plus

- The larger of the above or below space (if any) plus

- The rule space (if any) plus

- The inter-paragraph space (if any, and only if the two inter-paragraph spaces match).

Inter-paragraph spacing is the concept that gives the most trouble to beginners. It's best to think of inter-paragraph spacing as something that applies only when two identical tags follow each other. Usually you can safely ignore it. Use above and below space to add additional room before or after a paragraph.

In general, it is wise to add extra space that has a whole number relationship to the line spacing of the paragraph. For example, extra space of 6, 12, 18 and 24 points would be appropriate choices for a paragraph with 12 point line spacing.

♦ *Warning: Take care if you are using ruling lines, since the space above and below the rule(s) will be added to any space you create here. You could end up with more space than you want.*

Horizontal Spacing Between Letters and Words

Xerox Ventura Publisher has a wide range of typographical spacing controls. Horizontal spacing between letters and words is controlled in the TYPOGRAPHIC CONTROLS dialog box from the paragraph menu (Figure 8-4). Each choice made in this dialog box applies only to the paragraph that was selected at the time. Let's examine it from top to bottom to learn how it can help achieve professional-looking results.

Automatic kerning is the first option. Kerning reduces the spaces between selected pairs of letters to make them look better. The letters "A" and "V" provide an example:

The top example shows normal letterspacing. The bottom example has been kerned. Notice how the shapes of the two letters permit them to be pulled together slightly for a more attractive appearance.

Automatic kerning is accomplished by building a kerning table for each font. These lists contain all the different pairs of letters that need to be specially spaced. If a font has a kerning table, Ventura can take advantage of it. By selecting automatic kerning, you are telling Ventura to consult this table, and make minute adjustments in spacing if necessary.

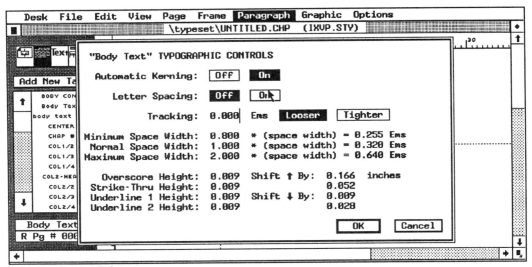

Figure 8-4
The typographic controls dialog box lets you perform sophisticated typesetting functions in Ventura Publisher.

Kerning tables must be supplied with the font. Ventura does not create them on its own.

Of the fonts supplied with Xerox Ventura Publisher, only the PostScript fonts have kerning information. However, some third-party font vendors include kerning information. Be sure to inquire before buying.

Kerning is most obvious in large display type, as shown above. It also subtly improves the appearance of body text. Its only disadvantage is that it may slow down the formatting of a long document. It is essential for good-looking headlines and display type. In fact, we recommend that kerning be used throughout most documents. To turn kerning on or off for every tag in the document, use PAGE LAYOUT from the page menu. It contains a button that will override any individual kerning choice you have made.

♦ *Note: Kerning takes effect only if Ventura has the necessary kerning information available. PostScript fonts contain this information; most others do not. Selecting kerning for a font that does not have the information will have no effect.*

When the user turns on kerning, Ventura offers a choice how to display it on the screen. SET PREFERENCES from the options menu includes a line specifying which type sizes should be kerned on screen. On-screen kerning slows down the display slightly and has little value. Unless the user has special screen fonts, Ventura uses its own generic fonts. These fonts are only an approximation of the printed versions. Their on-screen kerning, therefore, is only an approximation as well. In most cases, it makes sense not to show kerning on the screen. At most, select kerning only for large type sizes (24 and above). On-screen kerning is practically impossible to detect for smaller sizes even though it improves appearances on the printed page.

Letter spacing is the next option in the TYPOGRAPHIC CONTROLS dialog box. To understand its effect, you should grasp how Ventura justifies lines. It tries to fit as many words on each line as possible by adjusting the spaces between words. If the space between words falls below the preset minimum (shown in this same dialog box), then Ventura moves the last word to the next line. Likewise, it will add space between words if necessary to "stretch out" the type to fit between the margins.

Occasionally, this leads to "rivers," large gaps between words. Letter spacing cures this defect by adding space between letters as well as between words. It does not affect most lines. But "loose" lines— lines with an unacceptable amount of space between words— usually look better if a tiny amount of space is added between all the letters.

When should you use letter spacing? It is only required for tags that are justified. Generally you can do without it if you have only one fairly long column. Narrow columns, however, often need letter spacing. If you are unsure if it's needed, select SHOW LOOSE LINES from the options menu. This highlights all loose lines. You can correct these lines using the typographical controls described here, or by manually inserting words or hyphens.

To use letter spacing, click the ON Button, then move down to the space widths show in this same dialog box. Although it doesn't say so, these numbers refer to the spaces between words, not the spaces between letters. The numbers are expressed as a percentage of a normal space. To make letter spacing effective, you must make sure the correct values are entered for all three of the space widths:

- Minimum space width must be *less* than the normal, as in .80 (80% of the normal width).

- Normal space width should be set to 1.000.

- Maximum space width should be set to 2.000.

These width settings give Ventura the latitude it needs to compress or expand word spacing first, before it resorts to letter spacing.

The space widths can also be used to change the appearance of the text. For a tighter look, enter a lower percentage for the normal space width. (Don't do this if letter spacing is on). Ventura will then subtract more space between words *if needed to justify a line.* Anything less than 75% (.75) will

Table 8-1
Using Typographic Controls

Feature	Function	When to use
Automatic kerning	Moves certain pairs of letters closer together if their shape would cause them to look too widely spaced. Does not affect spacing between other letters and words	Recommended for most applications if available on your printer
Letter spacing	Allows Ventura to add space between letters if necessary to justify a line	Recommended for layouts with narrow columns of justified text. Not necessary for headlines or ragged right
Tracking	Loosens or tightens the space between all letters on all lines	For occasional use to make text fit a certain space
Normal space width	Specifies the spacing between words	For occasional use to tighten or loosen the look of text, or to make text fit a certain space
Minimum and maximum space width	Specifies how much Ventura can deviate from the normal space width if necessary to justify a line	To give Ventura more latitude in making its justification decisions

result in lines that are so crowded that they are difficult to read.

Ventura's letter spacing feature increases the room between letters if necessary to improve the appearance of a particular line. The tracking command, by contrast, forces Ventura to add or subtract space between each and every letter on each and every line. The most common use is to expand or contract display type to fit a given space:

CompuTh!nk
INCORPORATED

In the example above, tracking was used to spread out the lower line. It now fits with the rest of the logo, even though it is in a smaller type size. In a similar fashion, tracking is useful to make headlines fit column widths. It can even be used on body text. Tracking is specified in ems. One em is equivalent to the point size of the type. Thus, for 12 point type one em equals 12 points; for 24 point type, one em equals 24 points. It's best to experiment with tracking in units of 0.05 ems or so.

There's another valuable application for tracking: to improve display type. We have already explained kerning, which decreases the spacing between certain pairs of letters. Tracking applies to all the letters. The larger the type, the greater the likelihood the spacing should be reduced for an improved appearance. Spacing allows the eye to distinguish between letters. As type is enlarged, the proportional amount of space needed decreases. When 36 point type is spaced the same as 10 point type, it looks too loose, even though the proportional amounts are the same:

Spacing normal
Spacing tightened

Table 8-2
Keyboard Map for Symbol Font

Normal	1	2	3	4	5	6	7	8	9	0	−	=	\
	Q	W	E	R	T	Y	U	I	O	P	[	]t	
	A	S	D	F	G	H	J	K	L	;	'		
	Z	X	C	V	B	N	M	,	.	/			
Shifted Symbol Font	!	≅	#	∃	%	⊥	&	*	(	)	_	+	|
	Θ	Ω	E	P	T	Ψ	Y	I	O	Π	{	}	
	A	Σ	Δ	Φ	Γ	H	ϑ	K	Λ	:	∀		
	Z	Ξ	X	ς	B	N	M	<	>	?			
Unshifted Symbol Font	1	2	3	4	5	6	7	8	9	0	−	=	∴
	θ	ω	ε	ρ	τ	ψ	υ	ι	ο	π	[	]τ	
	α	σ	δ	φ	γ	η	φ	κ	λ	;	϶		
	ζ	ξ	χ	ϖ	β	ν	μ	,	.	/			

The amount to tighten varies with the typestyle and the size. Start by making tags with 24 point type .05 ems tighter and tags with 36 point type .1 ems tighter. Then experiment to find the values that look best to you. Unless you are already familiar with typography, this dialog box can be confusing. Table 8-1 offers a quick summary.

Although we've already covered a lot of ground, we still haven't finished with all the features found in the TYPOGRAPHIC CONTROLS dialog box. At the bottom of the box is a space for changing the width and position of the rules used for underlining and similar effects. If you don't like the width of the lines, you can make them bigger or smaller by changing the numbers shown here. Remember, however, that some laser printers have trouble creating anything much smaller than a 0.5 point rule. Likewise, you can alter the position of these rules. If, for example, the underline is cutting off the bottoms of the letters, you can shift its position downward.

Manual Kerning

We saw immediately above how Ventura implements automatic kerning. But many laser printers don't support this feature. In addition, even with automatic kerning there can be times it is desirable to change just the spacing between one or two letters. For these situations, Xerox Ventura Publisher provides a manual kerning feature. Manual kerning is accomplished by shifting the second letter to the left. Kerning takes place in text editing mode, since that is the only mode in which you can select individual letters. Highlight the letter to be moved, then select the set font button from the sidebar. The other letters on the line automatically adjust to the new position.

The dialog box also contains buttons for shifting up and down. Think of the KERN option as a third button labeled "Shift Left." As when shifting up and down, type in the amount you want the letter to move. We suggest choosing fractional points as the unit, since they provide the most precise measurement. Using enlarged view makes it much easier to position the cursor and to fine-tune the changes. Remember, however, that Ventura often uses generic fonts, so the screen appearance may not perfectly match the printed page. Experimentation and test-printing of pages is the only solution.

Manual kerning is too much trouble for anything but special applications like headlines and logos. But don't use manual kerning to reduce the space between letters of an entire logo or headline. In that case, the tracking feature is a much easier way to accomplish the effect. Reserve manual kerning for situations where one or two letters in a word need to be closer together. Manual kerning can also be useful to shift an entire word or phrase outside normal boundaries. To move that word up or down, use the SHIFT function in the font dialog box. To move it left, select the entire word and use the KERN function.

Using the Symbol Font

Chapter Six explained how to use the decimal code for the extended character set to access non-keyboard characters. Ventura has another option for generating symbols and unusual characters: the Symbol font. Here's the difference: the extended character set consists of extra, non-keyboard characters for the font you are using already. The Symbol font, by contrast, is an entire font composed of nothing *but* symbols and special characters. In essence, the keyboard is remapped. Each time you press a key, you are actually creating a symbol. With standard fonts, the top line of the keyboard produces these letters:

q w e r t y u i o p

When converted into Symbol font, pressing those same keys produces:

θ ω ε ρ τ ψ υ ι ο π

The Symbol font is particularly useful for foreign languages and scientific formulas. It can be selected just like any other font, either while in text editing mode or while in paragraph tagging mode. Table 8-2 gives a keyboard map for the Symbol font that will allow you to use a word processor to create extended symbol phrases. Using this map, type in the letters that correspond to the symbols you want. When the text is brought into Ventura, change it to the Symbol font. For example, here's a simple formula as it appeared when typed in the word processor:

w=1/2p

Here are the same letters converted to Symbol font:

ω=λ/2π

♦ *The correct symbol will not appear until the text is converted to Symbol font. Until that is done, Ventura assumes that you want a standard font.*

If you will only be using the Symbol font once or twice in a document, just use text editing mode to make the switch. But if you'll be using Symbol font more often, create a separate tag.

Hyphenation

Hyphenation can be turned on or off for any paragraph. The control is located in the paragraph menu under ALIGNMENT. In general, hyphenation should be off for headlines and other display type. It should be on for body text and justified paragraphs.

Ventura's hyphenation feature comes into play when text files are loaded. It looks at each word and adds discretionary hyphens according to preprogrammed rules. This method is often called logic-based hyphenation. Because English is not a consistent language, Ventura also contains an exception dictionary. The exception dictionary overrides decisions made by the logic function.

In addition, Ventura Publisher provides an exception dictionary for personal use. You can modify this ASCII file as you see fit. Add too many words and you will slow down hyphenation. But, within reason, you can add words if you find Ventura's logic does not hyphenate them as you like. To add a word, load the file C:\VENTURA\HYPHUSER.DIC Be sure to use ASCII mode. Enter words in lowercase, one per line, with a single hard return separating entries. Type in the hyphens where you want them. For example:

micro-Publish-ing

You can also enter words you do *not* want hyphenated. For example, you might want a multi-syllable company name to remain intact, so it will never be divided at the end of a line. To make it unavailable for hyphenation, enter it as described above *without any hyphens*. For instance:

microPublishing

You can even create separate hyphenation dictionaries for separate applications. For example, you might have one dictionary HYPHUSER.MED for medical terms, another HYPHUSER.LAW for legal terms, etc. In order to activate one of these application dictionaries, first make a backup copy of the original exception dictionary. Now put the new dictionary in the Ventura subdirectory and name it HYPHUSER.DIC.

In addition to exception dictionaries, Xerox Ventura Publisher provides access to foreign language hyphenation, plus three different choices for English hyphenation. The user may have two algorithms active at one time, one English and one foreign language (but only one dictionary, which must contain exceptions for both languages). When first installed, Ventura has only one active dictionary. Both buttons in the ALIGNMENT dialog box show USENGLISH as the choice.

To add a hyphenation for French, Spanish, or Italian, copy the appropriate algorithm from the Utilities disk to the Ventura subdirectory on the hard disk. All the algorithms have the extension .HY2. Now USENGLISH will show as the first hyphenation button and the new foreign language as the second. Do not copy more than one other algorithm to the subdirectory. Nor should you allow more than one file each with the extensions .HY1 and .HY2

Xerox Ventura Publisher also provides three options for English. Normally you should only have one English algorithm in the VENTURA subdirectory at a time. To replace the U.S. algorithm with the one for British English, first change the extension of the U.S. algorithm from .HY1 to .BAK. Now copy the UKENGLISH.HY1 algorithm to the Ventura subdirectory. Leave the extension as .HY1 so the British algorithm will show as the first choice in the ALIGNMENT dialog box.

American users have two choices. They can stay with the fast version that is installed originally. Or they can switch to a slower version that does a better job of hyphenation. The slower version is a good idea for magazines and others who create multi-column pages. Most other users will find that the original algorithm is sufficient.

To switch to the second version, change USENGLISH.HY1 to USENGLISH.BAK. Now copy USENGLISH2.HY1 from the Utilities disk to the Ventura subdirectory. USENGLISH2 is about four times as slow as the original algorithm, but it provides more hyphenation opportunities. You will notice the delay when loading text files.

Unusual or Difficult Formats

The previous chapters concentrated on simple, straightforward documents. Here are some tips on more complex formats.

Tables

Those of you with word processing backgrounds will associate tables with the use of tab stops. In Ventura Publisher, however, tab stops should be used only for tables like those in a spreadsheet— that is tables with only one line for each entry in each column.

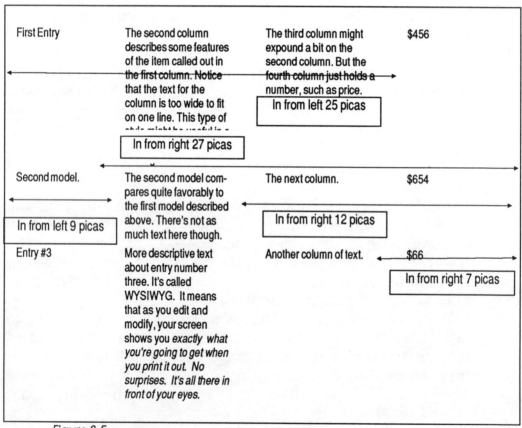

Figure 8-5
Example four-column table created with four different tags.

Create other tables by using *separate tags for each column in the table.* This is a very powerful technique that permits you to create tables with random-length, multiple-line entries (see Figure 8-5). Let's walk through the creation of a simple four-column table like Figure 8-5. With modifications for the number of columns, the same techniques apply to all tables.

Perhaps the most difficult changeover occurs while using the word processing program. If a table is the desired end product, the natural inclination is to create an imitation using tab stops. Instead, you should type each column as a separate paragraph, one after the other. Figure 8-6 shows how this same table looks in WordStar. The key point to note is that there are no tab stops whatsoever. Each time you are ready to type something for the next column, hit Return instead of the tab key. It's that simple.

Provided the text is properly typed, creating the table is relatively easy. You'll need four tags, one for each column. We use the names COL 1, COL 2, COL 3, and COL 4.

Figure 8-7 shows the complete attributes for all four tags should you like to create this format yourself. There are two main techniques to keep in mind. The first creates four tem-

```
        D:COLUMN.TXT   PAGE 1 LINE 6 COL 01          INSERT ON
L----!----!----!----!----!----!----!----!----!----!----!--------R
@COL 1 = First Entry                                             <
                                                                 <
@COL 2 = The second column describes some features of the item called <
out in the first column. Notice that the text for the column is too <
wide to fit on one line. This type of style might be useful in a comparison <
chart where flowing text is used.                                <
                                                                 <
@COL 3 = The third column might expound a bit on the second column. <
But the fourth column just holds a number, such as price.        <
                                                                 <
@COL 4 = $456                                                    <
                                                                 <
@RULE =                                                          <
                                                                 <
@COL 1 = Second model.                                           <
                                                                 <
@COL 2 = The second model compares quite favorably to the first model <
described above. There's not as much text here though.           <
                                                                 <
@COL 3 = The next column.                                        <
                                                                 <
@COL 4 = $654                                                    <
1REFORM 2SAVE    3Q MENU 4Q SYS  5UNDLIN 6DEL WD 7BEGBLK 8ENDBLK 9BEGFIL 10ENDFIL
```

Figure 8-6
The same table as it appeared in the word processor.

	In From Left (picas)	In From Right (picas)	Line Break
COL 1	0	27	Before
COL 2	9	16	None
COL 3	18	7	None
COL 4	25	0	After

Figure 8-7
Attributes for the four tags used to create the table in Figure 8-5.

porary columns so the text from each column does not over-lap the others. To produce temporary columns, use IN FROM LEFT and IN FROM RIGHT from the SPACING dialog box. As Figure 8-7 illustrates, the first column uses IN FROM RIGHT to keep the text restricted, the second and third columns use both IN FROM RIGHT and IN FROM LEFT to create a temporary center column, and the fourth column uses IN FROM LEFT to restrict the text.

The second key to creating tables is found in the BREAKS dialog box. By carefully manipulating our selections for each of the four columns, we can permit these four tags to peace-fully coexist on the same line. For the first column, select LINE BREAK: BEFORE. This means the first column will always be separated from the previous row. But since we did not select AFTER, other tags can also reside on the same line.

For the second and third columns, select a LINE BREAK of NONE. For the fourth column, choose AFTER. With these set-tings, the four tags can reside on the same line (while automatically excluding the rows that come before and after). Obviously, putting four paragraphs on the same line(s) works only if the tags have been structured so the text does not over-lap. As explained above, this is done with IN FROM LEFT and IN FROM RIGHT.

To prevent a table from breaking across a page, use the BREAKS dialog box to set allow within to no and keep with next to yes for columns one through three.

While in the BREAKS dialog box, make sure the NEXT Y POSITION is set to NORMAL for each of the tags. In Ventura Publisher, the Y position refers to the vertical position of the upper left corner of a page element. A normal Y position means the top line of each column will be even with the top line of the others. By contrast, if BESIDE LAST LINE of PREV. PARA were selected instead, the column would start even with the *bottom* line.

One good reason to use the tag method described here is that it permits you to build a table generator that automatically puts lines around each entry. Give each tag in the table a ruling line around. Set this ruling line to margin wide. The user must experiment with above, below and interline spacing to get the boxes from each tag to line up. Once this is accomplished, however, you have a table generator that automatically places rules around each entry.

Hint: When building a table inside Ventura, create just the first line, then copy it several times. Now you can simply edit the entries of each column, without the need to tag them.

Horizontal Tabs

Having explained why and how to use tags for most tables, we must now confess that there are certain applications that call for tab stops. Tabs permit certain formats that are difficult to achieve any other way, notably decimal-aligned columns and leader dots. Decimal-aligned columns are important to financial and scientific tables; they force all the entries to line up around a decimal point, like this:

A	123.456
B	12.3
C	12345
D	1.23

Leader dots are useful for product specifications, price lists, and directories, since they lead the reader's eye across the page:

John A. Doe..555-1212

J. Q. Doe 555-0011

If you need either of these effects, you should use TAB SET-TINGS to create the table instead of separate tags *as long as the entries do not exceed one line in each column.* For multiple-line columns, use the tag technique explained above.

Proper use of tab stops in Ventura Publisher starts with your word processing program. Review Chapter Three for complete details on inserting tabs into text. The two key points: (1) make sure the word processor inserts actual tab characters, not merely a string of spaces and (2) make sure you have just one tab stop inserted between columns. The temptation, once again, is to make the word processing screen imitate a table by inserting extra tabs to line up the text. Don't do it. As long as you have one and only one tab between columns, Ventura will format everything correctly once you load the file.

Although you can sometimes get away with bringing in spaced columns from a word processor (especially if each tabbed line is terminated by a hard return and not a soft

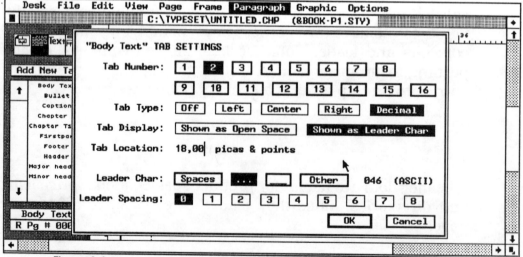

Figure 8-8
The tab settings dialog box allows up to 16 tab stops to be created.

return), the method recommended here is the most consistent and reliable.

♦ *To review: Hit the Tab key once to separate each column; hit the Return key once to end each row in the table.*

Once the text file is loaded into Ventura, create a single tag and apply it to each row of the table. Choose the font, alignment, spacing, and other characteristics from the paragraph menu just as you would for any other tag. When choosing alignment, do not select JUSTIFY. Ventura's justification feature overrides tab settings and will distort the alignment of the tab columns. Select LEFT so the first column will be aligned against the left margin (the tab settings will override this for the other columns). Also, you may want to set the overall width of the table wider than the body text if there are many columns in your table. For instance, you may want to align the tag to the margins of the page rather than to the column. To do so, choose FRAME-WIDE from the ALIGNMENT dialog box rather than COLUMN-WIDE. You must also turn column balance on using SIZING & SCALING from the frame menu.

Treat the new tag just like any other except to select TAB SETTINGS from the paragraph menu to specify the column widths

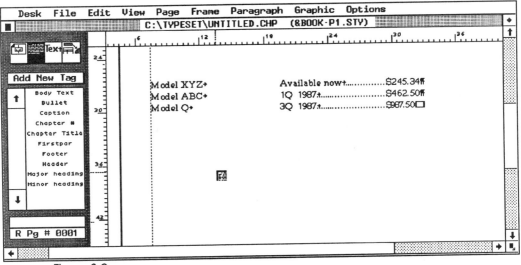

Figure 8-9
An example of a table created with Ventura's tab settings.

and other characteristics. The TAB SETTINGS dialog box (see Figure 8-8) lets you set up to 16 tab stops. Specify the characteristics one by one for each tab stop by clicking on the number of the tab stop and then on its attributes. When you have finished with all the tab stops, select OK.

Let's run through how it would work for the simple example shown in Figure 8-9. The left-most column does not require any tab setting (remember: you did not insert a tab character before the first column, but you did insert tabs between the first column and the second). The first tab stop will determine the location and alignment of the second column; the second controls the third column, and so on (see Figure 8-8).

TAB LOCATION determines where the tab stop will be *in relation to the left margin.* TAB TYPE determines how the text will be aligned around that stop. In the case of the first tab stop for Figure 8-9, TAB LOCATION is set to 12 picas, or 12 picas from the left margin of the column (if we had chosen to create a wider, frame-wide table it would have been measured from the left margin of the frame.) TAB TYPE is left. TAB DISPLAY is SHOW AS OPEN SPACE, which creates blank space between the first and second column.

♦ *Note: Since tab stops are measured from the left margin, you may want to reset the ruler point so it also measures from the margin. By default, the zero point begins at the left edge of the page. To set the zero point to the left margin, use SET RULER from the options menu or drag the hairlines down from the 0,0 corner box to the new settings.*

By specifying LEFT the text will be flush left with the tab location. If we had picked CENTER it would have been centered around the tab location. RIGHT would put the right edge of the text at the tab location. DECIMAL would put the decimal point at the tab location.

As you can see, the second tab stop uses leader dots. TAB LOCATION is 24 picas. TAB TYPE is right. TAB DISPLAY was set to SHOW AS LEADER CHAR. Since we chose a leader character, we had to specify which character to use. We chose periods by clicking ON ... in the dialog box. We could also have selected the underline Button, or we could have used any other character by clicking on OTHER and typing in the decimal equivalent of the character.

Tips on Using Tabs

Experiment with tab locations until you get them right. If you fail to leave enough space for lengthy entries, the text will wrap to the extreme left margin of the table, not the left edge of that column. As a result, you must adjust the tab locations to accommodate the longest entry in each column. You must also experiment (or do some quick addition and subtraction) to visually balance the table.

Consider using a line break to separate the rows in a table. A line break is created by pressing Ctrl-enter in text editing mode, or by typing <R> into the word processing file. *Advantage*: You will not have to tag each line separately. A Line Break tells Ventura to start a new line without starting a new paragraph. *Disadvantage*: The table will be harder to enter and read in the word processor, since each row will be separated only by the <R> symbol. The exception is Microsoft Word, which can not only enter line breaks that are read by

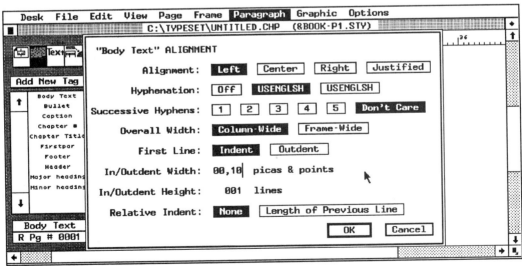

Figure 8-10
The alignment dialog box controls the horizontal alignment of text in a paragraph.

Ventura, but also displays them on separate lines in the word processing screen.

A sans-serif font (such as Helvetica or Dutch) and a point size smaller than body text are typical choices for tabular material.

To indent the first column use the SPACING dialog box to enter the desired indent under IN FROM LEFT. You cannot do this from TAB SETTINGS since there is no tab character preceding the first column in the table.

Use a smaller point size if you can't fit the table into the space.

To create lines to set off a table or chart, place a frame on the page and load the table into the frame. Format the table. After all formatting is complete and there will be no more changes, use the graphics drawing function to draw in the lines. Make sure the table's frame is selected when you start drawing so the lines will be tied to that frame. Now you can move the table anywhere in the document and the lines will move with it.

Indents

Indents are another special format worthy of extra consideration. Let's begin by getting the vocabulary straight. Many people use the word indent to refer to temporary margin settings where all the lines of the paragraph are set in on both sides (we're guilty of this ourselves). But Ventura uses *indent* to refer to the first line (or lines) of a paragraph. Indenting is accomplished in the ALIGNMENT dialog box (see Figure 8-10).

You cannot use this feature to set in all the lines of a paragraph. For example, if you need a special format for long quotes, you would create a special tag. That tag would use the IN FROM LEFT and IN FROM RIGHT settings in the SPACING dialog box to create an indent on both sides for every line of the paragraph.

But you can use Ventura's indenting to affect the first few lines of a paragraph. Because of Ventura's flexibility, you can

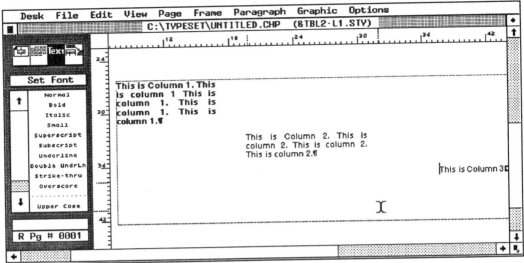

Figure 8-11
Relative indent, without a special line break setting, causes a staircase effect in text.

create some unusual and useful formats. Since the ALIGNMENT dialog box is a bit confusing, let's start by reviewing a run-of-the-mill single-line fixed indent.

Look at the ALIGNMENT dialog box in Figure 8-10 again and the IN/OUTDENT WIDTH setting. By default, Ventura always has indent specified here. But that indent does not take effect until you enter an amount into the FIXED INDENT line at the bottom of the dialog box. To indent the first line of a paragraph by two picas, simply go to the ALIGNMENT dialog box and enter 2,00.

If you have specified a frame-wide tag, those two picas will be measured from the left frame margin. For a column-wide tag, they are measured from the left column margin. And if you have created a temporary margin for this tag (using IN FROM LEFT from the SPACING dialog box), it will be measured from that temporary margin.

Occasionally, you may want to create an outdent, whereby the first line of a paragraph is pushed to the left of the margin. This format is useful for newsletter headlines and so-called hanging indents. Choose OUTDENT from FIRST LINE and type in the amount of spacing in the FIXED INDENT line. To cancel an indent or an outdent, simply type 0,00 into FIXED INDENT.

So much for a standard first-line indent (or outdent). Ventura also has a unique relative indent feature. By default, RELATIVE INDENT is set to NONE. Choosing LENGTH OF PREVIOUS LINE instead causes the first line to be pushed left exactly the length of the preceding line.

In and of itself, this is not very beneficial. As you can see in Figure 8-11, it merely creates a stairstep effect. To make use of a tag with a relative indent, you must also do two other things: (1) turn off the line break before the tag and (2) insert a small *fixed* indent.

The line break is set from the BREAKS dialog box. Choose AFTER, so the tag will start a new line after, but not before. But even with this adjustment, we still have one remaining problem. Since the relative indent is *exactly* the same length as the previous line, the text butts up flush. To create a small space between the two tags, use the FIXED INDENT feature. You will normally want to insert one em space (the equivalent of the point size).

Here's how we used this feature to format the "Tips" sections in this book. Figure 8-12 shows how a typical Tip looked in word processing format. As you can see, we specified the tags in advance in the word processor. Notice that there are

```
        D:VP5.TXT  PAGE 2 LINE 25 COL 01              INSERT ON
L----!----!----!----!----!----!----!----!----!----!---------R
formatting rules of that Tag will be applied to the highlighted Paragraph,
which will immediately change on screen to show the results.
                                                                      <
@HEAD5 = To highlight more than one Paragraph                         <
@HEAD5TEXT = at a time, select the first Paragraph normally. Move     <
the mouse to the second Paragraph and <MI>hold down the shift key
while clicking<D>. Repeat this for as many items as you wish to select
at the same time. If you accidentally select an item, deselect it
by clicking on it a second time <MI>while still holding down the shift
key<D>. Figures 3 and 4 show how you might use this function to
Tag all the items in a list at one time.                              <
                                                                      <
@HEAD3 = Tagging with the Function Keys                               <
Ventura permits you to assign Tags to the 10 function keys on the
left side of the standard IBM keyboard. You only need to assign the
keys once<197>from then on, they are available whenever you use that
style sheet. Once assigned, you can select a Tag by pressing a function
key (in place of clicking on the Tag name in the Assignment List).
More importantly, with the function keys you can Tag items while in
Text Editing mode as well as in Paragraph Tagging mode.               <
Tagging with the function keys presents several possible advantages.
First, it can eliminate the back and forth motion of the mouse, from
1REFORM 2SAVE  3Q MENU 4Q SYS  5UNDLIN 6DEL WD 7BEGBLK 8ENDBLK 9BEGFIL 10ENDFIL
```

Figure 8-12
The lead-in heads used in this book were created in the word processor with separate tags for the head and the following text.

two separate tags, even though these tags appear on the same line in the final version. We used these attributes:

HEAD5: Font: bold:
HEAD5TEXT: FIRST LINE: indent
RELATIVE INDENT: length of previous line
FIXED INDENT: 3 points

The paragraph below beginning with the words "Formatting headers" shows how Ventura translates these two tags. As you can see, HEAD5 has been printed in bold and HEAD5TEXT placed on the same line following it. The beauty of this method is that we have no need to concern ourselves with the length of HEAD5. Whether it is one word, two words or even two lines long, Ventura will automatically place HEAD5TEXT in its proper location following the boldface heading.

This same technique has numerous applications, including "Question and Answer" interview formats for magazines and newsletters and numbered section headings (see below under Numbering Techniques for more on this latter topic).

Headers and Footers

Chapter Five, Working with Style Sheets, gave details on how to create plain vanilla headers. To get the most of Ventura's capabilities in this area, you need to understand three more concepts: (1) how to format headers, (2) how to turn them on and off for individual pages, and (3) how to create live headers.

♦ *Note: Everything we describe in this section applies equally to footers.*

Formatting headers is simple once you understand that Ventura generates its own header tag. Like the special tags for captions, tables and figures (see Chapter Six, Page Design and Layout), this tag has a special, pre-assigned name that cannot be changed by the user. With this limitation, header and footer tags can be formatted just like any others. Headers are called Z_HEADER; footers are called Z_FOOTER. These names will appear in the assignment list provided you choose SHOW GENERATED TAGS from the SET PREFERENCES dialog box of the options menu. But whether or not the name shows on the assignment list, the Z_HEADER designation will show in the current selection box when you click on a header paragraph, and you can change its attributes just as you would change any tag.

To change the font of a header, then, move to paragraph tagging mode and click anywhere on the header. The entire paragraph will be selected. Go to the paragraph menu and choose FONT. Now proceed exactly as you would to reformat any tag. To change the spacing of a header, use the SPACING option. Add space above to push the header down toward the rest of the text. Add space below to push the header up away from the text toward the top of the page.

♦ *Key Note: ALIGNMENT options are inappropriate since the choice of what text goes where is done in the HEADERS & FOOTERS dialog box.*

Turning headers on and off is even more simple. When using the HEADERS & FOOTERS dialog box, you have the opportunity to select whether the header will appear on the left page, the right page, or both. But what if you want to turn off the header for an individual page? Simply go to that page

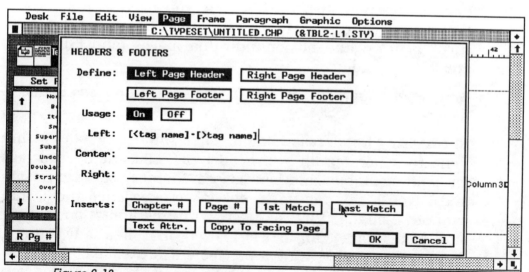

Figure 8-13
Live headers that extract their contents from the text on the page are created in the headers & footers dialog box.

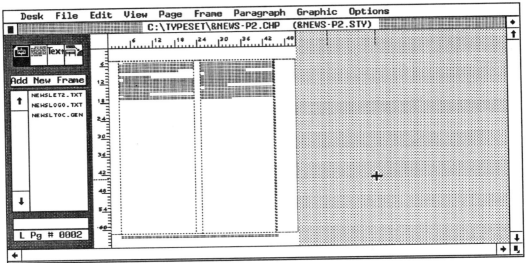

Desk   File   Edit   View   Page   Frame   Paragraph   Graphic   Options

C:\TYPESET\&NEWS-P2.CHP   (&NEWS-P2.STY)

Add New Frame

NEWSLET2.TXT
NEWSLOGO.TXT
NEWSLTOC.GEN

L Pg # 0002

Figure 8-14
Column balance on causes multiple columns to align vertically on the last page of a chapter.

and select TURN HEADERS OFF from the page menu. You will use this feature when creating books and manuals to turn off the header for the first page of a chapter or section. You will use it when creating manuals, reports, newsletters, and magazines when you need extra space to accommodate a large illustration or a bleed photo.

♦ *Warning: Don't turn headers off until you have the layout complete and final. If you make changes later, you could find the headers turned off for the wrong pages.*

Creating live headers occurs in the HEADERS & FOOTERS dialog box (see Figure 8-13). Live headers change for each page. Pick up any phone book for an example. You'll see something like "Smith-Snider" on the top of one page and "Snider-Socha" on the next.

You've previously seen how Ventura will automatically place the chapter and page number into the header. Live headers are created in a similar fashion. Let's recreate the phone book example used above. Suppose we want a live header at the left of each page. Go to the HEADERS & FOOTERS dialog box (Figure 8-13). Start by placing the text cursor in the correct location—LEFT. Now click on the 1ST MATCH. Ventura will place this

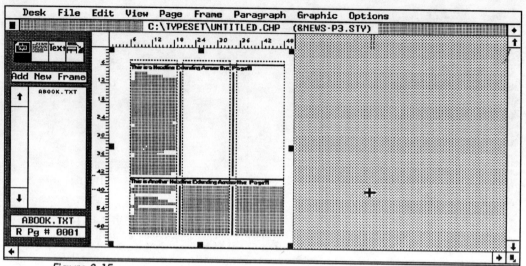

Figure 8-15
Without column balance on, newspaper-style layouts are not formatted properly.

designation on the line: [<tag name]. (If you prefer, you can type this phrase onto the line yourself.) Assuming that the surnames of the people in our phone book were tagged as LASTNAME, we'd replace "tag name" so the phrase would now read [<LASTNAME].

So far we've instructed Ventura to examine each page, find the first LASTNAME tag, and place the text with that tag on the left-hand side of the header. To finish, we would type a hyphen, click on the LAST MATCH button, and replace "tag name" with LASTNAME again. The end result would look like this:

Left: [<LASTNAME]-[LASTNAME]

This formula would create a different live header for each page containing the first and last surnames appearing on that page.

Although we used LASTNAME as our example, we could just have easily entered any other tag name, like SECTIONHEAD, HEAD1, CATEGORY, or whatever. Live headers make it easier for readers to find their way around a document. They have wide applications for directories, price lists, catalogs, proposals, reports, technical manuals, or any medium-to-long reference document with multiple categories and sections. Use the technique described here to place the name of departments, categories, or sections in the header.

♦ *In the example above, we separated the two last names with a hyphen. For a slightly better appearance, we could have entered an en dash instead of the shorter hyphen.*

Balanced Columns

Ventura can automatically balance columns. This feature is particularly useful for the last page of a multi-column book or manual. Without column balance, text will fill the left-most column all the way to the bottom. Only then will it proceed to the next column(s), and only if it has sufficient text.

Column balance forces Ventura to place equal amounts of text in each column, creating a visually pleasing result (Figure 8-14). Although the most common application is the last page in a chapter or section, column balance also helps when illustrations or sidebars are stretched across the entire width of a multi-column layout.

The COLUMN BALANCE button is found in the SIZING & SCALING dialog box. Choose ON to force the columns to balance horizontally, OFF to allow them to be uneven. We recommend ON for books and manuals and OFF for most newsletters and magazines. You can mix and match within the same document; for instance, you could have COLUMN BALANCE OFF on the underlying page, but ON for certain frames on top of the page. Column balance is of no value for single-column formats (there's nothing to balance), so turn it off to increase text formatting speed.

♦ *Warning: Column balance has certain limitations. It will balance columns as closely as possible, but you may be required to fine-tune the spacing on your own.*

If you have tags in a multi-column document that extend across the frame, such as a three-column-wide headline in a newsletter, you must normally set column balance on for the current frame. Otherwise, you will lose the "newspaper" effect you desire. Although the headline will extend across the frame, text subordinate to that headline will not necessarily

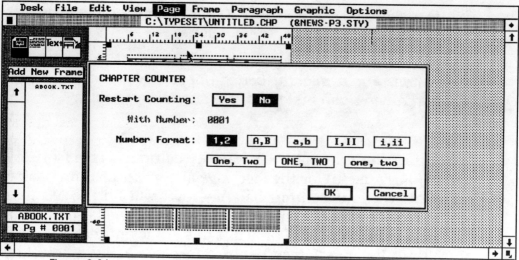

Figure 8-16
The chapter counter dialog box controls both the number and the numbering
format for chapter numbers.

line up in columns underneath the headline, but will jump to
the top of the next column. Figure 8-15 shows the effect with
column balance off.

Numbering Functions

We might have included numbering techniques under the
previous section, *Unusual and Difficult Formats*. But Ventura
Publisher has such powerful and useful numbering functions
we have placed them in a separate section. In fact, Ventura's
numbering capabilities are one of the attributes that set it dis-
tinctly apart from ordinary desktop publishing software.

Although Ventura's numbering options are powerful, they
are scattered over two menus and require a bit of study, particularly if you want to combine them with other advanced
techniques like relative indents. We've already seen in Chapter Six that Ventura Publisher can count tables and figures. It
will also count chapters, pages, and sections.

Chapter Counter

The chapter counter controls the numbering style of chapter numbers (see Figure 8-16). It comes into play only if you

have placed a chapter number symbol ([C#]) in either a header, a footer, a caption, or a section heading. RESTART COUNTING is used to correctly number a long, multi-chapter document.

If you use numbering styles that incorporate the chapter (as in 7-2 or 8-11), you must use CHAPTER COUNTER before you print. Go to each chapter in turn. Now use this menu option to tell Ventura the correct number. Ventura Publisher cannot sequentially number chapters when they are linked at print time. You must do this manually using this function.

Ventura's default option is for arabic numbering (the upper left Button under NUMBER FORMAT). To change to another format, you must load that chapter and select CHAPTER COUNTER from the page menu.

♦ *Caution: This must be done individually for every chapter in a multi-chapter document.*

Page Counter

This option controls page numbering exactly as CHAPTER COUNTER controls chapter numbering and works in the same fashion. It most often comes into play for multi-chapter documents with consecutive numbering. Some documents start the numbering at one at the beginning of each chapter (1-1, 2-1, etc.). Others, like this book, number all the pages consecutively from start to finish.

To number pages consecutively, you must use the PAGE COUNTER function just before you print. Go to the end of the first chapter to find out the last page number. Now load the second chapter and use PAGE COUNTER to enter the correct number for the first page of the second chapter. If the first chapter was 25 pages long, then chapter 2 will begin with 26.

♦ *If you restart at a number other than one, the new numbers apply only to the printed output. For all other uses, refer to the on-screen page counter, which appears at the extreme bottom of the sidebar. This on-screen display counts pages from the beginning of the chapter. For example, to use the GO TO PAGE function or to print selected pages, refer to the on-screen page numbers, not the artificial numbering you have created with* RESTART COUNTING.

Ventura's default option is for arabic numbering (the upper left button under NUMBER FORMAT). To change to another numbering style, select it from the PAGE COUNTER option of the page menu. All the page numbers in your chapter will change to the new format.

♦ *Note: You may mix multiple page number formats within the same chapter. To do this, go to the first page of your document and select the first number format. Then go to the first page that should have a different format and select it. All subsequent pages will share the second numbering format.*

Auto-numbering

This advanced technique has three major applications: (1) for section numbering (as in legal, military, and technical documents), (2) automatic numbering of outlines, and (3) automatic numbering of lists.

First the general principle: Using the AUTO-NUMBERING dialog box, tell Ventura which tag name(s) to watch for. Ventura will scan the document and number the tag(s) in order.

Seems simple enough. The first-time user, however, is apt to be confused by Ventura's ability to number multiple levels. Bear with us for a moment while we explain the multi-level concept before getting back to Ventura's implementation. Anybody who went to grade school is familiar with one type of multi-level numbering:

    I.
        A.
            1.
            2.
            3.
        B.
            1.
            2.

True, parts of this traditional outline use letters instead of numbers, but Ventura can handle alphabetical as well as

numerical sequencing. If you have been in the military, you
are familiar with another multi-level numbering style:

    1.

        1.1

            1.1.1

            1.1.2

        1.2

            1.2.1

            1.2.2

            1.2.3

This second example is a good place to introduce Ventura's
nomenclature. It is obviously a three-level numbering scheme
and it is easy to see which level is which. Level 1 has one number, Level 2 has two numbers, and so on. But our traditional
outline was also an example of three-level numbering.
However, the traditional outline showed only one level of numbering at a time. Here's how it would look if all the levels were
shown simultaneously:

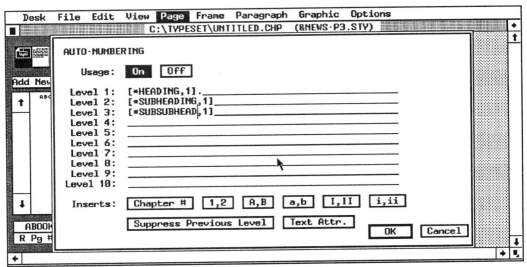

Figure 8-17
You can automatically number a portion of a document by assigning a tag to
each desired numbering level.

I.
   I.A
      I.A.1
      I.A.2
   I.B
      I.B.1
      I.B.2
      I.B.3

Whether or not all three levels are shown, Ventura would still refer to the Roman numeral (I) as Level 1, to the uppercase letters (A and B) as Level 2, and to the arabic numbers (1, 2, and 3) as Level 3.

Now let's see how multi-level numbering works in Ventura. Your first step is to decide which tags you want to number. To illustrate, let's assume we want two-level, military-style numbering for the tags HEADING and SUBHEADING.

To number any tag, select AUTO-NUMBERING from the page menu, and then take these three steps in the the dialog box (see Figure 8-17). First, put the text cursor on the level you want. Next click on the *numbering style* you want to use. Finally, type in the name of the tag.

Here's how it works for HEADING. We want this tag to be the first level, so we put the text cursor on the LEVEL 1 line. We want Arabic numbers, so we click on the 1,2 Button. At this point, Ventura inserts the code [*tag name,1] onto the line with the text cursor. We delete "tag name" and replace it with HEADING, leaving the rest of the code intact. LEVEL 1 will then read: [*HEADING,1]. Because Arabic numbers are easier to read when followed by a period, we will finish by typing a period on the same line immediately after the code. This period will also serve to separate the different levels. Without it, numbers such as 1.1 and 1.2 would read as 11 and 12.

To include SUBHEADING in the numbering scheme, repeat the same process on the LEVEL 2 line. When finished, the dialog box will look like Figure 8-17. If you look closely, you'll notice the periods that follow both codes.

If we did nothing further at this point, Ventura would insert Level 1 numbering for every HEADING tag and Level 2 numbering for every SUBHEADING tag. To do so, *Ventura generates its own tags and inserts them into the document on a separate line.* Like all tags created by Ventura itself, the tag names start with the letter Z and are visible on the assignment list only if you choose SHOW GENERATED TAGS from the Options menu SET PREFERENCES dialog box. The tag for Level 1 is Z_SEC1, for Level 2 Z_SEC2, and so on for the 10 levels permitted by Ventura.

Numbers and Paragraphs On the Same Line

Like all generated tags, the Z_SEC tags are initially given the same attributes as body text, *but you can change these attributes if you prefer.* Since body text is almost always set with a line break after, the Z_SEC tags will also have a line break. That means the numbers will appear on a separate line:

1.
First Heading
1.1.
first subheading
1.2.
second subheading

In practice, most documents call for the numbers to appear on the same line:

1. First Heading
1.1. first subheading
1.2. second subheading

This format requires us to change the attributes of the tags. To put the number on the same line with the heading, for instance, we must change both the Z_SEC1 tag and the HEADING tag.

Earlier in this chapter, we saw how to use RELATIVE INDENT from the ALIGNMENT dialog box to put two paragraphs on the same line one right after another. Review this section again to see how it would apply to numbers and headings. Here's a quick summary of the changes you must make:

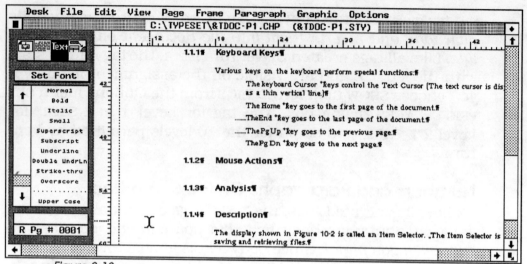

Figure 8-18
It's easy to make section numbers appear on the same line as the section head.

Tag	Dialog box	Change	Reason
Z_SEC1	Breaks	Line Break: Before (or None)	Allows it to appear on same line with following tag
HEADING	Breaks	Line Break: After	Allows it to appear on same line with preceding tag
HEADING	Alignment	Relative Indent: Length of Previous Line	Positions heading immediately to the right of the number, no matter how long the number is
HEADING	Alignment	Fixed Indent: one em space (equal to point size of Font)	Puts a space between the number and the heading

These are the changes you *must* make to the tags, and they must be repeated for every level of the numbering scheme. (In our example, Z_SEC2 and SUBHEADING must also be altered.) You can, of course, make other changes to either tag. For example, we would probably want to make the Z_SEC1 font match the HEADING font.

♦ *Warning: If you take these steps and do not get the results you want, check the SPACING dialog box for both tags. Space below the number (or above the heading) can throw off the alignment. Likewise, a rule below (or above) can cancel out the effect.*

Section Numbers in the Margin

Some document formats require that the section numbers appear on the same line as the text, but in the left margin (see Figure 8-18). You can achieve this format automatically in Ventura by making a few slight changes to the tags.

First the Z_SEC tags. Use the ALIGNMENT dialog box to create an outdent for the first line. On the FIXED INDENT line, enter the amount you want push the section numbers left. Be careful not to push them so far left that they disappear into the gutter margin.

Using this format requires one change to the text tag. The version explained above includes a fixed indent of one em space. Remove this fixed indent so the first line of the text will be flush with the left margin.

Adding Chapter Numbers

Chapter numbers can be added to any or all levels of a numbering scheme in the dialog box. Simply click on the CHAPTER # Button. Ventura will insert the chapter numbering code ([C#]) at that spot. To include chapter numbers in our example, we might place the code at the front of both entries, followed by a period (or any other punctuation). When we got to Chapter Seven, the numbering would look like this:

7.1. First Heading
    7.1.1. first subheading
    7.1.2. second subheading

Traditional Outline Style

With two slight modifications, we can use the techniques explained above to create a traditional outline style. The first change is simply to click on different number styles when in the AUTO-NUMBERING dialog box. For Level 1, then, we'd click on the I,II Button to get Roman numerals. For Level 2, we'd use A,B to get uppercase letters.

The second change will hide the numbers from the previous level so they are not printed. Type the tag name into Level 2 as previously, but before leaving the line, click on the SUPPRESS

PREVIOUS LEVEL Button. This will insert the code [-], which tells Ventura not to print the previous number.

♦ *Note: This code can appear at the very beginning or very end of the line.*

Without the code, the outline looks like this:
      I. First Heading
         I.A. first subheading
         I.B. second subheading
With the suppress code inserted, it looks like this:
      I. First Heading
         A. first subheading
         B. second subheading

♦ *Note: Clicking on the buttons at the bottom of the dialog box is merely a convenient way to enter codes. If you prefer, you can type them in directly.*

Renumber Chapter

This option from the page menu is the final important numbering option. Its name is deceiving. It has absolutely nothing to do with the chapter counter. It applies only to Auto-numbering.

When you number sections and later make changes, additions, or deletions, Ventura has to be told. By giving the RENUMBER CHAPTER command, you instruct Ventura to start from page one and count everything over again. A simple example: You have a chapter with four numbered sections:
      1   2   3   4

Later you decide to delete #3 and put #2 last. At this point, the section numbers look like this:
      1   4   2

By selecting RENUMBER CHAPTER, you force Ventura to recount from the beginning:
      1   2   3

Multiple Lists in One Chapter

Normally, the numbering system starts at the beginning of the chapter and counts sequentially all the way through. In some circumstances, you may want to start from one again within the same chapter. For example, perhaps you are compiling parts lists for a repair manual, and you have several lists in the chapter.

A simple trick will enable you to reset to one. To understand how it works, glance over this numbering scheme:

1.
     1.1.
     1.2.
     1.3.
2.
     2.1.
     2.2.
     2.3.
     2.4.

Notice how the Level 2 numbering started at one and proceeded sequentially (1.1, 1.2, etc.) *until it encountered a Level 1 number* (2.). At that point, it reset itself to one and started over (2.1, 2.2, etc.) To reset numbering, then, all you have to do is use Level 1 to contain a tag that will always precede your lists. When Ventura sees this Level 1 tag it will reset all the lower levels to one. You may want to use body text, since you will encounter body text throughout the document, and the numbering will always be reset to one.

But won't Ventura count this tag? Obviously, we don't want to number every body text paragraph. Fortunately, Ventura provides a way to count the paragraph (thereby resetting the lower levels to one) without actually printing the numbers. To keep Ventura from inserting the numbers, move the text cursor to the code line and erase the comma and number:

Before (numbers inserted):   **[*BODY TEXT, 1]**

After (no numbers):   **[*BODY TEXT]**

After inserting body text at Level 1 as a resetting device, you can proceed to construct a numbering scheme using Levels 2 through 8.

You can start at a number other than one. Simply replace the ",1" with the new value. To start numbering at zero, for instance, enter ",0."

File Management Functions

Normal DOS commands work on Ventura files, but they cause problems. Instead, use the special techniques explained below when moving, transferring, and archiving.

Several problems can arise when moving Ventura files. First, you may cause Ventura to "get lost." Ventura works by maintaining a chapter file that points to all the other files needed to build the document (text, pictures, style sheet, captions). These pointers are very exact— they tell Ventura just what disk and subdirectory to use. If you make any changes whatsoever, Ventura will not be able to find the files. It will open the chapter, but display a message that it cannot locate the files.

♦ *Tip: Should this happen for any reason, you can rebuild the chapter by reloading the files from their new location. Ventura will then know where to find them for future use.*

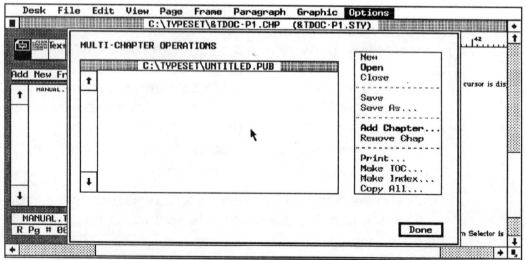

Figure 8-19
The multi-chapter dialog box lets you bind several chapters into one large document.

A second problem arises when using the DOS COPY command. It is very easy to overlook one or more of the files that go into making up a document.

♦ *Key Note: To avoid problems, always use MULTI-CHAPTER from the options menu to copy Ventura files.*

Moving Ventura Files

Moving Ventura files with MULTI-CHAPTER is a two-stage process. First, open a publication (even if you only want to move one chapter) to tell Ventura which chapter(s) are involved. Second, use the COPY ALL command to move the files.

The process is exactly the same whether you are moving a single chapter or an entire publication with many chapters. For illustration, let's see how it would work to back up a publication with two chapters, &BOOK1.CHP and &BOOK2.CHP from the hard disk to the A: drive.

Select MULTI-CHAPTER. If no publication was previously opened, the current chapter will automatically be shown alone in a publication. Otherwise, select NEW from the menu at the right of the dialog box (see Figure 8-19). You will get a blank list. Now select ADD to add the chapters to include in

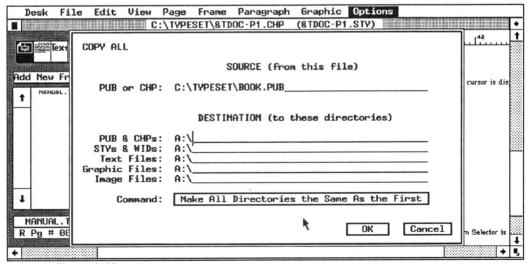

Figure 8-20
The copy all function archives an entire publication to a different disk or directory.

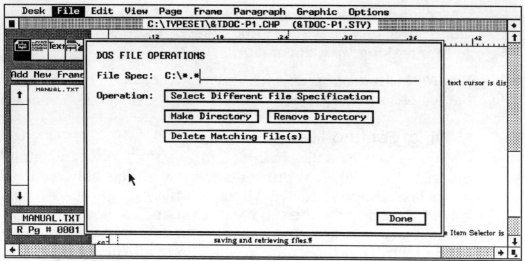

Figure 8-21
The DOS file operations dialog box gives you access to DOS functions without
leaving Ventura Publisher.

this publication (in this case, &BOOK1.CHP and &BOOK2.CHP).
Use the item selector to choose them (or type in the names).

♦ *Note: If the two chapters were already in a publication, you
could have skipped these two steps and chosen* OPEN.

Next choose SAVE AS... and give the publication a name. Now
that you have the two chapters in a publication, select COPY
ALL. Ventura will display a dialog box that gives you the opportunity to specify where you want the files to go. You can copy
everything to one location, or different types of files to different spots. In our case, we will copy everything to the A:
drive (see Figure 8-20).

♦ *Warning: When you copy files to a new location, you also
change the pointers in the copied files. If you open the new
&BOOK1.CHP from the A: drive, Ventura now expects all files to
be on that drive. If you open the old &BOOK1.CHP from the hard
drive, Ventura will expect to find the files in their previous
locations.*

To retrieve a publication that has been backed up onto floppy disk, use the identical process. Open the publication on
the floppy disk. Then use COPY ALL to move it onto the hard

disk. Be sure to specify the appropriate subdirectories on your hard disk where you normally keep text, chapter, graphics, and style sheet files.

♦ *Note: There is no need to create new subdirectories when using the* COPY ALL *function. If you specify a new subdirectory, Ventura will automatically create it for you before copying the files.*

Working with Non-Ventura Files and Subdirectories

On occasion you may need to delete files or subdirectories while in Ventura. This might occur, for example, if you run out of room on the disk. Use DOS FILE OPERATIONS from the file menu (see Figure 8-21). Type the name of the file or subdirectory onto the FILE SPEC line, then click on the action you wish to take. If you don't remember which file you want to remove, click on SELECT DIFFERENT FILE SPECIFICATION. This Button brings up the item selector so you can examine the disk directory and choose the file you want.

File Management Tips

To copy just one chapter from a publication, select MULTI-CHAPTER, then select COPY ALL. You do not need to create a publication for one chapter.

Floppy disks can contain subdirectories, too. If you can't locate a file on a floppy disk, you may have inadvertently put it into a subdirectory on a floppy. Use the item selector's backup button to find the subdirectory and view its contents.

To see a list of all the files associated with one chapter, click on the chapter name and then select OPEN. A temporary list will be displayed.

Miscellaneous File Techniques

Quick start-up technique. Ventura will load a chapter automatically if you specify its name and path at the A prompt. To open TEST.CHP on the TYPESET subdirectory, enter

VP \TYPESET\TEST.CHP

We have explored many of Ventura's advanced functions in this chapter. These functions demonstrate the superiority of this software for producing sophisticated documents in a short amount of time.

But this is not the whole story. You can extend Ventura's capabilities even further— *if* you know the tricks, tips, and inside secrets. In the final chapter of this book, we will present special effects and exclusive techniques for power users.

Chapter Nine

Special Tips & Techniques

This chapter presents a series of tips, tricks, and shortcuts that make Ventura faster and easier to use. Many of these techniques also come in handy for creating complex formats—formats that, in some cases, would be difficult (or impossible) to accomplish with any other desktop publishing program. We suggest you skim through this chapter to locate the techniques that can help with your particular job. Because there's so much to tell you about, we have made the explanations as to-the-point as possible. We have assumed that you've mastered the basic skills from earlier chapters. Our goal is to point you toward power techniques you might miss on your own.

At the end of the chapter, we've included some notes on various business documents. These notes give suggestions on which techniques to use for which documents.

Frame Techniques

Most desktop publishing programs are either batch-oriented (do all the pages at once) or interactive (do the pages one at a time). Ventura allows both modes. For this reason, some users have trouble deciding when to use the batch mode (the underlying page) and when to use the interactive mode (frames placed on top of the underlying page).

♦ *The key principles: Use the underlying page whenever possible—it speeds up repetitive operation. Use frames as required to keep material separated.*

There is obviously no substitute for the use of frames to separate pictures from text. But in many cases, what might originally seem to call for a frame can be accomplished on the underlying page instead. Yes, frames are easier to use in the short run. They are quick and simple and easy to visualize. In the long run, however, it is often better to experiment with ways to accomplish the same effect using a new tag on the underlying page. The fewer frames, the easier it is to speed production by throwing everything into a text file and loading the file onto the underlying page. Remember—Ventura automatically creates as many underlying pages as needed, but each and every frame must be drawn individually by the operator.

Still, frames are an unavoidable part of almost every Ventura document. Herewith, a collection of tips for their use.

Frame "Templates"

Magazines and newsletters often incorporate pictures that are the same size. For instance, a magazine might have a standard figure size of 27 picas square throughout an article. In this case, you can use Ventura Publisher's cut and paste feature to create a reusable template for this frame.

Create a new frame with the desired size and attributes. Now attach a caption. Select the position, label and numbering you want. When the frame looks right, copy it using the edit menu. Now the frame is in temporary memory where it can be pasted again and again into the document as needed. Ventura will not only place a correctly sized frame on the page, it will also number it correctly (assuming you chose to include numbering in the caption). All you will need to do is expand the caption frame and add the rest of the caption (if any).

Ventura's temporary memory can only contain one frame at a time. What if you have more than one standard size? Simply create empty frames as described above, and place all of them at the end of the document. If you need a size that is not already in temporary memory, hit the End key to jump to the last page, and copy the frame you need. Use GO TO PAGE to return to the page where you want to paste. You should put these empty frame templates at the end of the document where they won't throw off the page numbering. Be sure to delete them before printing.

Frames for Special Graphic Effects

The FLOW TEXT AROUND option is found in the SIZING & SCALING dialog box in the frame menu. Normal default is on. Turning text flow *off* makes it possible to create several special effects with frames.

Unusual text runarounds. To cause text to flow around a square, simply leave on the FLOW TEXT AROUND option. To create unusual shapes, turn it off after you load a picture into the frame. At this point, text will no longer flow around the frame and will overlap the picture. Now use a series of smaller frames to force the text to flow around the shape (see Figure 9-1). These smaller frames must have FLOW TEXT AROUND turned on.

Combining text and graphics is possible by turning off FLOW TEXT AROUND. The graphic can be as simple as a fill pattern, or as complex as a technical illustration. By turning off text flow, you can easily use a frame to put a screen over a section of text, without the need to put this text in a separate file and load it into a separate frame.

♦ *Note: In most cases, it's better to use box text to put text into drawings. Box text becomes attached to the frame. If you*

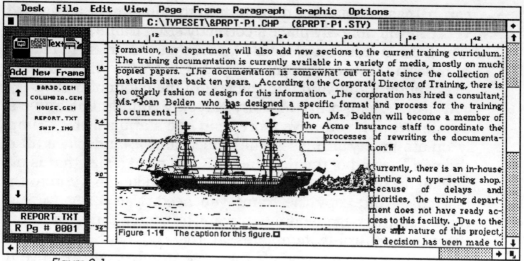

Figure 9-1
You can create text runarounds by placing small frames within a picture with flow text around off.

move the frame, the text moves with it and keeps its relative position.

Repeating Frames

Repeating frames are a powerful tool for a variety of advanced formats. Under most circumstances, any text or graphics placed into a repeating frame will repeat identically throughout the document. Use this feature if you will want a frame with the same size and contents on all or most pages. The trick is to create the frame exactly the way you want it: size, position, and contents (text, graphics, or both). Then choose REPEATING FRAME from the frame menu. The frame and everything in it will be reproduced throughout the document. The dialog box permits you to choose if you want the frame to repeat just on left pages, just on right pages, or on all pages. You can also go to an individual page and turn off a repeating frame just for that page, while leaving it on in the rest of the document.

Under one special condition, however, text in a repeating frame is *not* "cloned" throughout the document. This occurs if you place text from a file that is also on the underlying page.

To understand how this works, think back to newsletter style layout where frames on top of the underlying page hold the text. If a file cannot fit entirely into a frame, Ventura remembers where it left off. The next time you click on a different frame and then click on the name of the file, Ventura will take up where it left off and place more of the text file in the new frame.

This same effect occurs with repeating frames, provided the text file also appears on the underlying page. Under those circumstances, clicking on the repeating frame and then on the name of the text file will cause Ventura to pour as much of that file into the repeating frame as it can fit. The balance of the text will automatically continue onto the following pages.

In most cases, it's smarter to use the frame template technique explained above to create multiple frames. Repeating frames have to be the same size and in the same position; if you change one, you change them all. Still, they do come in handy for certain applications.

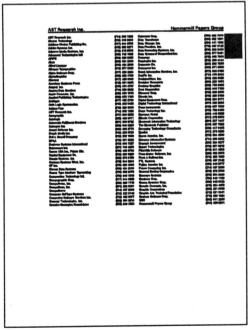

Figure 9-2
Thumb tabs at the edges of the pages make it easier for the reader to locate sections in a publication.

Logos can appear on every page of a document (or on every other page, since REPEATING FRAME lets you specify lefthand or righthand pages only if you prefer). An easier way to get the company name throughout the document is to place it in a header or footer, but for logos and other artwork, use the REPEATING FRAME technique.

Thumb tabs are small dark marks at the edge of directories and similar publications (see Figure 9-2). They make it easier to find specific parts of the document. They show up better if you print them on both sides of the paper, so use the LEFT & RIGHT option in the REPEATING FRAME dialog box. Create a small frame with an opaque black fill pattern at the upper right of the first (righthand) page and turn it into a repeating frame. Repeat the process for the next chapter, but place this repeating frame one notch lower. Use the rulers and enlarged view to get the size and position correct.

For an extra touch, put white text inside the black frame (A-F, or Suppliers, or the name of that particular section).

♦ *Most laser printers won't print to the edge of the page, so this method will only work when you are creating pages smaller than the maximum page size possible with your printer.*

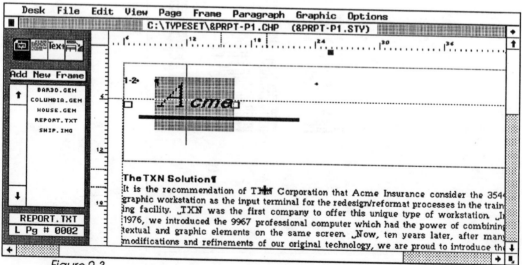

Figure 9-3
Ventura's repeating frame feature is useful for placing logos at the top of every page in a document.

Extra large headers (or footers) can be created using a repeating frame at the top (or bottom) of every page. However, this does not have the convenience of the easy-to-use automatic page numbering available with headers and footers. To get page numbers, overlap a normal header (or footer) with the repeating frame, leaving enough space for the page number to show. Be sure to leave space on *both* sides if you use page numbers that alternate from side to side (see Figure 9-3).

You can also create page numbers in a repeating frame using captions and TABLE/FIGURE COUNTER. Create a frame on page one and attach a caption. This caption should include automatic table (or figure) numbering. Now turn this frame into a repeating frame. Ventura will number the tables in order. Since there's one "table" on each page, the table numbers will correspond to the page numbers. Ventura permits captions to be above, below, or on either side, so you can position the page number anywhere you want it in relation to the rest of the header. However, this method only works if you want the same header (or footer) text on each page. This method also limits what you can do with picture captions in the rest of the document. Since you are already using one counter (either table or figure) to count pages, you will have only one left to count actual illustrations.

Page numbers not at top or bottom can be created with repeating frames. One possible format is to use the thumb tab method described to contain page numbers. Use figure/table numbering to generate the numbers, or you can place them manually.

To create page numbers for two 5 1/2 x 8 1/2 pages on one sheet of 8 1/2 x 11 paper, use the repeating frame technique described above. However, we do not recommend putting two small pages on a single sheet of paper. Those sheets cannot be folded into signatures because the page numbers will be out of order when the folded sheets are stacked inside each other. Since the sheets have to be cut anyway, it makes more sense to put each smaller page on a separate Ventura page.

This allows the user to make use of Ventura's standard page numbering features.

Unusual columnar formats can be built with repeating frames. Suppose, for example, that you want to create a three-column stairstep effect throughout the document. The left-most column could be created standard length on the underlying page. The next two shorter columns could be repeating frames. Using newsletter style layout, you could flow text from column to column.

Business forms can be created using a repeating frame to hold the blank form. This technique relies on turning off FLOW TEXT AROUND as described above. Here's the trick: The repeating frame resides on every page, complete with text, rules, screen, and whatever else is needed to make the form look right.

To fill in the blanks, load a text file. Load it onto the underlying page, not into the repeating frame. Normally, this text file would flow around the repeating frame—but not if you turn off FLOW TEXT AROUND in the SIZING & SCALING option of the frame menu. This allows the text to flow "on top" of the repeating frame.

To make the text line up with the form (the repeating frame) make sure to use the same line spacing for both. Also, make sure that the final tag on each page of the text file has PAGE BREAK AFTER selected from the BREAKS dialog box. That way one and only one form will appear on each page. Each time Ventura Publisher encounters the page break command it will start a new underlying page and create a new repeating frame, thereby creating a new form.

Notice that with this technique you do not need to know how many forms are required. Ventura will build new ones as needed. It's easy to see how you could instruct a database or accounting program to dump, for example, the day's orders into a text file. The database could also insert the tags as part of the report process. All the forms for the day could then be created by bringing this file into Ventura Publisher.

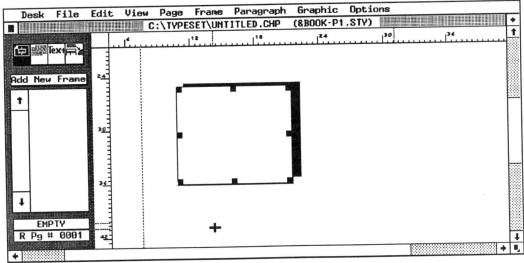

Figure 9-4
A shadow effect can be obtained by placing an opaque white rectangle over a black rectangle.

Graphic Techniques

The tips below will help you create sophisticated effects with Ventura's graphics drawing mode.

Vertical Rules

We have previously explained how to place inter-column rules using the VERTICAL RULES option from the frame menu. Ventura provides two methods for placing vertical rules elsewhere on the page. Only one of them is recommended.

The VERTICAL RULES dialog box provides the ability to place up to two additional rules on the page (in addition to any inter-column rules you select). However, we advise against using this feature. Rules created here have several disadvantages:

- They extend all the way from the top to the bottom of the frame, even if you want less.

- They cannot be drawn in; they must be positioned entering measurements.

- The rules remain stationary even if you move the frame.

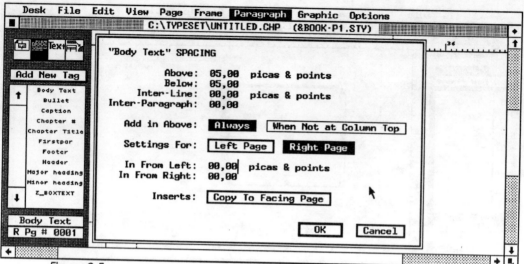

Figure 9-5
Attributes for a tag that reserves space for pictures.

It is far better to create vertical rules using Ventura's graphics drawing function. These rules have none of the limitations described above, and are tied to the frame so they move with it. Use GRID SETTINGS from the graphic menu to make sure graphics rules are perfectly vertical.

Custom Rules

The ruling functions of the frame and paragraph menus permit rules to be the width of the text, the margin, the column, the frame, or, for paragraphs only, a custom length. The last option provides many unique opportunities to the creative desktop publisher.

Special graphic effects are possible by varying the width and the vertical position. Don't forget the space below rule 3 function that permits you to move a rule down into the text below. We saw in Chapter Eight how this can create white type on a black rule. By varying the width and the indent of a custom rule, you can make it become part of a logo, for example. Or you can create rules to set off headings that are always the same size regardless of the width of the text. Or you can make square bullets by creating a custom rule that is exactly as wide as it is tall. You can make these "bullets" very large and noticeable by indenting the first few lines of the paragraph, and creating a custom rule that fills the space left by the multi-line indent—similar to a big first character without thĕ character. You can make these "bullets" dashed by selecting dashes on. Or you can fill these large square black bullets with a big first character whose color has been turned to white—the same as the reverse type effect explained in Chapter Eight, but only one letter wide.

Here are some of the possibilities:

A solid box can be associated with a paragraph, like this. To accomplish this, create a ruling line above the paragraph with a weight equal to two times the line spacing (28 points in this case). Set the custom width of the rule to the same amount. Then set a two-line indent for the paragraph using the ALIGNMENT option from the Paragraph menu.

A similar effect can be achieved by using the dashed rule option. In this example, we have moved the square into the margin by specifying a custom indent of negative 36 points for the rule.

A Thin Separating Rule

A thin, short rule can separate headlines from body text. Use the custom indent and width options from the RULING LINE BELOW dialog box.

Change Bars. Change bars are vertical lines placed in the margin to alert authors and editors that alterations have been made to the original manuscript. Certain legal, military, and technical documentation applications require change bars. To create a change bar, create a new tag called "Change" or something similar. This tag should be identical to body text except for a ruling line around. Give the ruling line a small height, and select custom width. Set the custom width to 0. To place the change bar in the margin, use the custom ident line. Usually a negative indent of about one pica is appropriate. Because the custom width is set to 0, the ruling line will not go around the text. It will appear as a vertical line in the margin next to the new text as the editor types it in.

To make change bars even more convenient, assign the new tag to a special function key. Now the editor can press this key whenever she adds new material and know that the change will be documented with a marginal change bar.

Some applications have stringent guidelines as to the appearance and location of change bars. If this is not the case, you can make the change bar concept even easier to use. Rather than creating a bar, give the new tag a different font. It could be bold, italic, larger, or in a different typestyle—whatever will stand out easily.

Dashed Rules

Dashed rules are not available in graphics drawing mode. If you need this effect, try to create it with a tag or a frame, since the ruling line functions of the frame and page menus allow dashed lines.

If you cannot get the effect you need in this fashion, create a frame with a dashed line around. Give it a width of zero to create a vertical dashed line. Give it a height of zero to create a horizontal dashed line.

Shadow Effects

Shadow effects are useful for setting off headlines, banners, pictures, and callouts, especially if they have a ruling line around. To create a shadow effect around a frame, create a graphic the exact size as the ruling box around the frame. Fill this graphic with black and move it slightly down and to the right (see Figure 9-4), then use SEND TO BACK from the graphic menu. Be sure the frame is selected when you create the graphic. That way the graphic will be attached to this frame, and will move when it moves.

The same technique works with two graphics, including box text. Use the copy function to create two identical graphics.

Fill the second with a dark fill pattern, move it down and to the right and send it to the back.

Some printers, notably the Laserjet Plus, are not able to print this effect.

Working with Graphics

Working heavily with graphics (especially small lines and boxes) creates some special challenges.

To link graphics select them all (using the graphics menu or the keyboard shortcut Ctrl-Q). Then when you move one graphic you move them all. If you don't want to move them all, deselect some of them. Graphics that are selected together move together.

To create several groups on the same page assign all the graphics in one group to a frame, all the graphics in the other group to another frame and so on. These grouping frames can be small, invisible (no ruling lines), empty and off in the margin. Their only function is to link a group of graphics. To choose one group, select the proper frame in frame setting mode, then switch to graphics drawing and press Ctrl-Q (select all).

To fine-tune the position of a graphic, link the graphic to a frame, and place the upper left corner of the graphic at the upper left corner of that frame. Now you can use SIZING & SCALING from the frame menu to adjust the upper left X,Y position of the frame— and, therefore, of the graphic.

To move a tiny line or box that is difficult to position, surround it with a larger box, choose select all and move the small graphic by dragging the larger one (you may have to deselect some of the other graphics on the page).

Using Tags to Create Space for Illustrations

Although this next technique is included in the graphics section, it does not use graphics drawing mode or frames. Rather, it is a means to use tags to avoid both graphics and frames.

Many publications routinely strip in illustrations. They use Ventura's frame and/or graphics drawing features only to create a blank space of the correct size. If your publication uses a few standard sizes for illustrations, you may be able to save time by using a tag to automatically create this blank space. This will save you from the trouble of creating frames on a page-by-page basis It will also allow authors to specify illustrations *and their locations* as they create the text, ensuring proper placement and saving time for the editor during layout. You can also create captions with tags, and have Ventura number the captions consecutively.

Let's begin with a simple example: a single-column format that has one standard illustration size. We could create a tag called PICTURE. Using the SPACING dialog box, we add enough space above (and/or below) to create a blank area of the correct size (see Figure 9-5). Next we go to the BREAKS dialog box and set ALLOW WITHIN to NO. This means that no line breaks are allowed within this tag, which will force it to remain together on one page. (It wouldn't be much help to have half of the picture space on one page and half on another). Also, make sure you select ADD IN ABOVE: ALWAYS in the SPACING option of the paragraph menu for the PICTURE tag. This will ensure that Ventura does not remove the white space when it happens to fall at the top of a column.

That's all there is to the basic technique—a tag that adds the correct amount of space for an illustration. Now let's consider some variations on the theme:

Apply the tag to a return (paragraph end mark) for a blank space with nothing inside.

Apply the tag to text if you want to create a message inside the space. This message could be a standard phrase such as "This space for illustration" or "Place illustration here." It could also be a special phrase typed in by the author or the editor, such as "Place Figure 7-1 here" or "This space reserved for Sales Chart." To center this message vertically, add an equal amount of space above and below. To center it horizontally, choose CENTER from the ALIGNMENT dialog box.

Use a margin-wide ruling line around to create a ruled area. This may make it easier for the lithographer to visualize the correct spacing. Remember to add space above the ruling line to create a white space buffer. Make this buffer space equal to the line spacing of the body text. If you fail to add space the text above and below will sit flush to the ruling line, creating a crowded, unattractive look.

Let authors insert the tag by typing it in where they want the illustration to appear in the text. To save time, program the phrase(s) into a keyboard macro program or the glossary function of the word processor. While they are at it, the authors can insert the name, figure number, or description of the illustration, if they know this information in advance.

To caption the illustration create a separate CAPTION tag. Change the tag until it has the font, spacing, alignment, ruling lines, and other attributes you want. Let authors type in the caption as they want it to appear. Have them place it immediately before the PICTURE tag (for captions above) or immediately after (for captions below). Use the KEEP WITH NEXT option from the BREAKS dialog box to keep captions and pictures on the same page.

For captions to the left side of the illustration use a ruling line around the PICTURE tag (set the ruling line to white if you don't want it to show). Select negative space below the third rule. Choose enough negative space to move the caption up where you want it. To push the caption left into the margin, use the OUTDENT function in the ALIGNMENT dialog box.

To automatically number the captions use the auto-numbering feature explained in Chapter Eight. With auto-numbered captions, you can move illustrations around and be assured that Ventura will keep track of the correct sequence.

♦ *Disadvantages: You cannot use auto-numbering for a caption tag if you also need it for outlining, section numbering, or numbered lists. In such a case you would have to insert figure numbers manually.*

Set up as many different size pictures as you need. Simply give each size a different tag name.

You can have different widths as well as different heights by varying the tags between column-wide, margin-wide, frame-wide, or custom width.

You may encounter spacing problems because ALLOW WITHIN is set to NO. The larger the illustration, the greater the chance that there will be a large amount of white space left if Ventura has to move it to another page to keep it intact without breaks. The solution is very simple. Move the PIC-TURE paragraph just as you would move any text element: with cut and paste. Experiment placing it slightly further down the page until the blank space fills with text. You'll find this much simpler than moving frames around.

Memory Management Techniques

Lack of available memory can in certain cases impact your use of Ventura Publisher. Because of the limitations of DOS versions 3.2 and earlier, it is restricted to the 640K of RAM. Fortunately, Ventura Publisher version 1.1 can automatically "swap" portions of a document between RAM and the disk drive, so that you can have a very large document.

Still, there will be times when you may run into memory problems. Two strategies will help you solve memory limitations. First, learn which elements are "memory-hungry" so you can avoid them when possible. Second, review our list of tricks and tips for overcoming memory shortages.

Memory Requirements

Three different factors can limit available memory. You need to know about all three, since any one of them can create problems. Each of these limitations acts independently of the others; the ones that you encounter will depend on the type of system you have and the kind of documents you create. We'll describe all three before explaining how to overcome them.

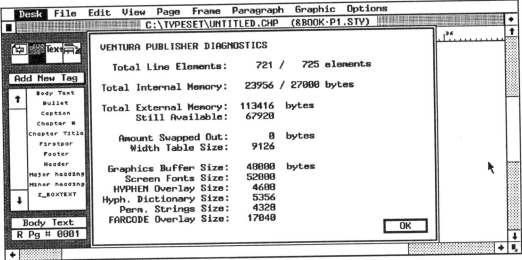

Figure 9-6
The Ventura Publisher diagnostic dialog box provides information on available memory.

System memory refers to the RAM memory available when Ventura Publisher loads a document. In general, you want as much as possible. The amount of system memory is determined by the total amount of RAM available to DOS (normally a maximum of 640K) minus the amounts consumed by:

- DOS

- Any drivers present in your CONFIG.SYS file

- Any RAM-resident utilities or desk accessories

- The hyphenation exception dictionary

- Font descriptions in the currently active width table. Depending on the number of typefaces and point sizes in the width table, this can consume another 9K to 35K

- Ventura Publisher itself

Anything left is available to Ventura Publisher documents. You know that you have run out of system memory if you see one of these error messages:

There wasn't enough memory to load and hyphenate all of the
text file you requested. If possible, remove some other file you
don't need anymore and try again.

You're out of memory. Save your document and quit the program
as soon as possible.

Frame memory. Ventura Publisher places a limit on the
amount of memory that can be consumed by one frame. You
will seldom encounter this limitation. If you do, you can
often overcome it by dividing your page into two or more
frames, using the frame-by-frame layout approach discussed
in Chapter Six. For example, in a three-column document,
you could create three one-column frames. If the problem is
chronic throughout a long document, create additional
repeating frames. We wish to emphasize that steps like these
are necessary only if you run out of frame memory and you
see this error message:

> This frame is too complex to completely format. Try splitting it
> into two frames or reducing the number of columns, tabs,
> leaders, and lines of text.

Page memory. Ventura Publisher places a limit on the number of lines on a page, regardless of how many frames are on
that page. You may run into this memory limitation if you
use a very small font, such as 6-point type, and more than
three full-length columns per page. If you run out of page
memory, an entire column of text may disappear from the
screen. The text has not been lost. Ventura is simply not
able to deal with it on this page.

Tips for Overcoming Memory Limitations
The following tips may help you overcome memory limitations so you can create larger documents.

Avoid memory-hungry page elements. Certain page elements eat into available memory. In particular, tabs, tags
and leader dots are memory hungry.

Eliminate unneeded tags from your style sheet since they
consume memory whether used or not.

Use the body text tag for the most common page element. Ventura Publisher always has a body text tag. You cannot eliminate it, so make good use of it. Each time you add a tag you consume another amount of memory. You can minimize the use of additional tags by making sure the preexisting body text is assigned to the page element that appears most often.

Link chapters at print time. This suggestion is not a memory management technique *per se* but a reminder that Ventura can link multiple chapters into a publication. This publication can be printed at one time. Since Ventura prints a publication by sequentially opening and printing each individual chapter, this approach requires no more memory than does the largest chapter in the publication. Perhaps the simplest way to overcome memory problems in a long chapter is to split it into two parts and then link them when you print. It is also much easier to deal with 50 to 60 pages than with documents of more than 100 pages.

Don't use memory-resident utilities unless they are partitioned in aboveboard memory, or (with 80386 computers) in a separate virtual 8086 partition. Even if they are not activated, they eat up precious memory.

You may be able to increase DOS memory to 704K if you have an extended memory board such as the JLaser Plus AT board. Insert the command:

DEVICE=JBOOT.BIN 704K

in your CONFIG.SYS file, and the JLaser board will allocate an additional 64K of memory to DOS. Ventura Publisher will recognize this additional memory.

♦ *Note: The JLaser printer driver uses less than 10K, compared to as much as 30K or more for a PostScript driver. When this extra 20K is combined with the additional 64K of DOS Memory, the JLaser board makes an extra 84K available to Ventura Publisher—a substantial amount. In version 1.1, more memory equals faster performance since Ventura does not have to go to the disk as often. However, extra memory does not help if you have problems with frame or page memory.*

DOS 3.0 uses about 15K more than DOS 2.0. Likewise, an EGA board consumes slightly more system memory than a Hercules card.

You can diagnose memory problems by accessing a little-known dialog box. Select PUBLISHER INFO from the desk menu. You will see an informational dialog box (see Figure 9-6). Click on the word "Ventura" in the "Ventura Software Inc." box, even though this word is not shown as a button. Doing this will bring up a second dialog box, as shown in Figure 9-6.

The entry labeled LINE ELEMENTS is an indication of how many more lines of text can be placed on the current page. If this figure is much lower than 100, you will soon need to break text to a new page to avoid running out of page memory.

The EXTERNAL MEMORY line refers to the amount of system memory remaining in your document. If the AMOUNT SWAPPED OUT value is greater than 0, this indicates that Ventura Publisher has made use of its disk swapping capability, as mentioned earlier.

Use a RAM disk to eliminate the delays of swapping to disk with large documents. Create a RAM disk greater than 500K using a separate utility program. To tell Ventura to swap to the RAM disk (instead of to the hard disk as it does normally), add a few characters to the end of the second line in the VP.BAT file.

The VP.BAT file resides on the root directory of the hard disk. It is created automatically by the installation program. You can change it using the ASCII option of any word processor or text editor. The exact wording varies depending on the type of computer and display you use. Regardless of the wording of the line, you must append the code "/O=D:" to the end. (This assumes that your RAM disk is set up as the D: drive. If not, substitute the actual letter.) For example:

DRVRMRGR VP %1 /S=SD_X6655.EGA/M=32/0=D:

Adding a RAM disk will dramatically improve Ventura'a performance with large documents.

Experiment with disk caching software. Depending on the type of computer and the speed of the hard disk, this step may provide performance improvements.

For power users only. Xerox Ventura Publisher includes one more switch that can improve memory management. Use this tip only in 640K systems (512K is not sufficient). Proceed at your own risk as results cannot be guaranteed.

Modify the second line of the VP.BAT file to add the switch "/A=n" where n is any number between 1 and 32. This switch transfers the stated number of kilobytes to the area used for text. This RAM is taken from an internal memory buffer used for printing and screen graphics. On the down side, this trick may increase screen drawing time for large graphics and/or prevent the use of the Alt key panning function. On the plus side, it will greatly reduce disk swapping and thereby boost performance.

Notes on Different Document Types

Before we bring this book to an end, we want to include one final section devoted to practical applications. This section gives advice and ideas for applying the techniques we've been describing to the business documents users produce every day. For more detailed information about specific business documents, refer to the coupon at the back of this book referencing the *Ventura Publisher Document Gallery*, or write to Micro Publishing at the address in Appendix A. This book/disk set includes disk and paper versions of style sheets for the kinds of documents described below, plus many others.

Document "Templates"

Our first tip applies to virtually any complex document. As long as you are creating *simple* documents— those with most of the text on the underlying page— you'll do fine just by saving the style sheet and reusing it. But if you work with *complex* documents— those with most of the text in separate frames— you'll be wise to create a reuseable template. Making the template is quite simple. Create your first document. Fine-tune it until it looks just right. Print it out. Now unload all the files from all the frames and save this empty document *under a new name*. We suggest incorporating a word like "bare," "empty," or "blank" into the name to distinguish it from real documents.

To create another document using this template, load the empty chapter. Before you do anything else, save it under a new name— whatever name you want to use for the document you are creating. Now you can proceed to load files and layout the document as you normally would.

♦ *Don't ignore this technique just because the publication varies from issue to issue. It's much easier, for example, to adjust the size of a sidebar frame that to create it from scratch.*

Advertisements

Though Ventura Publisher's unique strength is creating long documents, you can also easily create one-page documents such as advertisements or flyers. For this type of document, you may want to create the text within Ventura Publisher, since there is generally not too much to write. You will probably want to use individual frames or box text to hold the text within the ad. Logos and unusual typestyles (stretched, angled, pi fonts) can be created in outside graphics programs and then brought into Ventura as pictures.

Books

Books are a prime application for Ventura Publisher. Its batch processing capabilities make it ideal for long documents that would be a headache with other desktop publishing programs. To make best use of this batch processing power, minimize the use of separate frames. Keep as much of the activity as possible on the underlying page.

Camera-ready art for book pages needs crop marks to show the printer where to line up the negatives on the masking sheets. These marks are reference points that keep the pages of the book from ending up crooked or off center. They also indicate the final size of the page. Crop marks are printed along with the rest of the page, then trimmed off when the book is bound. Although you could use a ruling line around the entire frame as a crop mark, lithographers prefer tiny, faint lines just outside the live area.

Ventura has a built-in crop marks feature that is turned on and off in the PRINT dialog box. However, it works only for certain sizes. (Hint: try clicking on the underlying page, then using SIZING & SCALING to reduce the area where crop marks print).

You can easily create your own crop marks for any page size up to the printing limits of your laser printer. Make sure grid settings are on, and use the thinnest possible graphics line to draw the marks on the underlying page. By putting them on the underlying page, you guarantee that they will be reproduced on every page of the document.

♦ *Caution: Most laser printers can't print all the way to the end of an 8 1/2 x 11 page, so you may not be able to use this technique for pages larger than about 7 x 10.*

For more ideas on books, turn to the Colophon in Appendix B of this book, which gives full details of use of Ventura Publisher for the production of this book.

Directories

Perhaps no other type of document demonstrates the amazing power of Ventura Publisher. Most directories consist of repeating elements that are consistently formatted. For example, in a product directory, the product category names might always appear at the top of a column in 12-point Helvetica Bold and company names in 8-point Helvetica Light.

```
        D:DIRPROD  FC=477 FL=18 COL 01                    INSERT ON
/SUBHEADER1                                                                      <
@Categ = __@__                                                                   <
/SUBHEADER2                                                                      <
@Comp2 = _@_____ <9>__@_____                    <
/BODY                                                                            <
@Prod = _@_____                                    <
 _@                                                                              <
 _@_____ <9>__$2__@___.__ _@_                    <
@End =                                                                           <
/*                                                                              <
OPEN MANUF                                                                       <
OPEN PROD INDEX.2                                                                <
OUTFILE                                                                          <
MOVE 0 TO PAGEEND                                                                <
REPORT PROD BY INDEX.2 BREAK PROD.CODE PROD.COMP                                 <
INDICATE BLANK AS PROD.COST EQ 0                                                 <
[BLANK] INDICATE NOT BLANK AS PROD.RQMTS GT ' '                                  <

INDICATE VAPOR AS PROD.F2 MATCH 'N'                                              <
SECTION SUBHEADER1                                                               <
        PRINT PROD.CODE                                                          <
        OUTPUT SUBHEADER1                                                        <
SECTION SUBHEADER2                                                               <
1REFORM 2SAVE  3Q MENU 4Q SYS 5UNDLIN 6DEL WD 7BEGBLK 8ENDBLK 9BEGFIL 10ENDFIL
```

Figure 9-7
This report format from DataFlex automatically creates tagged text for Ventura Publisher.

An intelligent approach to directories is to use a database management program such as dBase III or DataFlex to generate both the text *and* the tags. It is then just a matter of loading the resulting ASCII file into Ventura Publisher. If you have previously created a style sheet for the directory, you will see the document instantly formatted according to your specifications.

The key to this technique is to devise a report format for your database that creates an ASCII file with Ventura Publisher tags inserted in it. For instance, you might instruct the program to print the character string "@PROD_CAT = " before outputting the contents of the Product Category field. Figure 9-7 shows a report format from DataFlex that automatically generates a formatted Ventura Publisher file.

Forms

Ventura Publisher was not really designed for the creation of forms. Nevertheless, it is so powerful that you may find use for it in this application. And because of its style sheets, you may be able to merge data from another program into a Ventura file. In this fashion, you can print both the form and the data in one pass.

Simple, one-page forms that will be filled out by hand don't need much discussion here. Use any and all graphic drawing and frame techniques you need to get the right look. Box text is the easiest way to create simple forms like invoices. Use grid snap to make sure the boxes line up with each other. Fill some of the boxes with a pattern to set them apart.

But if you want to attempt to merge the form with data from another computer application, use tags as much as possible to create graphic effects. If graphics are needed, put them on the underlying page so they'll be reproduced on every page. Separate logos and address information from the data by putting them into a repeating frame that will appear on every page. The idea is to create a format and a style sheet that can reproduce as many forms as needed just by pouring in tagged text.

♦ *Key note: Make sure that the last tag on the page includes a page break. This will force Ventura to a new page where it will start the next form.*

This method won't work, of course, unless you can get the other application to generate the tags. Many accounting programs, for instance, are limited in their reporting abilities. Others, however, are based around database management software, and may have the capabilities you need. And most popular database programs can do what you want— namely, pull out specified information, insert tags before it, and put them together into an ASCII file.

The preceding section about directory publishing gave additional thoughts on getting other software to generate tags. And the final section of Chapter Three, Creating Text, gave a full explanation of how to preformat files by inserting tags and other information.

Here is just one way you might use these ideas: Create a simple database program to capture ordering information as it comes in. At the end of every day (or more often if needed), print a database report to disk. This report will insert the proper Ventura tags in front of all the data elements. Now load the report file into Ventura, which will automatically format the data into forms. This technique could work for invoices, packing slips, picking slips, statements, and similar applications. Better yet, set up the system so that all necessary forms are printed out at the same time.

Magazines

Ventura Publisher can be a powerful tool for producing magazines, especially trade and technical magazines that follow a consistent format from month to month. For this type of publication, you might well use a combination of batch and interactive pagination to produce your pages. For example, you might use the underlying page to produce each feature article, letting the articles run as many pages as necessary. Departments such as shorter news articles and briefs could be accommodated within frames placed on the page.

If there are advertisements in your magazine, you can use frames to indicate where they will be placed so that your lithographer can strip in the right negative from each client. Use Ventura Publisher's box text function to place a label in the empty frames that indicate which ad goes there, and any other pertinent information about the ad.

Photographs within the editorial pages should be handled using the techniques described in Chapter Seven.

Memos

Standardized memo formats can improve your image if they incorporate good design. They can cut cost if you are able to use the laser printer to put the company logo on the same page (without the need to reload the printer with letterhead). They can convey more information if graphics are combined with text on the page. And they can increase productivity if information is in a standard format, so readers always know where to look for the facts they need.

One approach to creating memos with Ventura Publisher is to put the logo/letterhead material into a separate frame at the top of the page. Use this as the document template as described above— load the template then bring in the text file. Rename the document if you want to save an electronic ver-

FROM: J. Berst

DATE: April 12, 1987

REGARDING: Inside Xerox Ventura Publisher

PROBLEM: Not enough books to meet demand

OPTIONS: Print more; recall from warehouses

RECOMMENDED ACTIONS: Enter second printing

Preliminary indications from our distribution centers indicate that the supply of books is insuffi-

cient to meet the demand from users of Ventura Publisher. This shortage could become a crisis if

not corrected within three to four weeks. I recommend we move our schedule up for the second

printing. Calling books back from warehouses at this point could be a cause other problems in

supply.

Figure 9-8
A "prefab" memo created with Ventura Publisher.

sion of the memo, or simply abandon it after printing if you do not.

A second approach uses a word processing file as a template. This standardized file can be handed out to all the people who write memos. (If they use different word processors, create it once and use Chapter Three's technique to convert it to different formats). This file will have the correct tag names inserted. It can also include text that you want to appear in every memo. All the writers need to do is fill in the blanks. For instance, here's a word processing file that creates memos like Figure 9-8 when combined with a logo:

@HEAD1 = To:
@HEAD1 = From:
@HEAD1 = Date:
@HEAD1 = Regarding:
@HEAD2 = Problem:
@HEAD2 = Options:
@HEAD2 = Recommended Action:

Once you master this simple template technique for memos, you'll find ways to adapt it to other, more complex documents.

Newsletters

There are as many different approaches to newsletter design as there are newsletters. Once again, Ventura is ideal for this type of application because of its flexibility. Some newsletter editors like to use boldface lead-ins rather than separate headlines. As explained earlier in this chapter, Ventura's relative indent feature lets you make the lead-in as long as you want. Whatever the length, Ventura will automatically place the text that follows at the right spot.

Other newsletters place headlines out in the margin to the left of the main text. To accomplish this effect, turn breaks before off for the first paragraph following a headline and use the IN FROM LEFT setting to make the main text appear side-by-side with the headline.

Still other newsletters use a magazine or newspaper approach, running headlines across two or three columns of main text. Use the frame approach to pagination discussed in Chapter Six to produce this type of newsletter. Alternatively, you may want to use a "running galley" approach to design where the headlines appear in the same column as body text. With this style, you may want to place all your articles in one large text file and then load the single file into the underlying page to accomplish batch pagination. You can then use graphic frames and other devices to ensure the text precisely fills the required number of pages.

Proposals

Since proposals are usually intended to get business, they are vitally important. Appearance and readability are crucial. This is one application where it might pay to hire a professional help to create a graphic design you can reuse over and over again. As an alternative, search for outstanding proposal samples you can imitate.

Consider using a repeating frame to place the company logo on every other page. You may want to include the date in the header or footer as well. Live headers can also be a good idea. Key them to the section heading, or even to the subtitles, so readers can glance at the top of the page to know exactly where they are.

If your customer is susceptible to subtle flattery, try using Ventura's fonts to create an imitation of the customer's corporate logo style. Incorporate the logo throughout the document whenever appropriate. If the logo cannot be imitated with type alone, you can scan the logo and bring the scanned image into the document just as you would bring in any other picture.

Reports

The longer the report, the more important it is to use Ventura's table of contents and indexing capabilities. Consider adding live headers as well, to make reference easier.

Drawings and charts can be incorporated through the standard means: by saving the desired illustration to a file, then loading that file into a frame. Spreadsheets can be incorporated using the technique from Chapter Three for converting and inserting tab characters into spreadsheets.

Technical Documentation

Organization is one key to useable, effective documentation, and Ventura has several valuable features to aid organization, including table of contents, indexing, footnoting, and live headers.

You may also find that you can enforce a degree of standardization upon your authors by supplying them with template documents for their word processors. If they are given the organization in advance, their job becomes one of filling in the blanks. And if the template incorporates tags, the editor's job becomes one of simply loading the pretagged text files into Ventura and fine-tuning the end result.

Those who document software may be able to benefit from DoubleDOS, DesqView, and other programs that provide the ability to switch back and forth from one application to another. The idea is to keep the word processing program in one partition. In another partition, the writer keeps the software being documented along with a screen capture utility like HotShot. The writer works in tandem: He or she uses the software in one partition, switches to the word processor to write about it, switches back to the software again, and so on. When the writer needs a screen to illustrate his or her point, he or she invokes the capture utility to put the screen into a file. Then the writer jumps back to the word processor and inserts that file name at the spot where the illustration belongs. The writer can also insert the caption at the same time.

When laying out the document, the editor has merely to stop at each reference and load the screen file into a frame. If the screen illustrations are a standard size, the editor can keep a frame in temporary memory and paste it in as needed.

We hope the advice in the preceding section will serve as a starting point for bright ideas of your own. We also hope you'll share those ideas with other Ventura Publisher users. This book is periodically revised, partly to keep up with new revisions of the product, but also to stay up-to-date with creative new ways to apply the power of Ventura Publisher. Please send us the tips and tricks you develop on your own to the Micro Publishing address in Appendix A. Those with broad application will be included in the next edition, with full credit to the originator.

Manufacturers and Products

Adobe Systems Inc.
1870 Embarcadero Rd.
Suite 10
Palo Alto, CA 94303
415 852 0271
PostScript
Illustrator

Allied Linotype Co.
425 Oser Ave.
Hauppauge, NY 11788
516 434 2000
Linotronic 100 and 300

Ann Arbor Softworks
2393 Teller Rd., Ste. 106
Newbury Park, CA 91320
805 375 1467
FullPaint

Apple Computer
20525 Mariani Ave.
Cupertino, CA 95014
408 996 1010
Macintosh
LaserWriter
LaserWriter Plus
AppleShare
MacPaint

Ashton-Tate
20101 Hamilton Ave.
Torrance, CA 90502
213 329 8000
dBase III
Chart Master
Diagram Master

Autodesk, Inc.
2320 Marinship Way
Sausalito, CA 94965
415 332 2344
AutoCAD

Borland International
4585 Scotts Valley Dr.
Scotts Valley, CA 95066
408 438 8400
SideKick

Canon, USA Inc.
One Canon Plaza
Lake Success, NY 11042
516 488 6700
IX-12 scanner

Centram Systems West, Inc.
2372 Ellsworth Ave.
Berkeley, CA 94704
415 549 5900
TOPS network

CompuScan, Inc.
81 Two Bridges Rd., Bldg. 2
Fairfield, NJ 07006
201 575 0500
Model 245 PCS Page Reader

Computer Associates International, Inc.
2195 Fortune Dr.
San Jose, CA 95131
408 942 1727
SuperCalc 4

Cricket Software
3508 Market St., Ste. 206
Philadelphia, PA 19104
215 387 7955
Cricket Draw

Data Access Corp.
8525 SW 129th Terrace
Miami, FL 33156
305 238 0012
DataFlex

Datacopy Corp.
1215 Terra Bella Ave.
Mountain View, CA 94043
415 965 7900
Model 730 scanner

Dataviz Inc.
16 Winfield St.
Norwalk, CT 06855
203 866 4944
MacLink

Desktop Graphics
213 W. Loockerman
Dover, DE 19901
302 736 9098
DrawArt

Dest Corp.
1201 Cadillac Court
Milpitas, CA 95035
408 946 7100
PC Scan
PC Scan Plus
Publish Pac

Digital Research Inc.
60 Garden Court
Monterey, CA 93942
408 649 3896
GEM Desktop
GEM Draw Plus
GEM Paint

Enabling Technologies
600 S. Dearborn St., Ste. 1304
Chicago, IL 60605
312 427 0386
Easy 3D

General Parametrics Corp.
1250 Ninth St.
Berkeley, CA 94710
415 524 3950
VideoShow

IBM
900 King St.
Rye Brook, NY 10573
914 934 4488
Model 3117 Scanner
Cadwrite
IBM PC/XT
IBM AT

ISSCO
10505 Sorrento Valley Blvd.
San Diego, CA 92121
619 452 0170
ISSCO Displa

Hewlett-Packard
P.O. Box 15
Boise, ID 83707
208 323 3869
Laserjet
Laserjet Plus
Laserjet II
ScanJet

Imagen Corp.
2650 San Tomas Expressway
Santa Clara, CA 95051
408 986 9400
DDL

Innovative Data Design, Inc.
1975 Willow Pass Rd., Ste. 8
Concord, CA 94520
415 680 6818
MacDraft

Lifetree Software Inc.
411 Pacific St., Ste. 315
Monterey, CA 93940
408 373 4718
Words & Figures

Lotus Development Corp.
55 Cambridge Parkway
Cambridge, MA 02142
617 577 8500
Lotus 1-2-3
Symphony
Graphwriter
Freelance Plus

Media Cybernetics
8484 Georgia Ave., Ste. 200
Silver Spring, MD 20910
301 495 3305
Halo Desktop Publishing Editor

Mentor Graphics
8500 SW Creekside Place
Beaverton, OR 97005
503 626 7000
PicEd

Micro Publishing
21150 Hawthorne Blvd., Suite 104
Torrance, CA 90503
213 376 5724
microPublishing Report Newsletter
Document Gallery Style Sheets for Ventura Publisher

Micrografx, Inc.
1820 N. Greenville Ave.
Richardson, TX 75081
214 234 1769
*In*A*Vision*

MicroPro International Corp.
33 San Pablo Ave.
San Rafael, CA 94903
415 457 8990
Wordstar

Microrim, Inc.
3925 159th Ave., NE
Redmond, WA 98052
206 885 2000
Rbase 5000

Microsoft Corp.
10611 NE 36th St.
Redmond, WA 98073
206 882 8080
Word
Chart
Excel

Microtek Lab
16901 S. Western Ave.
Gardena, CA 90247
213 321 2121
MS300A Scanner
Eye-Star

New Riders Publishing
P.O. Box 4846-V
Thousand Oaks, CA 91360
(818) 991-5392
Inside Xerox Ventura Publisher

QMS, Inc.
P.O. Box 81250
Mobile, AL 36689
205 633 4300
Concept Designer
Concept Equation Setter

Ricoh Corp.
5 Dedrick Place
West Caldwell, NJ 07006
201 882 2000
IS30 Scanner

RoseSoft Inc.
P.O. Box 45880
Seattle, WA 98145
206 282 0454
ProKey

Shape Inc.
Biddeford Industrial Park
Biddeford, ME 04005
207 282 6155
ShapeScan scanner

Software Publishing Corp.
1901 Landings Dr.
Mountain View, CA 94043
415 962 8910
Harvard Presentation Graphics

Software Research Technologies
2130 S. Vermont Ave.
Los Angeles, CA 90007
213 737 7663
   SmartKey

Solutions International
29 Main St.
Montpelier, VT 05602
802 229 0368
   Glue

Symsoft
P.O. Box 4477
Mountain View, CA 94040
415 962 9500
   HotShot

T/Maker Co.
2115 Landings Dr.
Mountain View, CA 94043
415 962 0195
   Click Art

Tall Tree Systems
1120 San Antonio Rd.
Palo Alto, CA 94303
415 964 1980
   JLaser Plus

3D Graphics
860 Via de la Paz
Pacific Palisades, CA 90272
213 459 7949
   Perspective

Velo-Bind, Inc.
650 Almanor Ave.
Sunnyvale, CA 94036
408 732 4200
   Binding Systems

Ventura Software, Inc.
675 Jarvis #C
Morgan Hill, CA
(408) 779-5000
   Ventura Publisher

WordPerfect Corp.
323 N. State St.
Orem, UT 84057
801 227 4000
   MathPlan 3.0
   WordPerfect

Xerox Corp.
Xerox Square, 5th Fl.
Rochester, NY 14644
800 832 6979
   Star Workstation
   Documenter System
   4020 Color Inkjet
   Model 4045
   Interpress

Xerox Corp.
Palo Alto Research Center
3333 Coyote Hills Dr.
Palo Alto, CA 94304
415 494 4000

ZSoft Corp.
1950 Spectrum Circle, Ste. A-495
Marietta, GA 30067
404 980 1950
   PC Paintbrush
   Publisher's Paintbrush

Colophon

As we've made abundantly clear in the course of this book, Ventura Publisher is a productive publishing tool for all kinds of documents. This book is yet one more example.

While the procedures we used to write, edit, and design this book are by no means the final word for book publishers, readers may find it interesting to learn how we did things.

Each of us wrote our respective portions of the manuscript using WordStar 3.3 from MicroPro International Corp. Jesse used the AST Research Premium Publisher computer, while James used the PCs Limited AT machine. Using SmartKey, from Software Research Technologies, we devised a set of keyboard macros that automatically inserted tags and character attributes right into the word processing files (see Chapter Three for more details on this process). We then edited each other's text—in several passes—using WordStar, and Move-It, from Wolff Software, to transmit copy over the modem.

Some of the artwork was generated using GEM Draw Plus from Digital Research, Inc. Other pieces came from PC Paintbrush Plus, the Z-Soft graphics package. This program also served as the scanner control software for images brought in from our Canon IX-12 scanner. Still other graphic images were reduced versions of Ventura Publisher documents brought into our chapter files using the Encapsulated PostScript format (see Chapter Four). But the majority of the graphic images in this book consist of screen shots captured from Ventura Publisher, as well as several character-oriented and graphics programs. For this task, we found the HotShot program from SymSoft, Inc., to be an invaluable aid.

When all of the text and graphics were finished, we assembled them into pages using Ventura Publisher. Unfortunately, just as we began this task, James' AT computer crashed and was put out of commission for a few weeks. As a result, the majority of the pages in this book were produced with Ventura Publisher running on an IBM-XT clone. We are pleased to report that Ventura Publisher performed quite respectably on an XT-class computer, even when our chapters reached 30 pages or more in length with several graphic images included.

During the course of the layout process, we used two large-screen displays, the Xerox Full Page Display and the Cono-Vision 2800 from Conographic Corp. Both of these products perform very well with Ventura Publisher, and make the layout process much easier than it would be with a smaller-format display. Because these displays can show a full page of text at 100 percent size (the ConoVision 2800 can show facing pages), we were able to make last-minute edits and insert index entries from within Ventura Publisher.

We used Ventura Publisher's index and table of contents features to generate the index and Table of Contents for this book. These two functions undoubtedly saved us several days of labor.

When the layout was finished, we used the JLaser printer controller from Tall Tree Systems Inc. to produce proof copies of the pages. This printer option was able to output pages very quickly, even though the font availability was not as great as with the Apple LaserWriter Plus.

Finally, we made the required corrections to the pages directly within Ventura Publisher, and output the final, camera-ready pages using the Apple LaserWriter Plus. The fonts used in this book are 12-point ITC Bookman for body text, Avant Garde for page headers and captions, and Helvetica Narrow for tabular material. Every page of this book, with the exception of the front and back covers, was created entirely with Ventura Publisher. The cover was designed and produced using traditional graphic arts methods. The cover design represents the combined efforts of Jon DeKeles, Todd Meisler, Carolyn Porter, and Wendy Staroba.

This book was printed by Griffin Printing Company of Glendale, CA, using a web offset press.

Index

A

Alignment 142
Archiving
  See publication files
ASCII 55
  creating with WordStar 60
  editing files 58
  format for caption files 202
  from a database program 310
  hard returns in 58
  option in spreadsheet software 65
  output from database 63
  output from other programs 59
  tab character 51
  with tab-delimited columns 66
AutoCAD 90, 94, 97, 117

B

Backup button 35
Balanced columns
  See column balance
Binding 230
Box text 168, 195
Boxes
  See rules
Breaks
  controlling 182
  in tables 258
  purpose 147
Bullets 241
Business forms 310
  creating with repeating frames 294

C

Calculated width of columns 137
Cancel button 32
Captions
  adding 198
  as page numbers 293
  attaching 198
  CAP file 202
  created as tags 301
  enhancing 200
  spell-checking 203
Chapter files
  elements of 41
  saving 71, 169, 205
Collated pages 213
Column balance 167, 270
Column guides 167
Column widths 136
Copying
  frames 185
  text 170
Cursor
  shapes 26
  text 31
Cutting
  frames 185
  tabs, returns, and line breaks 174
  text 170

D

Dashes
  See rules

Database software 50, 63
Desktop publishing 2
    benefits 4
    defined 3
    history 3
    limitations 7
Displays
    high-resolution 3
Distribution
    electronic 221
DOS
    See MS-DOS
Double-sided documents 132
Downloading fonts
    See fonts

E

Em dash
    inserting in word processor 177
Extended character set 175, 177

F

Facing pages view 132
File conversion 116
File filtering 34
File management 282
    moving files 283
    tips for 285
Fill patterns
    used to create patterned type 243
First line indent 142
Flow text around 289
Fonts 226
    changing 173
    choices for tables 263
    defined 140
    downloaded 227
    screen 226
    serif 47
    size 140
    symbol 71, 77, 252
Footnotes
    inserting 177
    inserting directly in text file 79
Frame menu 135
Frames
    adding 185
    adjusting margins 187
    anchoring 82, 204
    captions 289
    combining text and graphics in 289
    containing Ventura graphics 196
    copying 203
    creating 168
    cutting, copying, and pasting 185
    default margins 167
    defined 41
    fine-tuning 186
    moving 189
    padding 188
    sizing & scaling 187

    special techniques 288
    templates 288
    tips on adding 189
Function keys
    assigning 123, 124, 127
    choosing the order of 127
    tagging with 122
    using 125
Function selector 37

G

GEM 25
    role within Ventura Publisher 24
Graphics
    capturing screen images 110, 112
    creating 89
    cropping 109, 192
    Drawing mode 40, 89, 90, 138, 193, 194, 195,
        243
    editing 189
    enhancing with graphics drawing mode 193
    from outside Ventura Publisher 43
    images 92, 93, 100, 103
    leaving windows 95
    line art 91, 94, 98, 99
    loading 91, 100, 104, 185
    placing 189
    scaling 95, 103, 190, 191
    special techniques 295
Grids
    layout 10
Gutters
    between columns 136

H

Headers & footers 134, 157, 267
    extra large 293
    formatting 267
    live 269
    turning on and off 268
Hints
    tips 125
Hyphenation 253
    dictionary 54
    exception dictionaries 254
    missed opportunities 54
    suppressing 55
    suppressing in dictionary 254
    turning on and off 142
    when loading text 162, 254
Hyphens
    discretionary 54, 61

I

Illustrations
    See graphics
Indents 264
Index
    creating 81, 219
    inserting entries 178
    inserting marks in headers and footers 181

inserting references directly in text file 79
naming generated files 219
see and see also references 179
sort keys 179
tips for 180
Installation 14
Interpress 211

K

Keep with next 150
Kerning
   automatic 246
   global override 133
   information in font files 247
   manual 251
   on-screen 248
Key assignments 28
Keyboard macro programs 71, 84
   as used by authors 84

L

Layout 159
Line breaks
   See breaks
Lines
   See rules
Lithography
   color 209
   color separations 234
   defined 208
   guidelines for offset printing 231
   printing press 11
   working with 236
Logos 244, 308
   on memos 313
   used with repeating frames 292
Lotus 1-2-3 64, 65, 66, 90, 91, 96, 97, 101

M

Macintosh 3, 8, 103
Macro programs
   See keyboard macro programs
Margins & columns 135
Memory
   error messages 304
   management techniques 302
   used by files 163
Menus
   purpose of 27
   used for creating style sheets 130
Mouse 3
   choosing a file 33
   dragging 26
   selecting with 26
   tagging with 121
   use within Ventura Publisher 25
MS-DOS 14, 34
   changing file names 120
   copy command 282
   file operations 285
   increasing memory to 704K 305

limitations of 302
memory usage 306
Multi-chapter operations 213, 283-285

N

Numbering
   adding chapter numbers 279
   auto 274-276
   captions with auto-numbering 301
   chapter 272
   information in chapter file 42
   multiple lists in one chapter 280
   numbers and paragraphs on same line 277
   outline style 279
   page 273
   renumber chapter 280
   style 273

O

Offset lithography
   See lithography
Outdents 265
Outline
   See numbering
Overall width 142

P

Page counter
   See numbering
Page description languages 209
   defined 211
   printers with 210
Page menu 130
Pages
   inserting 166
Thomas Paine 1
Paper sizes 131
Paragraph
   as term is used by Ventura Publisher 23
Paragraph menu 139, 140
Paste-up 10
Pasting
   frames 185
   text 170
Patterns
   fill 194
PC Paintbrush 92, 102, 103, 104, 107, 108,
   109, 111, 116
Photographs
   color separations 234
   cropping 11
   gray scale required 105
   leaving windows for 231
   negatives 11
   proof 233
   stripping in 7, 11
   tips for 234
Pictures
   See graphics
PostScript 99, 140, 211, 225, 322
   point sizes recorded in width table 228

printers 223
Printers
  laser 105
Printing
  a publication 215
  a single chapter 212
  imitating another printer 225
  switching printers 222
  to a file 215
  to disk file 229
  using more than one printer 221
  with manual feed 213
Printing press
  See lithography
Publication files
  archiving 220
  copying one chapter of 285
  creating 213
  defined 213
  printing 215, 305
  saving 214, 284

Q

Quotation marks 46, 175

R

Relative indent 143
Repeating frames 131, 290, 315
Reverse type 242
Revisions
  in traditional publishing 10
  to paste-up 11
Rivers 51
Rulers 139
  resetting zero point for setting tabs 262
Rules
  adding 188
  associated with tags 150
  dashes 153
  effect on paragraph spacing 245
  function in frames and paragraphs 139
  in traditional paste-up 11
  inter-column 137
  range of sizes 137
  setting pattern 153
  spacing above and below 154
  vertical 137, 295
  width 152
  with graphics drawing mode 138

S

Scanners 44, 102, 104, 105, 107, 108, 109, 232, 322
Scrolling 26
Shadow effects 298
Sidebar 37
Spaces
  after punctuation 51, 57
  discretionary 51
  em 45
  hard 51

non-breaking 54
thin and figure 47
Spacing
  above and below a paragraph 144
  above and below rules 154
  from left and right margins 146
  function of dialog box 144
  horizontal 246
  letter 248
  line 173, 244
  line spacing 48, 145
  minimum and maximum between words 249
  paragraph 244
  suppressing at the top of a column 145
  vertical 244
Special characters
  search and replace for 85
Special effects 240
Spreadsheet software 50, 64
Style sheets 44
  applying 22, 121
  changing 128, 162
  defined 8
  loading 22, 119, 129, 160, 161
  maintaining 155
  menus used 130
  saving 155, 162
  saving under a new name 120
  tips for 156
  width tables in 226
Symbol font
  See fonts
Symbols
  inserting 175

T

Table of contents
  creating 216, 217
  formatting 218
  naming file 218
Tables
  creating 256
Tabs
  in tables 259
  in word processors 51
  inserting true characters 52
  key 31
Tagging 39, 71, 169
  adding a new tag 155
  defined 22
  generated tags 201
  inserting as you type 71
  multiple paragraphs 122
  removing a tag 155
  tips 125
  with the function keys 122
  with the mouse 121
Technical documentation 9, 14, 86, 315
  numbering in 274
Templates 308
Text
  attributes 47, 53, 62, 68, 71, 75, 76, 171, 173,

174
  capitalization 73
  creating 49, 51, 53, 55, 57, 59, 61, 62, 63, 65,
    67, 69, 71, 73, 75, 77, 79, 81, 83, 85, 87, 181
  editing 68, 163, 169, 183
  editing mode 39, 53, 125, 170, 173, 174, 176,
    177, 201, 244
  file conversion 55
  files 43
  loading 16, 162, 294
  placing 18, 163, 164, 165, 167, 169
  preformatting files 68, 86
  rotated 100
  tagging 169
Tips
  for creating text 56
  for editing text 183
  for faster tagging 125
  for graphics drawing 196
  for loading text 162
  for overcoming memory limitations 304
  for photos 234
  for placing text 169
  for scaling pictures 191
  for style sheets 156
  for using scanners 109
  for working with bit-map graphics 103
  for working with captions 202
  on adding frames 189
  on file management 285
  on indexing 180
  on using tabs 262
  using item selectors 36
  working with AutoCAD 97
  working with dialog boxes 31
  working with Lotus graphs 96
  working with object-oriented graphics 99
Tracking 250
Typefaces
  See fonts
Typesetting 4, 9
  cost of machines 4
  in traditional publishing 10
  output from Ventura Publisher 208, 210, 225
  PostScript machines 211

  service bureaus 221
Typographic functions 239

U

Underlying page 19, 41, 135, 159
  loading text into 288
  margins 131
  putting crop marks on 309
  rules on 138
  text on 163
  text placed on 164
  typing text on 181
Units of measurement
  applied to rules 137
  changing in dialog box 32
  ems and ens 46
  for tracking 250
  use of space character 54
User interface 24

W

Widows & orphans 133
Width tables 223, 225
  changing 224
  in style sheet 226
  provided with third-party fonts 228
Word processors 43, 50
  dot commands 61
  editing caption files 202
  inserting non-keyboard characters in 177
  proper use of tabs 260
  search and replace function 85
  supported by Ventura Publisher 54
  tagging paragraphs in 125
  using spelling checkers 55
WordStar 51, 53, 321
  nondocument mode 60
  vari-tabs 62

X

Xerox Corporation 3

Yes, please send me the productivity-boosting benefits of the preformatted, professionally-designed Document Gallery Style Sheet Collections checked below. Make check to New Riders Publishing.

☐ **Check enclosed.**

☐ **Charge to my credit card:**

☐ **VISA** ☐ **MasterCard**

Card #:_____
Expiration:_____

Signature:_____

Name:_____

Company:_____

Address:_____

City:_____

State:_____Zip:_____

Charge Orders: Call (818) 991-5392.

Quantity of Style Sheet Collections	Total at $39.95 each
Shipping: $3.50 per Collection	
Sales Tax: Caifornia Residents add $2.80 each	
Total	

Document Gallery Collections

☐ **Sampler Collection**
Turn your PC into a design department with this versatile collection of our most popular document types and formats.

☐ **Newsletter Collection**
Put the persuasive power of professional design to work for your publication. Choose from one, two and three column layouts. Incorporate advanced formats like multi-line marginal headings, TOCs, run-in headings and more.

☐ **Tech Doc Collection**
Get your tech doc department up to speed with this productivity-boosting collection of manuals, spec sheets, parts lists, reports and military documents with advanced features like auto section numbering, live headers, auto figure and table numbering, auto outlining and much, more.

☐ **Marketing Collection**
Add pizazz with attention-getting brochures, flyers, ads, press releases, pamphlets and order cards.

☐ **Book Collection**
Includes Tags and style sheets for all important parts of a book — front matter, TOC, body text, headings, captions, appendix, index and more. Includes separate style sheets for all the most popular page sizes.

☐ **Corporate Collection**
Give yourself and your documents a boost up the corporate ladder with professional-looking reports, proposals, memos, letterheads, reply forms, and more.

☐ **Directory Collection**
Produce directories, price lists, catalogs and more. Slash days from traditional production methods by feeding database reports into one of these Document Gallery formats. Incorporates power techniques like live headers, leader dots and multi-line tabular formats.

☐ **Forms Collection**
An electronic forms library. All the most-wanted forms, including invoices, purchase orders, expense reports, personnel records, phone logs, message/reply forms and many more with room for the company name, logo and address.

☐ **Want More Information?**
I don't want to order right now, but please send more information about Document Gallery Style Sheet Collections.

Document Gallery Style Sheet Collections

Custom-Designed by the Experts on Ventura Publisher

Point. Click.

That's all it takes to create documents that look like they came from a high-priced design studio. Because that's all it takes to combine the amazing power of Xerox Ventura Publisher with high-performance Style Sheets designed by Micro Publishing.

Document Gallery Style Sheet Collections were designed, precoded, and preformatted by James Cavuoto and Jesse Berst, authors of *Inside Xerox Ventura Publisher*. Each disk in the collection holds over 20 Style Sheets and associated files.

Document Gallery Style Sheet Collections are for businesspeople who don't have time to become a professional graphic designer.

- *Save time.* Access entire libraries of top-notch designs. Twenty per disk.
- *Get professional results.* Created, analyzed, and fine-tuned by experts.
- *Use advanced features.* Incorporate advanced Ventura functions simply by loading a Document Gallery Style Sheet.
- *Get more value from Ventura.* Create virtually any kind of document — without stopping to code a style sheet.
- *Improve the appearance of documents.* Each style sheet rigorously adheres to professional design principles.
- *Upgrade your skills.* Complete instructions on loading and use, plus tips and tricks for getting the most from each one.

To order: Fill in the reverse, fold, and mail.

Please send me the following INSIDE books:

☐ **Copies of INSIDE XEROX VENTURA PUBLISHER @ $19.95 US**
(Supports Xerox Ventura Publisher Version 1.1) ISBN 0-934035-13-X

☐ **Copies of INSIDE AutoCAD @ $34.95 US**
(Supports AutoCAD 2.5) ISBN 0-934035-08-3

☐ **Please add my name to your list for more information on desktop publishing.**
I understand that I may return any book for a full refund if not satisfied.

Name_____

Address: _____

City: _____State: __ Zip: _____

Telephone: _____Ext.: _____

Californians: Please add 7% sales tax per book.
Shipping and Handling: $3.50 for the first book and $1.00 for each additional book.

☐ **I can't wait 3-4 weeks for Book Rate Mail. Here is $5.00 per book for Air Mail**
Make check payable to New Riders Publishing, P.O. Box 4846-V, Thousand Oaks, CA 91360
(818) 991-5392

Please send comments to ATTN: PRODUCT REVIEW.

COMMENTS (Suggestions for improvements to INSIDE XEROX VENTURA PUBLISHER):

_____

_____

_____

_____

_____

WISH LIST (Topics you would like to see covered):

_____

_____

_____

_____

_____

_____

To order: Fill in the reverse, fold, and mail.

- -

BUSINESS REPLY MAIL
FIRST CLASS PERMIT NO. 53   THOUSAND OAKS, CA

POSTAGE WILL BE PAID BY ADDRESSEE

NEW RIDERS PUBLISHING

P.O. Box 4846-V

Thousand Oaks, CA 91360